TRANSLATING THE COUNTERCULTURE

TRANSLATING THE COUNTERCULTURE

THE RECEPTION OF THE BEATS IN TURKEY

ERIK MORTENSON

Southern Illinois University Press
Carbondale

Southern Illinois University Press
www.siupress.com

Cover design by Jack Prange

Printed in the United States of America

21 20 19 18 4 3 2 1

Library of Congress Cataloging-in-Publication Data
Names: Mortenson, Erik, 1970– author.
Title: Translating the counterculture : the reception of the Beats in Turkey / Erik Mortenson.
Description: Carbondale : Southern Illinois University Press, 2018. | Includes bibliographical references and index.
Identifiers: LCCN 2017031354 | ISBN 9780809336548 (pbk. : alk. paper) | ISBN 9780809336555 (e-book)
Subjects: LCSH: American literature—20th century—History and criticism. | Beat generation. | American literature—Appreciation—Turkey. | American literature—Translations into Turkish—History and criticism. | Turkish literature—20th century—History and criticism. | Counterculture in literature. | Counterculture—Turkey.
Classification: LCC PS228.B6 M68 2017 | DDC 810.9/005071056—dc23 LC record available at https://lccn.loc.gov/2017031354

Printed on recycled paper. ♲

To my daughter, Zelda

CONTENTS

ILLUSTRATIONS

PREFACE

We rarely acknowledge the role chance plays in the world. It is far more satisfying to think of ourselves as directors controlling the course of events than as spectators watching them unfold before our astonished eyes. This unwillingness to accept circumstance is even truer when it comes to our work. We tend to think of the act of creation as a sacrosanct expression of personal will that makes something new come into being. Yet chance is always a present, if often overlooked, factor.

It was chance that brought me to Turkey. In 2006 I left a Fulbright position in Germany to take a job at Koç University in Istanbul. The administration needed someone to help establish a program in English and comparative literature, and I jumped at an opportunity that I probably would not have received in the United States. I had never been to Turkey, I did not speak one word of Turkish, and like most Americans, I could not have located Istanbul on a map. But I settled in, built a program from scratch with my colleague Gloria Fisk, slowly learned Turkish, and enmeshed myself in the culture.

Chance also helped create *Translating the Counterculture*. While teaching a humanities course at Koç, an engineering student of mine, Burak Polater, handed me a copy of a journal. He had heard I was a Beat scholar, and he thought the publication might be of interest to me. It was an issue of *Underground Poetix*, a journal done in fanzine style that among other things collected translations of Beat texts and articles about the lives of Beat writers. I had assumed that my research on the Beats would be done from afar, going back to the States in the summer to collect materials and working on them in Istanbul during the school year. But here was the potential to explore the Beats in Turkey, a connection I had never thought existed. My interest was piqued.

As more material kept surfacing over the next ten years, I realized that I had inadvertently stumbled on an interesting, previously overlooked dynamic. More than half a century after their postwar debut, the Beats and their countercultural message were resurfacing in Turkey as what was being called underground literature. Translations of Beat texts were on the rise; editors and critics debated this new type of literature in journals and magazines; and fans eagerly devoured this novel form of Western protest. It fascinated me how the Beat struggle to live their lives as they saw fit found resonance in a country that was vastly different from the United States in so many ways. *Translating the Counterculture* thus became a means of documenting, analyzing, and trying to understand the Beat's continued importance for readers in Turkey.

To write this book, I needed help. While my Turkish was steadily improving, I was still by no means fluent in either the language or the culture. So I began to do something I had never done before: to collaborate. As someone who fits the stereotype of the quiet, bookish scholar, I preferred to spend my time working independently in libraries. But I quickly realized that the only way to write this book was to talk, and to work, with others. I was fortunate to receive a prestigious grant from the Turkish government to conduct quantitative research on underground literature and its youth readers. The grant allowed me to work with several graduate students to conduct interviews and create focus groups across Turkey. As part of a summer research group composed of undergraduate students, I read and discussed the various translations of Allen Ginsberg's *Howl.* And with numerous student research assistants from our department, I received help gathering materials, summarizing articles, and producing translations. This book owes its existence to these students, and I cannot thank them enough for their enthusiasm, support, insight, and hard work.

Chance made this book possible, but chance cuts both ways. By the summer of 2016, the manuscript was basically complete. Returning home from the office, I was met at the door by my partner Lia McCoskey. "Have you heard the news?" she asked excitedly. I had not, I told her, but huddled over the glare of the computer screen, I soon discovered the source of her agitation—Turkey was in the middle of an attempted coup. It was a tense night. We got our baby daughter to sleep, and sat away from the windows in a darkened room wondering what morning would bring. Fighter jets screamed overhead, and the muezzin by our apartment, normally the source of melodic prayer, issued shrill exhortations every half hour throughout the night. While morning brought some relief with the news that order was restored, it was only the beginning. A series of purges and arrests were in store, and academics were among the main targets. A week later, after witnessing a series of unsettling demonstrations, a string of uncertain announcements, and an armada of screaming Recep Tayyip Erdoğan supporters anchored in the waters of the Bosporus outside our apartment, we decided it was time to go. Erdoğan had announced that academics would not be allowed to leave the country, and though we were not sure if that ban included foreigners, we did not wait to find out. We caught a taxi to the airport for an immediate departure to London. Fortunately, my manuscript was complete and tucked safely into my carry-on baggage.

Now I watch events in Turkey unfold from afar, wondering what will happen to friends and colleagues. I also find myself thinking about the future of the Beats and their texts in a country that apparently is becoming more and more autocratic and conservative. Can such oppositional literature still have a role to play? Will readers still be willing to read and discuss texts that might end up landing them in trouble? While *Translating the Counterculture* cannot predict the future, it is my hope that this book might outline some of the many possibilities for the counterculture across the globe as such texts encounter new moments of reception.

I realize that no work that generates broad claims about a field as diverse as Beat studies is going to please every scholar, fan, or reader of the Beats. Nor will a work that seeks to make sense of a country and its people avoid criticism. The difficulty inherent in examining how a provocative set of writers like the Beats are received in a country undergoing drastic changes like Turkey, however, is precisely why a book like this is important. *Translating the Counterculture* is meant to provoke thought, to spark debate, and to open up the oftentimes unspoken assumptions about the Beats for review and discussion. The premise here, then, is that disagreement can be good; if it does not lead to an eventual reconciliation of viewpoints, then at least it offers us a better understanding of our positions and the assumptions under which they operate. Chance has made the Beats once again timely, and it makes sense to use that chance to help in understanding the nature, function, and ongoing relevancy of their countercultural message.

ACKNOWLEDGMENTS

No book could ever reach completion without the support of colleagues, friends, and loved ones who offer their support, and so I take a moment here to thank them.

As someone who arrived in Turkey with no knowledge of its culture, history, and language, I owe an enormous debt to all of my Turkish friends, colleagues, and research assistants; they helped me better understand the contexts for this work. Sinan Ünver offered friendship as well as explanations when I was puzzled about what was going on around me. Our quiet talks as dusk fell will always be cherished. Canan Akgökçem kindly shared her invaluable experience with and research into the topic. I also profited immensely from discussions with a colleague in sociology, Murat Engin, as well as with my history colleague Aslı Niyazioğlu, whose critical readings of chapters at early stages helped curtail generalization. Raoul Motika was gracious enough to invite me to present part of this work at Istanbul's venerable Orient Institut, where I had the good fortune to meet Timour Muhidine, who has likewise been a helpful correspondent and collaborator.

I am grateful to my colleagues in the English and Comparative Literature Department at Koç University. Although I did not always agree with poet, scholar, and translator Nazmi Ağıl on some of the finer points, Nazmi was always willing to help with feedback and advice, and I miss our discussions over meze and raki. The Ottoman translator and scholar Sooyong Kim provided essential feedback, helping me to better grasp the intricacies of Ottoman and Turkish culture. Meliz Ergin was kind enough to read sections of the manuscript and lend a sympathetic ear to an often confused foreigner. The quick-witted and convivial Megan MacDonald willingly read my introduction at an early stage. And the feedback of supportive colleagues Georgia Axiotou, Rossen Djagalov and Nergis Dolcerocca was invaluable.

I owe an even larger debt to the numerous undergraduate student assistants who worked with me through all stages of the project. One of the first was Hazel Merve Aydin, who helped me to understand the nuances of reader-written Turkish poetry. The translations and explanations of Rafet Karaoğlu were instrumental throughout this book. Hard-working and supportive, he is certainly a bright young man with a promising future. Cansu Soyupak, who I am proud to see embark on her own academic career in Beat studies, lent her insight to numerous parts of this book and could be counted on to track down an obscure text, reference, or interviewee. Burak Polater was the first to bring underground literature to my attention and the insightful, enthusiastic, and ambitious young students in my seminars American Culture and the Cold War and The "Underground" in Literature, Film, Comics, and Music were a joy to teach and pushed my thinking on the topic forward. The two months I spent discussing the various translations of Allen Ginsberg's work with students who participated in our Summer Research Program for Undergraduates working group were not only essential for the book but also a huge amount of fun.

This book would have been impossible without a research grant from the Scientific and Technological Research Council of Turkey (Tübitak); I thank both the governing board of the institution and the Turkish government for funding my research. The grant allowed me to work with Cem Bico, Selen Erdoğan, and Duygu Ergun, whose hard work showed their dedication to the project. Işıl Baş, Ahmet Beşe, Zafer Parlak, and Tanfer Tunç graciously allowed Cem and me to conduct focus groups at their schools, and I am grateful for their generosity and time as hosts. Tanfer, in particular, has been an extremely supportive colleague. Cem worked hard on the project, handled the logistics of these trips, and simply was a lot of fun to be around.

Koç University was kind enough to make available the time and funding for me to spend one summer at Harvard University and another at the University of Michigan. I thank the staff at both institutions for facilitating my research. And I wish the best for my previous dean, Sami Gülgöz, and the current dean, Ahmet Içduygu, who supported and made such research trips possible.

The Turkish translations included in this book form a palimpsest, with numerous assistants, friends, and myself revising and amending them over a considerable period. I thank all who helped produce these translations throughout their various stages. Umur Çelikyay was gracious enough to go over the book's final Turkish-English translations. His work hides a plethora of translators who contributed everything from a suggestion for a new word to the translation of an entire passage. It is the grossest understatement to say that this book could not have been completed without the support of all these translators.

Karl Kageff, who helped me with this, my third book project, has been a wonderful editor, and it was with deep regret that I learned of his retirement. He will be sorely missed. The entire staff of Southern Illinois University Press has been helpful and considerate, making publishing at the press a joy. Project editor Wayne Larsen, in particular, provided essential feedback on the book and helped guide me through the publication process. Both of my unknown readers offered valuable insight and feedback.

Part of this book resulted from a research trip to the Sohm Archive at Stuttgart's Staatsgalerie, made possible by funding from the German Academic Exchange Service and fruitful by help from the archive's staff. Heike Paul supported my application and gave me a chance to present my work in both Erlangen and Munich. Marc Priewe kindly invited me for a talk in Stuttgart, and Josef Raab did the same in Essen. Fellow Beat scholar Alexander Greiffenstern helped me in researching the archive as well as graciously hosting me in Freiburg and Essen.

Parts of this manuscript were published previously. Portions of chapter 1 appeared in a special "The Beat Generation and Europe" issue of *Comparative American Studies: An International Journal*, edited by Polina Mackay and Chad Weidner, both of whom provided helpful editorial comments. Another section of chapter 1, about underground literature's readership, was written with Selen Erdoğan and Duygu Ergun and published in *New Perspectives on Turkey*. My colleagues at Koç, Deniz Yükseker and Fatoş Gökşen, were instrumental in helping a literature colleague make the temporary switch to sociology, and I thank them for taking the time to introduce me to their field. Fatoş was also extremely helpful in my capturing the Tübitak grant. I was truly blessed with wonderful colleagues at Koç. Yet another portion of chapter 1 appeared in the collection *Out of the Shadows: Beat Women Are Not Beaten Women*, edited by Frida Forsgren and Michael J. Prince, both of whom provided useful comments that made for a better manuscript. An early version of chapter 3 was published in *The Transnational Turn in American Studies: Turkey and the United States*, edited by Tanfer Tunç and Bahar Gursel. I thank both of the editors for their beneficial comments. The bulk of chapter 4 has appeared in *Arizona Quarterly: A Journal of American Literature, Culture, and Theory*, and I thank the editors and readers for their useful comments as well as Steven Belletto for suggesting the journal.

Finally, a section of chapter 5 appears in *CLCWeb: Comparative Literature and Culture*; I thank European Beat Studies Network president and founder Oliver Harris along with vice president Polina Mackay for their editorship. Oliver in particular has always been there with advice and support, and it was a pleasure to host him during his visit to Istanbul.

The quiet wisdom of John Alff has always helped to put things into perspective. Gerald MacLean and Donna Landry, veteran Turkophiles, explained why a military intervention might be seen as a positive development. I thank them both for their friendship and advice. Mark Huston gave me hospitality and spirited discussions, and Christopher Kramer has always been there to offer understanding. Heidi Eichbauer was kind enough to read the manuscript, and Barrett Watten, as usual, has been a constant support in both academic and personal matters. Jeffrey Kahrs and Julie Doxsee provided helpful feedback as well.

A penultimate thanks to my Istanbul neighbors and the Turkish people. I was always made to feel welcome because of the warmth and hospitality of those I met. My decade spent in Turkey was a blessing, in large part due to the warm and accepting atmosphere of the country. I look back on my time spent in the country with nothing but fondness.

Last, but certainly not least, I thank my family for their unflagging support. My wife, Lia McCoskey, has been patient and willing to read the manuscript throughout its various stages. My daughter, Zelda, has been an unending source of joy, and has helped me to focus on the important things in life. My entire family, both immediate and extended, have been there with love and support. I certainly could not have written this book without them.

Any errors in the text, of course, remain my own.

TRANSLATING THE COUNTERCULTURE

INTRODUCTION
WHY THE BEATS? WHY TURKEY? WHY NOW?

As recently as 2012, William S. Burroughs's novel *The Soft Machine* underwent a trial for obscenity in Turkey. The Committee for the Protection of Minors from Harmful Publications believed the book was an affront to Turkish morals, claiming it was "an account of an undisciplined sex addict that holds no moral principle dear" ("Bir kararımız"). Despite this blanket condemnation, the trial was really about the sensitive topic of homosexuality in Turkey. Not only did Burroughs's highly graphic homoerotic depictions rankle the committee, but in Turkish, the word *soft* is also slang for passive homosexual practices. While the legal dynamics of the Turkish trial had many similarities to the various censorship battles the Beats were embroiled in during the early postwar period in the United States, cultural and temporal differences have lent new meaning to the proceedings. Rather than backing down, the publisher and translator of the book, along with various supporters, chose not only to fight the allegations in court but also to publicize the proceedings in blogs, on websites, and through Facebook, thus raising awareness of government repression and combatting Turkish homophobia. The stakes were real: the publisher faced heavy fines and even jail time, while the book's supporters risked public condemnation and harassment. The trial demonstrates that despite cultural and temporal gaps, the Beats and their countercultural questioning of social norms are still useful to those interested in challenging the status quo in Turkey.

If countercultural literature is meant to "counter" a culture, what happens when another culture borrows that critique? *Translating the Counterculture* addresses that question by examining the reception of the Beat Generation in Turkey. In their own cultural moment, the Beats were seen as direct threats to both social and literary propriety. The Beat lifestyle, stereotyped in the popular media as a dropping out of "normal" society, was a clear rejection of the middle-class consumerist lifestyle of the 1950s. The Beats were also seen as literary iconoclasts challenging staid academic critics and the traditional canon with poetry infused with the language of popular culture and the street. Today the Beats are less iconoclastic than iconic, and while their works still inspire many to question the society in which they live, they are far more likely to be seen as nostalgic reminders of a time when "us versus them" seemed easier to define. Yet in Turkey, the Beats and their message of dissent are once again socially relevant. Although Allen Ginsberg and Peter Orlovsky were the only Beat writers to actually visit the country, publishers, editors, critics, readers, and others dissatisfied with conditions in Turkey have turned to the Beats and other countercultural forebears for alternatives. This unexpected return of Beat nonconformity and protest into new cultural and temporal conditions offers a unique opportunity to rethink both the cultural logics that made the Beats possible in the first place as well as the possibilities they might still hold for social critique in our highly globalized twenty-first century.

This study challenges and unsettles the American understanding of the Beats, their message, and their legacy in both popular culture and academic discourse by focusing on the ways in which their texts are used, disseminated, and discussed. An examination of countercultural literature's function outside the time and place of its own production calls into question the assumptions that have accreted around Beat texts. The Beats in Turkey are still the Beats, but their use is specific to local conditions and particular needs, reminding us of the contingent nature of meaning as texts traverse both geographical space and generational time. This adaptability has important ramifications for the Beats, mired as their reception has been in the cult of personality surrounding their lives and exploits. For those who were "there" during the Beat heyday or feel nostalgia for an unrecoverable moment of postwar reception, an examination of how texts are used by those who have never actually met a "Beat" offers exciting insights into how new readers receive Beat texts.[1] *Translating the Counterculture* likewise questions the idea of a univocal Beat message, arguing instead for a Beat Generation capable of generating numerous, if at times contradictory, meanings. An examination of the Turkish cultural translation of the Beats ultimately reveals that their power to raise issues, spark debate, and motivate reconsiderations of the status quo remains very much alive.

To fully understand the reception of the Beats in Turkey, *Translating the Counterculture* not only examines textual translation and its concomitant issues but also delves into paratextual materials that are essential to understanding how the Beats function in their displaced cultural context. It also codifies reader response by drawing on an empirical study of reader demographics and opinions conducted by the author. The function of the obscenity trial of Burroughs's text for both the government and its critics, for example, can be understood only through an analysis of court documents, press releases, jacket blurbs, journal articles in mainstream media, and in-depth interviews with those involved in the debate. Given that the appropriation of *The Soft Machine* and its trial in Turkey are taking place more than half a century after the book's initial publication, the trial highlights what is at stake when Beat texts are translated across both temporal and cultural gaps. Those using the book to combat what they believe are faults in Turkish society have been savvy in their use of the Internet, disseminating court documents and social commentary outside censored media channels to reach and gain support from a wider, and international, audience. *Translating the Counterculture* examines this online dissemination by exploring how medium affects the Beat message. Ultimately, this book explores how Turkish readers, editors, translators, and others interested in the Beats redeploy these texts in ways that are meaningful to local concerns. It is interested in *use*.

The investigation of how the Beats are appropriated in Turkey requires a transnational lens. There is no unanimous consensus on a definition of transnationalism, with each field approaching the term uniquely. But there is a broad sense in which the bordered, especially in regard to nation-states, is no longer adequate for understanding social processes. Transnationalism is characterized by a rejection of the idea that flows of people, goods, images, and cultural products are best understood by bound notions of space, region, or government. The term is perhaps best understood through a comparison with its competitors, the "international" and the "global."[2] *International* retains the idea of the nation as the final unit of measurement. Internationalist perspectives are thus concerned with how individuals, groups, movements, businesses, and texts circulate among national entities. The *global*, by contrast, transcends the nation-state as the unit of measurement but does so by positing a worldwide perspective that tends to universalize its subjects of inquiry. Such an approach, however, can easily result in homogenization, as local conditions are elided in favor of larger concerns. The transnational focuses on a smaller unit of measurement, examining how processes and flows affect particular areas in particular ways.

The transnational turn began in U.S. American studies in the 1990s as a means of critiquing the American-centeredness of the field.[3] This decentering of America as the main locus of discussion led to a thinking of American studies through other rubrics and constellations, such as the transnational, hemispheric, or Pan-American, with Paul Gilroy's *The Black Atlantic* being a paradigmatic example. This rethinking of the United States outside the borders of the nation-state was meant to raise questions of exceptionalism and imperialism that had been largely ignored in U.S. American studies.[4] Thus, in his book *American Studies in a Moment of Danger*, George Lipsitz argues that the "hegemony of the nation-state as the ultimate horizon in American studies leaves us poorly prepared to understand the ways in which culture functions as a social force or the ways in which aesthetic forms draw their affective and ideological power from their social location" (17). The hope is that displacing texts, writers, movements, and forms outside a strictly U.S. framework will illuminate the problems inherent in America-centric approaches and can point the way to other possibilities for thinking through the problematics in the field.

Reading its subjects into the gaps and tensions between cultural formations allows transnational inquiries to raise previously unexplored questions. Discussing the transnational mode in *Virtual Americas: Transnational Fictions and the Transatlantic Imaginary*, Paul Giles argues that "the subject must play off what is inside a framework defined as 'American' against what is outside it, thereby illuminating the ways specific local conditions and cultural landscapes reconstitute transnational networks in different ways" (11). The transnational works through a double move. Although the Beats are very much a product of the American society that produced them, their dissemination outside U.S. borders challenges the foundational myths ascribed them by providing a glimpse of other possible trajectories for their interpretation and deployment. Today, thanks in part to the rise of English as a global language and the instantaneous dissemination of information via the Internet, the Beats have become a worldwide phenomenon accessible across the world at the stroke of a key. But the Beats are not received in the same manner everywhere, as this book will demonstrate. An examination of the Turkish reception of the Beats thus provides insight into the possibilities of culturally translating an imported counterculture while simultaneously revealing the unquestioned assumptions underpinning the American countercultural model.

While the transnational turn is clearly an important development in American studies, it has been more difficult to pinpoint what constitutes this new approach. What exactly is the object of study here? In his introduction to *Re-Framing the Transnational Turn in American Studies*, Donald Pease discusses the extreme fluidity of the term, writing,

> The transnational enables such a wide range of articulations, ideas, and practices that are everywhere and universally incomplete that it requires the attribution of additional points of choice and strategies of purpose. Each contextualization of the transnational supplies a provisional meaning for a signifier whose significance solicits endless recontextualization. (6)

The term *transnational* is a signifier for an array of theoretical approaches and formulations, including but not limited to globalization, migration, influence studies, modernity, and diaspora. In addition, its objects of inquiry are equally diverse. The transnational can encompass a multitude of possible entities such as corporations, migrants, diasporic communities, and political organizations, as well as textual products. This study examines the repurposing of a group of Beat texts that have been collected under the banner of "underground literature" in Turkey. To understand this reception, *Translating the Counterculture* is concerned not only with the translation, marketing, and editorial commentary on the Beats but likewise with the attendant myths, conceptions, memes, and reappropriations that have followed in their wake. The point is not to compare the U.S. and Turkish receptions invidiously but to explore how the signifier "Beat" does cultural work. It is precisely in these ruptures and disjuncts where a better understanding of what we mean when we say "Beat" can emerge.

There is a danger, however, that reading the United States from outside its borders can result in a reification of the very exceptionalism that the transnational seeks to avoid. Pease's work, in particular, has been on guard against this very real threat. A discussion of the Beats' appeal outside the United States does run the risk of reifying their message as an exceptional moment of countercultural struggle. Although they provide a critique of U.S. capitalism and its social norms, an insistence on the universality of the Beats or their work as a premier site for dissent raises the specter of imperialism in an inverted form—the American counterculture becomes *the* model for countering the neoliberal order inaugurated by the United States itself. Transnational approaches often end up reinforcing the very notions of American exceptionalism and center-periphery models that they sought to critique. This study offers a novel way of thinking through questions of cultural appropriation and difference by focusing on the agency of readers, editors, translators, and others who adapt the Beats to local needs and thus make them their own. While most transnational Beat critiques are interested in how the Beats influenced or were influenced by postwar events, movements, and writers, this reception study looks at the Beats from the other side of the fence, exploring the possibilities for their work to be used in future moments of countercultural struggle rather than past questions of influence. The Beats are not here to "save the day" once again with their countercultural critique, but they offer an array of strategies, or tool kit of ideas, that users can select or discard according to their needs. These tools may, at times, seem particularly American, but their deployment in other contexts demonstrates the malleability of the Beat critique.

In Beat studies, this rethinking of the field beyond national borders has already begun. Unsurprisingly, perhaps, it was European Beat scholars who first undertook an examination of the Beats outside the American context. Jaap van der Bent explored Beat influence on European writers and movements even before transnationalism gained ground in the field. In his contribution to the coedited volume *Beat Culture: The 1950s and Beyond* (1999), for example, van der Bent traces the "reception and the assimilation of Beat literature in four countries: France, England, Germany and—last but not least—the Netherlands" (50). A. Robert Lee has likewise argued for what he terms a "Beat International." In *Modern American Counter Writing*, Lee discusses a Beat aesthetic that transcends national borders, claiming Beat was "an international phenomenon, and virtually from the start" (70). Collections such as Rudi Horemans's *Beat Indeed!* (1985) and Kostas Myrsiades's *The Beat Generation: Critical Essays* (2002), while not entirely devoted to transnational concerns, included numerous chapters dealing with the Beats beyond U.S. borders. While more studies could be named, thinking beyond the confines of the nation clearly has a firm foundation in Beat studies, in large part due to scholars working outside the United States.[5]

With the advent of the transnational turn, monographs dedicated to the subject began to appear. The focus of these volumes is varied, but they are all united in their attempt to draw on transnational concerns to help rethink the Beats and their contributions. Timothy Gray's *Gary Snyder and the Pacific Rim* (2006), for example, examined Snyder's relationship to Asia and its importance for the San Francisco writing community; Todd F. Tietchen's *The Cubalogues* (2010) looked at the Beat travel narratives of Lawrence Ferlinghetti, Amiri Baraka, and Allen Ginsberg; and Jimmy Fazzino's *World Beats: Beat Generation Writing and the Worlding of U.S. Literature* (2016) continues this trend of examining the Beats outside U.S. borders. The importance of Tangiers for the Beats, especially for William Burroughs, has inspired volumes like Greg Mullins's *Colonial Affairs: Bowles, Burroughs, and Chester Write Tangier* (2002), which examines the link between homosexuality and colonialism, and Brian T. Edwards's *Morocco Bound: Disorienting America's Maghreb, from Casablanca to the Marrakech Express* (2005), which explores the importance of Tangiers' political situation on *Naked Lunch*. Collections such as Davis Schneiderman and Philip Walsh's *Retaking the Universe: William S. Burroughs in the Age of Globalization* (2004) and special issues such as Chad Weidner and Polina Mackay's collection of essays in *Comparative American Studies* (2013) are further examples of this transnational impulse. Not all of these studies are laudatory, however. Manuel Luis Martinez's *Countering the Counterculture* (2003), for example, invidiously compares Beat mobility to that of the migrant. Nevertheless, Beat studies has embraced the transnational, and based on conference presentations and calls for papers, the trend seems to be continuing.[6]

The most emblematic of these studies of Beat transnationalism is Nancy M. Grace and Jennie Skerl's edited collection *The Transnational Beat Generation* (2012). The editors' introduction justifies and explains the importance of the transnational rubric for the field. The editors argue that the Beats were living in a time when the United States took on an active role internationally and, thus, Beat writing is very much responding "to globalizing forces, colonialism, US neo-imperialism, and postwar conformist repression" (7). This claim is undeniable—not only were the Beats absorbing, refracting, and reconfiguring the narratives of American exceptionalism prevalent in the Cold War, their work was also extensively influenced by their travels and sojourns outside the country. This expatriate experience had a lasting impact on both their own work and that of the artists and intellectuals with whom they came into contact. Given that the Beats and their work were bound up in the international, the editors rightly claim that the transnational approach is a necessary addition to existing scholarship on the Beats, as it helps us to think about Beat texts beyond existing paradigms.

Grace and Skerl's volume is an important contribution to the field, but it also highlights a problem rampant in Beat studies as a whole—its limited temporal approach. Though the editors claim to have a stake in the "trans-generational dimensions of Beat literature" (11) and argue that such texts have "continued to resonate for post–World War II generations around the world" (5), the focus remains exclusively on the early postwar period. Unfortunately, as in most scholarly studies, Beat influence here seems to end in the early 1970s, though the Beats and their texts continue to enjoy brisk sales and cultural circulation worldwide. What is lacking in the field is a consideration of what Beat means *today*. As important as past encounters and border crossings are for understanding the Beats and their work, the function that these texts serve in the present is equally relevant if we want to understand how their work can be appropriated for other generations in other parts of the world.

The tendency in Beat studies to focus on the postwar moment of the Beats' emergence runs counter to the myriad of trade publications designed to understand the lasting importance of the Beat legacy. A search of Amazon's website reveals over a hundred pages of books devoted to the Beats. Setting aside works by the Beats themselves, scholarly studies, and collections of primary sources, many of these works are cultural histories of the Beat movement and memoirs and biographies of Beat writers and fellow travelers that often rely heavily (or sometimes exclusively) on photographs in a nostalgic bid to preserve the Beats and their cultural milieu for posterity.[7] But a substantial number of books also seek to explain the continual relevance of the Beats. The titles, blurbs, and reviews of these books are telling. The reviewer of Mel Ash's *Beat Spirit* (1997), for example, claims the book is an "'interactive' self-help book aimed at Generation Xers who find themselves drawn to the philosophical and spiritual principles that inform Beat literature and art." The blurb for Stephen D. Edington's *The Beat Face of God: The Beat Generation as Spirit Guides* (2006) reads, "We need the Beats—now more than ever! They still guide us on our journeys of the spirit. Learn from these Holy Mis-Fits—and come alive!" Perhaps most emblematic, the back cover of John Leland's provocatively titled *Why Kerouac Matters: The Lessons of* On the Road *(They're Not What You Think)* (2008) argues that Kerouac's novel "still matters because it lays out an alternative road map to growing up." These texts, and others like them, make a pitch for the ongoing importance of the Beat legacy. The Beats are clearly being reproduced, and thus it makes sense to turn a scholarly eye to the ways in which the Beats are reentering the social field, both in the United States and outside its borders.

Beat scholarship has tended to focus on individual Beat authors and their contributions to particularly American postwar issues. When transnational issues do emerge, they revolve around studies of influence, cross-hybridization, and the impact of international experience on the Beats themselves. There has been, unfortunately, a dearth of scholarship that directly addresses how the Beats are received by larger readerships or the role translation plays in reception. This work seeks to redress that lacuna. Shelley Fisher Fishkin, in her often-cited presidential address to the American Studies Association, includes studies of cultural translation in her call for a more transnational approach to the field: "We need to understand the cultural work that forms originating in the United States do in cultures outside this country, studying their reception and reconfiguration in contexts informed by a deep understanding of the countries where that cultural work is taking place" (33). If the Beats are still a potential force for social and cultural change, as I believe they are, then it behooves critics to examine how the Beats' texts function in various contexts.

The Turkish reception provides an interesting example of what can happen to Beat ideas and concepts when they are received outside a strictly Western framework. A country that geographically, historically, and culturally seems to straddle East and West, Turkey has been burdened by two competing paradigms that seek to explain its global position. The more positive of these formulations sees Turkey as a "bridge" between the East and the West, while the more negative claims that Turkey's inability to reconcile these twin perspectives results in a land of "contradictions."[8] While it is certainly true that the West plays a crucial role in Turkey, these positions do not adequately capture the country's relationship to the West. As Sibel Irzık and Güven Güzeldere argue in their introduction to the important *South Atlantic Quarterly* special issue on Turkey, "Turkey is neither caught between nor a successful synthesis of an 'East' and a 'West.' It is, rather, a country in which many of the fundamental social divisions have been experienced, articulated, concealed, or displaced in a cultural/ideological vocabulary mobilizing 'West' in different power and justification strategies" (285). The Turkish situation therefore challenges easy notions of transnational flows. Western culture is not simply absorbed wholesale but is displaced and refracted through particularly Turkish concerns, systems, and institutions. This unique situation makes Turkey ideal for an examination of the Beat legacy. As we shall see, Beat concepts such as freedom, mobility, and the importance of the individual that may seem self-evident in a Western context become rearticulated when deployed in the Turkish context, and these cultural and temporal differences have an effect on the ways in which Beat texts are received. Reading the Beats into such gaps creates an opportunity for new perspectives to emerge.

While a detailed discussion of the history of Turkey is beyond the scope of this book, a brief sketch of several important historical developments is essential for developing the social context for understanding the Beat reception in Turkey. One figure stands at the center of modern Turkey: Mustafa Kemal. Known as Atatürk or "the father of Turkey," Mustafa Kemal was a highly successful military leader in the First World War who came to power in 1923, effectively ending autocratic rule by an Ottoman elite and establishing modern Turkey. Mustafa Kemal embarked on a vast modernization project that not only included a revamping of Turkey's political and economic structures but delved into cultural affairs as well. In addition to establishing elections and encouraging Western economic reforms, Mustafa Kemal gave women the right to vote, replaced the Ottoman script with the Latin in a bid to improve literacy, and separated religion and the state by dissolving the caliphate. This program drastically changed Turkey, and Kemalists, as supporters of such secularization policies came to be known, continued Mustafa Kemal's program of reforms after his death in 1938.

Despite Mustafa Kemal's success at modernizing the country along Western lines, Turkey's often turbulent history allowed few opportunities for the sort of cultural revolution that the Beats helped to foment in the postwar period in the United States. Mustafa Kemal and his party brooked little dissent, and multiparty democracy was allowed only in 1945, seven years after his death. With the advent of open elections came unrest, as political conflicts often boiled over into violence. The first of three major coups over the following years came in May 1960, when a group of military officers overthrew Adnan Menderes's Democrat Party. Menderes, a fairly popular ruler who beat the Kemalist Republican People's Party in an uncontested 1950 election, was driven from office and eventually executed despite international outcry. According to Feroz Ahmad in *Turkey: The Quest for Identity*, the officers were driven to action by "spiraling inflation, political instability, and a general sense of discontent in urban areas," a pattern that would become familiar in Turkish politics (117). Unfortunately, the new government fared no better, and the military again intervened in March 1971. Continued violence and economic collapse caused the military to step in yet again on September 12, 1980, dissolving parliament and declaring "a curfew, a ban on foreign travel and martial law throughout the country" (Pope and Pope 142). Such a climate of instability and the governmental repression that followed it disallowed any flourishing of the type of cultural politics the Beats promulgated.

The 1980 coup, however, was a watershed. A crackdown on demonstrations, political rallies, and propaganda sought to curtail direct insurrection. As Nurdan Gürbilek notes, "over five hundred people were sentenced to death, fifty of them executed; over a hundred died under torture; thousands lost their citizenship. Books, magazines and films were destroyed by the thousand" (4). Yet at the same time the Turkish government became more repressive, it also jettisoned its state-centered economy and entered the global marketplace. Along with greater economic exchange came an increased cultural exchange, and a new generation was able to connect with the world, allowing for the importation of both Western products and ideas. Despite attempts to reinforce Kemalist ideology through appeals to the nation and to the concept of a shared Turkishness, subversive material and ideas began making their appearance, and with the exception of a few limited translations in the 1960s and 1970s, it was during this opening to the West that the Beats first arrived through informative articles and translations of individual texts in 1990s rock-and-roll fanzines. With the rise of globalization and the Internet, access to the Beats increased exponentially, and today Western countercultural literature is readily available and enjoys a fairly widespread circulation. The importance of the 1980 coup cannot be overstated, and the event remains a touchstone for those discussing recent Turkish cultural history.

With direct political action suppressed, attention gradually moved toward the cultural as the realm for challenging the establishment. The 1980 coup was particularly important for marginalized groups who could now voice their concerns through nonpolitical channels. Followers of various Islamic practices, for instance, reemerged in the public sphere. Richard Tapper discusses how Mustafa Kemal suppressed Islam in his bid for a modern Turkey, arguing, "With the abolition of the Caliphate, the outlawing of the powerful Sufi *tarikats* (orders / brotherhoods) and the discouragement of the mystical forms of Islam, Turkish Islam in effect became more standardized, circumscribed and compartmentalized, while republican ideology and associated institutions came to dominate much of everyday life" (2). The Kemalists understood the utility of Islam in Turkey, and actively used it to solidify national identity. Yet resistance to such attempts remained, and after the 1980 coup Turkey saw "an apparent shift in government attitudes and a remarkable proliferation of religious newspapers, periodicals and other literature" (2–3).[9] Kurdish minority groups, whom Mustafa Kemal had sought to absorb under a broad banner of Turkish nationalism, asserted their own cultural, ethnic, and linguistic identities as well.[10] Women, too, began to voice their own concerns, and as Gürbilek adds, even "[h]omosexuals, almost never heard of in public, began to speak for themselves" (9).[11] All of these voices challenged the dominance of Kemalist discourse that purported to speak for each and every Turkish citizen.

This new form of cultural protest is very much alive in Turkey today, and can be clearly witnessed in the response to Recep Tayyip Erdoğan and his Justice and Development Party (AKP). Erdoğan rose to power as mayor of Istanbul (1994–98) by capturing the middle-class vote, and went on to become prime minister in 2003 in large part through his strong Anatolian base of religious voters. Opponents claim that after switching from the role of prime minister to that of president with another strong showing in an August 2014 election, he is now in the process of revising the constitution. But resistance to what many believe to be a growing

Islamicization of Turkey and a clampdown on personal freedoms has led to a continued protest against government policies and actions. As Ahmet Insel notes, "The AKP's defense of social justice is based on the strengthening of traditional relationships of charity and cooperation rather than the strengthening of individual and social rights. The AKP brings its conservatism to the foreground by emphasizing such traditions, especially those related to the family" (298). Insel's analysis was published in 2003, and since then the AKP has demonstrated an increasingly religious bent. Resistance to Erdoğan crystallized in the 2013 Gezi Park protests, which were composed of a broad range of social and cultural groups that sought to challenge Erdoğan's policies not in the political arena but rather through a public condemnation of what they saw as the ruling party's suppression of their freedom to live their lives as they saw fit.[12] The failed coup attempt by the Turkish military in 2016, however, has only emboldened Erdoğan and his followers. In such a climate of identity politics, the Beats have gained an afterlife, and provide an active optic to reflect on Turkish society and culture at a crossroads.

To complicate matters further, the majority of Turkish readers of Beat and other underground texts are youth whose world is different from that of those who received the Beat message in the twentieth century. Globalization and the widespread dissemination of information via the Internet and social media have changed the ways in which texts and writers are encountered and used. This phenomenon raises important issues for thinking about the reception and legacy of the Beat message. As James Clifford notes in *Routes: Travel and Translation in the Late Twentieth Century*, the globalized world produces uneven effects, "sometimes reinforcing, sometimes obliterating cultural, regional, and religious differences, gendered and ethnic divisions. Flows of immigrants, media, technology, and commodities have similarly uneven effects" (9). Unfortunately, Beat studies has mainly neglected to discuss the role technological change plays in understanding reception. As we have seen in light of the Arab Spring and Gezi Park events, social media plays a huge role in the ways in which information flows. Despite cultural and geographical distance, Turkish readers have much in common with worldwide youth due to the accessibility provided by new technology. As Irzık and Güzeldere observe, "the sense of belatedness and the fear of inauthenticity that accompanied the traumatic late-nineteenth-century encounter with the Western model have become complicated by a bewildering sense of simultaneity with the rest of the world" (285). To fully understand the possibilities for the Beat Generation given the prevalence of more easily digested and distributed forms of social media, an investigation of how the

Beats are articulated within the Internet and how generational differences impact social protest is an essential, if undeveloped, task.

These differences inflect the Beat message. Much has been made of the "in-between" spaces that erupt when cultures come into contact. These interstitial zones are often seen as the places where new meaning announces itself. Contrasting his approach to Jacques Derrida and Paul de Man, Homi Bhabha writes in *The Location of Culture*, "I am more engaged with the 'foreign' element that reveals the interstitial; insists in the textile superfluity of folds and wrinkles; and becomes the 'unstable element of linkage,' the indeterminate temporality of the in-between, that has to be engaged in creating the conditions through which 'newness comes into the world'" (326). Despite the importance of Bhabha's work in theorizing such cultural gaps, the Beat reception in Turkey operates under logics of *selection* rather than hybridity or newness. As we shall see throughout this work, while there are moments of gaps and slippages that offer the possibility for new concepts to enter Turkish cultural discourse, for the most part, the Turkish reception of the Beats is a matter of selecting certain readings over others, depending on immediate needs and interests. The ways in which the Beats are received in Turkey thus calls attention to the polyvocality of texts and their range of possible uses.

Turkey is the perfect site for conducting an inquiry into the relevance of the Beats because it allows us to see beyond the mainly Western reception that followed quickly on the heels of the Beat explosion in the late 1950s and that still tends to dominate the field. The European Beat reception, of course, has its own particularities, but as western countries largely sharing similar economic, social, and cultural institutions, the Beats were far more readily absorbed there. Turkish culture provides a sharper set of differences that allow for a more nuanced discussion of reception. More important, there is a resurgence of interest in Turkey, and this belatedness of reception offers a unique glimpse of the Beats entering the social field outside the moment of their postwar reception. Finally, the Beats are entering a contested and polarized social space that helps to reveal the viability of their countercultural message today. In Turkey, the Beats are being read, referenced, and used in ways that go beyond the purely literary. Such a unique situation offers the perfect opportunity to think about the Beats' global reception and lasting legacy to countercultural struggle, as well as the ways local reception can change the way we look at texts.

To fully understand the Beats' relevance to Turkey requires an objective appraisal of who is reading this material and why they are reading it. Thus a methodological approach novel to literary studies is called for. Typically, literary analysis proceeds from close readings of texts coupled with a theoretical framework that helps to make sense of the work. This book goes a step farther by employing the more quantitative methods of the social sciences as well as appeals to paratextual materials such as online discussions, government documents, personal interviews, and news reports. *Translating the Counterculture* is also informed by sociological research conducted as part of a Turkish-government-funded study designed to elucidate the readership of underground literature.[13] This novel approach is crucial for gaining a better understanding of how the Beats are received. According to John Carlos Rowe in *The New American Studies*, "We should acknowledge that a great deal of work in American Studies is conducted without statistical, clinical, demographic, and other forms of empirical evidence that would make this work both more convincing and more conversant with disciplines in the social, natural, physical, and health sciences" (xxvii). Understanding reader response can come only through a mixed method of inquiry that combines both traditional literary analysis with other modes of sociological investigation to provide a clearer picture of the role the Beats and their texts are playing in Turkey.[14]

This broadening of the scope of inquiry is not unheard of in literary studies. *Translating the Counterculture* follows in the wake of studies such as Janice Radway's classic work on Romance readers, Wendy Griswold's discussion of the writers and readers of Nigerian fiction, and Maria Damon's conception of the "micropoetic," all of which attempt to understand texts within a particular moment of cultural reception. Radway, whose book *Reading the Romance* is perhaps emblematic of the approach, is a touchstone for those interested in discussing reader response in a detailed and critical way. Employing interviews and questionnaires to examine reading habits, Radway relies on quantifiable data to understand "the way such cultural forms are embedded in the social life of their users" (8). While Radway is quick to admit that readers are by no means homogenous and each has their own particular and unique concerns, nevertheless "there are patterns or regularities to what viewers and readers bring to texts in large part because they acquire specific cultural competencies as a consequence of their particular social location" (8). This book employs a similar array of approaches to understand the reception of the Beats in Turkish culture, but is united with Radway and others who believe that uncovering how readers read is crucial for a full understanding of the "meaning" of texts. Ultimately, this study seeks to understand the ways in which Beat texts are used by Turkish readers, and to use those insights to examine U.S. and Western assumptions about the Beats, their work, and their legacy.

The reception of the Beats in Turkey is *interested*. Of course this is true of any translation. Beginning in the 1990s, the field of translation studies began to take an interest in the cultural and social dimensions of translation. Drawing on the poststructuralism of the period as well as developments in cultural studies, critics began to analyze the social effects of translation and its attendant ethical ramifications.[15] As Lawrence Venuti argues,

> Translation never communicates in an untroubled fashion because the translator negotiates the linguistic and cultural differences of the foreign text by reducing them and supplying another set of differences, basically domestic, drawn from the receiving language and culture to enable the foreign to be received there. The foreign text, then, is not so much communicated as inscribed with domestic intelligibilities and interests. The inscription begins with the very choice of a text for translation, always a very selective, densely motivated choice, and continues in the development of discursive strategies to translate it, always a choice of certain domestic discourses over others. (482)

Translating the Counterculture provides a concrete example of Venuti's point by examining how Beat texts are "brought over" both literally as texts to be read and figuratively as a concept that does a certain type of social work. "Beat," after all, is a strange term, signifying both a group of writers and their texts as well as an attitude or stance toward society.[16] While there are undoubtedly those reading the Beats as "literature" with a capital "L" or as examples of American cultural history, most readers, in both Turkey and the United States, read the Beats as part of an intervention into personal and social issues. Moreover, the Beats are not just a textual phenomenon. The foundation of Turkish reception is, of course, the texts of Beat writers, but a full understanding of their impact requires a broader discussion of how their cultural image has been received as well. The Beats exist as memes—nostalgic photographic images or quotes lifted from texts and interviews, to name only a few instantiations—that are repackaged yet again by editors, translators, fans, and others who circulate them for further consumption. *Translating the Counterculture* explores how the Beat message of resistance becomes translated into Turkish culture.

To understand the role Beat texts play in Turkey, it is crucial to trace their initial reception through the concept of the "underground." While some Beat poetry was translated as early as the 1960s in Turkish literary journals, the Beats' increased visibility in the culture really began much later, in the early 1990s. Following the easing of restrictions and access to foreign materials in the wake of the 1980 coup, nascent rock-and-roll fanzines provided readers with access to information about the Beats and translations of their works. But because the Beats were interspersed among other countercultural texts, editors needed a catchall term to describe this new form of cultural import; they settled on the "underground." This reception history is important for understanding the subsequent appropriation of the Beats in Turkey. The term *underground*, borrowed directly from Western countercultural tradition, describes a range of countercultural products, from bands like Led Zeppelin and Nirvana, to critical theorists such as Guy Debord, to film mavericks like David Lynch, as well as to the Beats and other postwar American countercultural writers and figures. In addition, while earlier underground products were exclusively Western imports, over time a home-grown Turkish variant has flourished, drawing on Western models while amending and updating them for a contemporary Turkish audience. The first chapter examines this Turkish reception to provide a context for the chapters that follow by unpacking a term that continues to provide a lens for understanding Beat texts in contemporary Turkey.

The importance of the term *underground* is that it signals a challenge to social, cultural, and artistic norms. Underground works are those that are hidden from "normal" society, and chapter 1 attempts to understand this challenge by examining the demographics and opinions of the genre's readers. The results of our study on the readership of underground literature helps to illuminate not only who is reading this material but, more important, what they are reading and their reasons for doing so. But the underground did not remain so for long. As readership increased, underground literature gained more widespread attention. While most coverage in the Turkish media dealt with reviews of new Beat translations, two prominent literary journals, *Varlık* (2005) and *Notos* (2011), ran a series of articles by publishers, editors, critics, and underground writers attempting to define "underground" and establish its importance. Two critical tendencies emerged from these dossiers (*dosyalar*): The underground was seen either as a group of texts with "dark" themes, characters, and storylines that transgress established norms or, as in the Soviet *samizdat* tradition, as illegally distributed clandestine material. Even as underground literature moves evermore firmly into the mainstream with each passing year, both of these interpretative strategies continue to foment debate in the press and among readers.

An examination of these key positions and their impact for Beat reception allows us to rethink the function of countercultural literature like Beat Generation texts and their possibilities and limitations for social critique today. Not only does the recourse to the adjective *dark* frame the reception of the Beats in more nihilistic terms, but by the mid- to late-2000s a fear emerges that underground literature has developed beyond a point of no return. Whereas earlier the influx of subversive material signaled the potential for underground resistance, now the predominance of commodification is seen as having rendered such forms of rebellion moot in Turkey. For many, this change is due in large part to the rise of the Internet, which helped destroy fanzine culture and undermined a sense of shared solidarity. This discussion impinges directly on our understanding of the Beat legacy. Is there still hope for the sort of countercultural struggle the Beats waged, or has that moment passed? Many older Turkish critics, who think of rebellion in terms of direct social action, view underground literature as a useful but ultimately insufficient instrument for change. But for a burgeoning youth culture that is the primary audience for the Beats, underground literature's ability to foment a revolution in cultural attitudes and opinions is the real engine of social amelioration.

To better understand the attraction of underground literature, the second chapter examines the preeminent Beat journal in Turkey and the readers who support it: *Underground Poetix*. Put out by the important Beat publishers 6:45 (also spelled out Altıkırkbeş), *Underground Poetix* draws on earlier countercultural publications in terms of themes, style, and layout but updates the Western alternative press for their contemporary Turkish audience. To do so, the editors rely on a punk-inspired, anything-goes, do-it-yourself fanzine style. The result is a journal that offers an eclectic stance against the mainstream. The Beats figure prominently but are also placed alongside other countercultural figures from a variety of temporal periods and geographical locations. Readers can go from Ralph Waldo Emerson to punk rock to an analysis of Turkish pornography to the Beats in the span of several pages. This "cocktail" of rebellion is meant to both educate those unfamiliar with the countercultural tradition and simultaneously inculcate a shared sense of transgression against cultural, artistic, social, and in some cases, legal norms. *Underground Poetix* places the Beats at the center of a desire to form a community of like-minded individuals who feel that their thoughts, opinions, and beliefs cannot be adequately expressed in existing Turkish forums.

An examination of *Underground Poetix* reveals the ways in which the Beats have been repurposed for a contemporary Turkish audience. But the journal's heavy reliance on reader-generated poetry also reveals what Beat fans have done with this countercultural message. The underground press in the West was meant as an "alternative" to mainstream media outlets that many believed were unsympathetic to countercultural concerns.

These journals, newspapers, and pamphlets were designed to build solidarity among those outside the mainstream culture by disseminating information, sharing views, and allowing those with similar interests to join together for mutual causes. *Underground Poetix* follows this spirit of camaraderie by offering its readers a chance to voice their own concerns in the pages of the journal. Publishing poems exactly how they were written from readers spread throughout Turkey, *Underground Poetix* creates a textual community within its pages where readers feel free to express their emotions, thoughts, and beliefs without fear of reprisal or rejection. Given the countercultural thrust of the journal, most of these poems are assaults on Turkish social and cultural norms. Analyzing the sorts of issues raised in this reader-driven poetry provides insight into the preoccupations of Beat enthusiasts in Turkey, as the social critiques contained within the journal's pages become reworked by readers into critiques of religious fundamentalism, unequal gender relations, and the plight of Turkey's ethnic minorities, among other touchstone issues.

Having laid the foundation for an understanding of the cultural complexities at work in the Turkish reception of the Beats, *Translating the Counterculture* now turns its focus to the reception of the Beat texts that have received the most attention. Chapter 3 examines the ways in which that postwar countercultural classic of exuberance, Jack Kerouac's influential *On the Road* (1957), has been received in Turkey. Through an analysis of student and reader responses, interviews with translators and publishers, an examination of both online and print media, and comparisons with the Turkish road film, this chapter explores what Turkish audiences make of this particularly American novel. *On the Road* is well known and well respected in Turkey but often encounters resistance or bewilderment, as cultural differences render some of its countercultural messages difficult to implement in the Turkish context. Ultimately, however, such difficulties are productive, as they provide an opportunity to understand how the logics of a particular cultural moment become translated into other contexts. Taking *On the Road* to Turkey allows us to better see the assumptions that both the novel and its readers are making.

For many living in the containment culture of the 1950s, reading Kerouac's novel was a transformational event. *On the Road* opened up a new way to live, a new way to write, and even a new way to think. Despite its revolutionary nature, the novel nevertheless draws on particularly American themes that are not always so easily transferable to other cultural moments. Take, for example, Kerouac's stress on individuality. Through the character of Dean Moriarty, *On the Road* replaces postwar social expectations involving work, marriage, and family with the freedom to pursue personal desire in every moment. But the novel's reception in Turkey provides an opportunity to reexamine the nature and function of this "freedom." Dean's extreme individualism meets resistance in this more collectivist culture. The idea of personal mobility, as the title suggests, draws on a history of U.S. territorial expansion and is one of the lasting legacies of *On the Road.* Yet here again the notion of the "freedom" of movement is problematic in Turkey, as the numerous extratextual discussions of the term *hobo* in the Turkish reception makes clear. Finally, *On the Road* is an optimistic book. While the carefree and pleasure-driven lifestyle Dean epitomizes becomes more and more problematic upon subsequent re-readings (usually later in life), Kerouac's novel was nevertheless written in a particularly affluent period of U.S. history and is infected with the optimism of the times. Given Turkey's volatility, and indeed the increased economic uncertainties worldwide, the novel's Turkish reception complicates *On the Road*'s anti-consumerist stance in interesting ways.

Translating the Counterculture is not interested in simply recording the places where *On the Road* breaks down in Turkey. The argument here is that it is precisely these disjuncts, where cultural translation comes to the fore, that allow everyone, Turkish and Western readers alike, to think about the assumptions behind our reading. The meaning of these difficulties in reception is instructive. For some readers, the difficulty of implementing the sort of lifestyle changes chronicled in Kerouac's novel means that *On the Road* becomes read as a spiritual rather than a literal quest. For others in the underground scene, it is precisely these moments of cultural dissonance that offer a chance for Turkey to become more individualistic, more mobile, or perhaps even more optimistic. One of the most interesting aspects of *On the Road* is its provocative nature—readers seem forced to take a stand on the book. For many women and ethnic minority readers, Kerouac's novel is extremely problematic in its character depictions. In Turkey, many women readers have voiced similar concerns, allowing us to talk not only about cultural differences but also about similarities in interpretation across cultures. Finally, such a displacement is by no means unidirectional—Kerouac himself maps his anxieties and concerns onto a mythic "East" throughout the novel as he registers unease about Dean's lifestyle. Thus reading *On the Road* in the space between cultures makes the assumptions that have accreted around the novel, and the cultural work those assumptions perform, more visible.

Chapter 4 continues this strategy of reading the Beats into the space between cultures by examining the obscenity trial of William S. Burroughs's novel *The Soft Machine* (1961) and the cultural response it has created. The trial began in 2011 when the Turkish government's Committee for the Protection of Minors from Harmful Publications decided that Burroughs's work posed a threat to Turkish youth. While the committee claimed it was protecting the interest of minors, appeals to courtroom proceedings, government reports, and media coverage of the trial demonstrate that the trial was an attempt to police the morals of the country. In the end, the trial was really about the controversial topic of homosexuality. The committee sought to uphold cultural values founded on family, fatherhood, and nation, and Burroughs's text, replete with homoerotic depictions, presented a challenge to Turkish norms established on heteronormative principles. In many ways, the obscenity trial of *The Soft Machine* is analogous to the sort of reception Burroughs's famous book *Naked Lunch* (1959 in France, 1962 in the United States) received in the States roughly a half century earlier. The Turkish trial process followed logics similar to those of the censorship trials of *Naked Lunch* and Ginsberg's *Howl* and, like those earlier trials, has also led to increased publicity for and sales of the book. But *The Soft Machine*'s Turkish reception also presents important differences. While promoters of the book have helped Burroughs's text achieve an afterlife in Turkey, they have done so by highlighting certain aspects of his life and work over others in an effort to harness *The Soft Machine* to their cause. While the result is not inaccurate, it is also, like all cultural translations, interested.

The increased visibility of Burroughs's text is due to a dedicated group of publishers, translators, and readers who have taken it upon themselves to publicize the trial of *The Soft Machine* in order to raise awareness of both government censorship and Turkish homophobia. Through press releases, Facebook pages, book jacket blurbs, and other media outlets, supporters of the book have used the committee's own words against it by publishing its statements and reports in an effort to raise awareness of the problematic nature of its claims. But the ways in which Burroughs and his text are framed for a Turkish audience shed light on what is at stake in such appropriations. The trial has sparked interest in Burroughs, and the media has responded with biographies of the man and his work. For the most part, Burroughs receives deferential treatment. He is typically represented as the older, more respectable leader of the Beats rather than as the homosexual, drug-taking rebel who challenges all manner of authority and control. This portrayal makes sense, given that supporters want to make Burroughs a sympathetic figure while shifting culpability to the committee. Such decisions, however, have ramifications for how his work is received. While all those involved in the Turkish discussion of Burroughs agree that his work is important, his literary contributions are downplayed in favor of the social messages of his texts. *The Soft Machine* is important in Turkey because it opens up discussions of homosexuality, not because its "cut-up" style is innovative.

The role that the Internet has played in supporters' attempts at disseminating information about the trial also factors into the reception of Burroughs's work. Not only does the Internet allow supporters to circumvent media outlets that might be unsympathetic to their message, but it also provides a forum for a delicate topic like homosexuality to be discussed in Turkey. This change in the medium of delivery is an important consideration that remains undiscussed in Beat studies. The importance of the Internet for the future dissemination of the Beats and their texts to their primarily young audience will only increase, and thus it is worth considering how medium affects the Beat message. The obscenity trial of *The Soft Machine* thus offers a useful case study of what happens when Beat texts are repurposed with specific goals in mind.

Key to understanding the Beat reception in Turkey is an appreciation of the ways in which local conditions and needs determine the particular aspects of the Beats that become highlighted. The final chapter of *Translating the Counterculture* examines both the textual and the cultural translations of Allen Ginsberg to reveal why particular versions of Ginsberg and his texts are promoted at particular times as well as what these selections have to tell us about the possibilities for his legacy. In many ways, Ginsberg is the perfect figure for appropriation. Through his long and multifaceted career, he cultivated a variety of personae that are highly amenable to adaptation and translation. An analysis of which of these personae are picked up and which are ignored is telling. In the Turkish context, almost all aspects of Ginsberg are borrowed at some point, but those appropriations are highly dependent on the needs of the moment. The same holds true for translations of Ginsberg's poetry. Translations have received little attention in Beat studies, but an analysis of the choice of poems to be translated as well as the decisions of the translator have much to tell us about the potential the Beats hold for those outside the English-speaking world who want to harness the Beat message for social change.

Chapter 5 begins with a discussion of three translations of Ginsberg's famous poem *Howl* (1956) and the paratextual materials that accompany them. Ginsberg was translated early, but the first book-length translation, Orhan Duru and Ferit Edgü's 1976 *Amerika* (*America*), bundled a selection of Ginsberg poems with those of Lawrence Ferlinghetti to offer Turkish readers a political Ginsberg that drew on his leftist and antiestablishment credentials. As interviews with those involved in the translation indicate,

Ginsberg's work offered Turkish intellectuals of the period a means to be both socially engaged and literary. But as direct political struggle changed over to more cultural critique with the 1980 coup, the presentation of Ginsberg's *Howl* in Turkish changed as well. Hakan Arslan's 1991 version, while acknowledging this earlier, political Ginsberg, offers more intimate access to Ginsberg the man. Arslan is committed to the communist cause, but he filters that commitment through his personal relationship to Ginsberg's texts. The Ginsberg that emerges from his translation is therefore more personal. Şenol Erdoğan's 2013 translation draws on Ginsberg's hipster credentials and spiritual concerns to offer his readers a portrait of Ginsberg as guru. Fusing Ginsberg's spiritual interests with the Eastern mysticism of Jalāl ad-Dīn "Mevlana" ar-Rūmī's Sufism and drawing out the transgressive moments in *Howl* such as (homo)sexuality and drug use, Erdoğan harnesses Ginsberg to the publishing house 6:45's countercultural cause. As local conditions change over time, so do versions of Ginsberg.

This chapter broadens the notion of translation beyond that of transferring a text from one language to another, examining how Ginsberg is "brought over" to Turkey in ways other than literary. The career of küçük iskender, or "little Alexander," provides an illuminating example of Ginsberg's influence on a younger Turkish poet. Küçük iskender is perhaps the best-known underground poet in Turkey. He is also the country's most notorious. Openly gay, küçük iskender flaunts his homosexuality as well as his use of drugs and alcohol. The poet draws on the Beats, especially Ginsberg, for both his literary inspiration as well as his assault on Turkish social values, mentioning them explicitly in interviews and referencing Ginsberg in poems such as "Türkiye" ("Turkey"), which borrows directly from Ginsberg's "America." Given the attention küçük iskender receives in Turkey, his constant referencing of Ginsberg and the Beats functions as an inadvertent advertisement for their countercultural position, raising their profile as iconoclasts for both readers of his work and those who condemn him.

Ginsberg's presence in Turkish culture is felt in other ways as well. Though references to Istanbul are found throughout many Beat texts, interestingly enough Ginsberg is the only Beat writer, besides his partner, Peter Orlovsky, to have actually visited the country. In all his travels, Ginsberg made a point of engaging local writers and artists in an attempt to fully understand the country, and his visit to Turkey was no exception. Ginsberg met with several Turkish poets and ended up collaborating with Can Yücel on a poem during one of the evenings. Despite some miscommunication—Ginsberg wanted to discuss human rights and drug issues, while his hosts were interested in poetry—Ginsberg's visit was productive and resulted in several articles in the Turkish press as well as fodder for anecdotes and fond reminiscences for the Turkish poets present. Ginsberg's visit demonstrates that despite the difficulties in cross-cultural exchange, such moments of cultural translation offer unique opportunities for everyone to reassess their thoughts and assumptions.

When the Beats first burst onto the postwar scene they were branded as rebellious outsiders who purposely transgressed social and literary standards. While the Beats' original moment of reception has passed, that image has lingered. Those of us in the academy have fought hard for acceptance, acknowledging but often downplaying Beat iconoclasm to recuperate the Beats and their texts as legitimate objects of literary study. This battle seems to have been won, as Beat titles are now reissued as "modern classics" and have found their way onto college syllabi and into scholarly monographs and articles. Yet it is undeniable that many readers (and critics as well) consider these texts as blueprints for action. The reason the Beats have remained so visible is that they offer readers a chance to rethink their relationship to the world around them, providing new models for living, thinking, and resisting. To understand the Beats in all their complexity, we must critically examine not only how Beat texts function as literary objects but also how they enter into the social field to do cultural work. How exactly do Beat texts help negotiate responses to ongoing social problems and issues? And how do they respond to frighteningly new problems that the Beats themselves could not have anticipated? What fate is in store for a mid-twentieth-century countercultural model as it enters a new moment of reception: renewed relevancy, nostalgic longing, or fading obscurity? Examining the Turkish reception of the Beats allows us to raise those questions and, in the process, begin to think about the cultural legacy of the Beats in the globalized twenty-first century.

1. LABELING A PHENOMENON
THE BEATS AS "UNDERGROUND" FIGURES

The act of naming something is an attempt to fix meaning and stabilize interpretation. But the associations that accumulate around names are never so easily contained. The history of the term *Beat* itself provides an illustration. The term's most obvious reference is to music. Given the Beat Generation's veneration of the jazz lifestyle and aesthetic, this connotation makes quite a bit of sense. But *Beat* was also used to refer to the idea of being beaten by society. Drawing on the underworld associations of the term taught them by the junky and hustler Herbert Huncke, Beats such as Jack Kerouac, William Burroughs, and Allen Ginsberg chronicled this demimonde in their work. But the term's allusions were easily malleable. As the Beat Generation became more visible in U.S. culture during the late 1950s, *Beat* entered the popular lexicon. San Francisco journalist Herb Caen, in order to disparage this new movement, added a Russian suffix to arrive at *Beatnik*, a term that was then appropriated by the mass media and the counterculture alike. To combat this negative stereotype, Kerouac countered that *Beat* comes from the Biblical beatitudes, adding a spiritual dimension to the movement. Even within the Beat Generation, there is no consensus on the term's meaning, and many writers deny they are "Beat" at all. The debate continues in academia. Despite there being both a European Beat Studies Network and a U.S.-based Beat Studies Association, many scholars are uneasy with an overarching term that includes such different writers within its rubric. While the term *Beat* has been in wide circulation since the late 1950s, its meaning is still the subject of debate.[1]

In Turkey the reception of the Beats has been influenced by their refraction through yet another label. The Beats are seen as examples of "underground literature" (*yeraltı edebiyatı*), a broad term borrowed from American countercultural discourse after the 1980 coup in an attempt to classify texts that were challenging social and literary expectations. The term began as a means to categorize imported foreign texts, but Turkey quickly developed its own underground scene, and the concept now denotes both foreign and domestic works. Underground literature is meant to provide an expansive rubric that can collect all manner of transgressive works that have no other generic classification in the culture. That the term is borrowed from the West itself and appears in both English and in Turkish is a sign of the amorphous nature of the concept. While the Turkish term is a literal translation of the English (*yer* is "ground," *alt* means "under"), the cultural translation of the Beats through the prism of the underground concept has created intense debate in Turkey as critics, writers, editors, and fans debate the term's meaning, relevance, and function.

The discussion that surrounds the term "underground literature" and its use demonstrates that the concept, like the term *Beat* itself, is far from stable. Readers and critics wonder how the Beats compare with their own local underground literary products, and what Beat texts might have to contribute to larger social issues under consideration in Turkey. Many involved in the debate even question the underground's very existence. Yet it is precisely this volatility that allows a rethinking of what *Beat* signifies as a classificatory rubric and the functions such texts can serve. The fact is that we need labels. There needs to be a means of categorizing and explaining, if only to allow the beginning of a discussion about what the term itself struggles to encapsulate. This chapter examines the debate over the underground in Turkey and the Beats' place within this rubric. Such a discussion is beneficial not only because it provides a glimpse into Turkish preoccupations but also because it offers the possibility of taking another look at the assumptions typically made about the Beats and the potential impact they hold for cultural change. An examination of the reception of the Beats as "underground" figures in Turkey thus provides a new frame for examining the Beat legacy.

THE AMERICAN UNDERGROUND

What exactly does *underground* mean? The term needs unpacking. As a spatial notion, the "underground" is clearly meant to project the image of the hidden or the buried. If the ground is the space on which humans live, that which is under it must represent something outside normal, quotidian existence. Yet this hiddenness quickly becomes overdetermined with possible implications. Is this material hidden underground because it is unacceptable, or because there are factions or individuals who do not want it revealed? Here the insinuation is that underground literature is dangerous and volatile, like nuclear material not meant to be unearthed. Or is it something desirable to be unearthed and consumed later, hidden away from prying eyes that might want to appropriate it for themselves? Perhaps the underground is simply the only place where clandestine thoughts or opinions can live. The metaphor itself provides no answer, and one wonders whether the popularity of *underground* as a term stems from its ability to allow so many divergent approaches to find a single, common label.[2]

The ambiguity begins with the term's history. While the underground is most often associated with the countercultural 1960s in the United States, the "hippies" in fact reappropriated the term from earlier political discourse. Sean Stewart, in his *On the Ground: An Illustrated Anecdotal History of the Sixties Underground Press in the U.S.*, makes this link explicit. For Stewart, *underground* is a word that "identified anti-Fascist forces behind enemy lines of the Second World War" (x). Such resistance was initially glamorized by Hollywood, but after the war the "Cold War mood minimized the role of the underground, insisting that Allied troops had little assistance from behind the lines" (x), partly to bolster the image of a successful military campaign and also because the Resistance was tainted by communist sympathies that had become ideologically suspect. In the spirit of 1960s dissent, the counterculture picked up the term and applied it to a movement that criticized containment culture. Just as an earlier Resistance movement worked behind enemy lines, the 1960s counterculture sought to undermine the mainstream from *within*.

What came to be called the underground press was a crucial component of this assault on the established order, because it formed an ancillary information distribution system. Abe Peck, in his foreword to *Voices from the Underground*, traces the countercultural underground press to 1964 and the *Los Angeles Free Press*, and then to the *Berkeley Barb* and the *Paper* in Lansing, Michigan. Others soon followed, and the underground press became an important voice of the counterculture until at least 1973. At the time, the mainstream press had a stranglehold on information. According to John McMillan in *Smoking Typewriters: The Sixties Underground Press and the Rise of Alternative Media in America*, "By 1962 twelve managements controlled one-third of the circulation of newspapers in the United States" (8). The underground press challenged this hegemony by allowing small groups in local places to produce their own news that was better suited to their outlook and concerns. Due to a technological change in printing, producing a newspaper came within reach of the public. According to McMillan, "all one needed was a competent typist, a pair of scissors, and a jar of rubber cement" (6). This do-it-yourself attitude allowed countercultural voices intimately involved in the struggles against mainstream culture direct access to a small, but growing, segment of the U.S. public.

Yet the exact implications of the term *underground* are still the subject of debate. Though he discusses their underground distribution, McMillan claims that the term *underground* was used for these publications not because they actually circulated as illegal *samizdat* but rather because the first of them "appealed to self-styled cultural outlaws" (6). Mimeographed publications, broadsides, campus newspapers, and "underground comix" were sold predominantly in head shops and local bookstores that catered to a young crowd fed up with Cold War culture and who questioned many of the assumptions handed to them by an earlier generation. Stewart concludes that this "underground press provided real news and insight on the war in Viet Nam, events abroad, and protest movements at home that could not be published" (xiv). It also became the vehicle for those whose voices were silenced by the mainstream: "black power, Indian, Asian-American, and Latino movements given only hostile treatment within the mainstream, and after 1970 in most places, feminist, gay, and lesbian movements and personalities as well" found vent in the underground press (xiv). McMillan argues that these papers were very subversive, "flouting society's conventions and, by the late 1960s, championing the revolutionary overthrow of the United States government" (6). This era also gave rise to the "New Journalism," which purported that only those participating in the events as they unfolded could legitimately comment on them. Underground, here, also signifies an emerging attitude and belief system directly at odds with the mainstream.

But the concept of the underground traveled, informing other contexts, and this process of translation reveals the slippery nature of the term. In his book *An Introduction to Underground Film*, Sheldon Renan attributes the term to film critic Manny Farber's essay "Underground Film" (1957), which defends the B-films made in Hollywood from the 1930s through the 1950s. Renan goes on to attempt an updated explanation of the term's meaning: "It is a film conceived and made essentially by one person and is a *personal statement* by that person. It is a film that dissents radically in form, or in technique, or in content, or perhaps in all three. It is usually made for very little money, frequently under a thousand dollars, and its exhibition is outside commercial film channels" (17). Renan's definition is anything but precise. Underground film is a personal statement and is thus in tune with the highly subjective nature of the counterculture. But more important, underground film "dissents." How exactly does it dissent? Renan is unclear, and goes on to qualify the definition by discussing the term's connotation of low-budget production, as well as its distribution and consumption outside mainstream channels. Such confusion over how to define the term is not the fault of Renan, however, since "underground" is quickly overdetermined by the multifarious possibilities it invokes. As we shall see, there are many ways for something to be underground, and not all of them are mutually exclusive.

Underground was also a useful term for the counterculture, since it implied a more indirect form of resistance. Juan A. Suárez, writing approximately thirty years later than Renan, attempts to come to terms with the label of underground in his work *Bike Boys, Drag Queens, and Superstars: Avant-Garde, Mass Culture, and Gay Identities in 1960s Underground Cinema.* Suárez sees the underground cinema of the 1950s and 1960s as an "echo" of the European avant-garde in the 1920s and 1930s but ultimately differentiates the former by its concern with the role of "commodified cultural forms" as well as its gay sensibilities (xvi–xvii). Despite filmmaker and critic Jonas Mekas dating the origin of the term to a 1961 speech of Marcel Duchamp in which the master of surrealism claims that "the only solution for the artist of tomorrow is to go underground," Suárez notes that the term had its own U.S. trajectory (81–82). Suárez claims that the "notion of an 'underground scene' had been put forward by some of the beats themselves," referencing Kerouac's novel *The Subterraneans* and quoting Andrew Ross's claim that the Beats' desire to go underground "had as much to do with the recent McCarthyist victimization of the identifiable left as it had to do with a romantic infatuation with the nihilist vanguardism of Dostoyevsky's *Notes from Underground*" (82).[3] The underground, in Ross's view, was also a site of shelter. As with the Beats' refusal to directly engage politically, the underground in cinema became a site for resistance, challenging the mainstream by turning their own cultural forms against them. This is the beginning of the postmodern, where reference to popular culture becomes just as important as invoking canonical texts. Citing experimental filmmaker Stan Van Der Beek's claim that "artists, poets, experimenters in America, must work as if they were secret members of the underground," Suárez concludes that these postwar artists were engaged in a sort of clandestine "guerilla warfare" against the popular culture occurring above them (83).[4] In the most extreme cases, such as the 1960s revolutionary group the

Weather Underground, dissent can and did become violent. But for the majority, remaining underground offered protection from the vicissitudes of early Cold War culture.

The rise of the term *Beat* masks the extent to which the Beats were themselves involved in the underground. As Suárez notes above, the term appears in Kerouac's work and finds echoes in Ginsberg's "mad ones" who live underground lives in the "negro streets" of his poem *Howl.* The Beats were familiar with many of the underground figures in the New York cinema scene, and even contributed to film projects like *Pull My Daisy* (1959; dir. Robert Frank and Alfred Leslie) and the cult classic *Chappaqua* (1966; dir. Conrad Rooks). Even less documented is the Beats' connection to the underground press. Bob Hippler, in his contribution to *Voices of the Underground* titled "Fast Times in the Motor City: The First Ten Years of the Fifth Estate, 1965–1975," lists some of the names included in a 1973 issue called "The Roots of the Underground" and includes Beat authors Lawrence Ferlinghetti, Ginsberg, Kerouac, LeRoi Jones (Amiri Baraka), Burroughs, and Diane di Prima (30). As we shall see in the next chapter, some Beats like Di Prima, Ginsberg, and Gary Snyder contributed directly to the underground papers of the time. The underground press, in its turn, lauded these countercultural "stars." Hugh Fox, in his "The Living Underground" column in the *North American Review*, claims that "Charles Bukowski is the acknowledged King of the Underground" and was "elected 'Outsider of the Year' by *Outsider* mag[azine]" (57). The idea of an underground space existing outside the mainstream where like-minded individuals could fully express their dissatisfaction with Cold War culture was partly a result of Beat challenges to the dominant culture in the 1950s. As the 1960s counterculture solidified, these earlier Beats were hailed as predecessors who helped to map out this underground terrain that later dissenters found so useful.

The repackaging of the Beats under the "underground" label is important because it demonstrates the continued viability of the Beats' antiestablishment message. While the term *underground* is difficult to define, all of its permutations involve the idea of a challenge to the established order "above ground." In their own moment of reception, the iconoclastic Beats intersected with other underground figures and movements because of a shared desire to challenge the Cold War containment culture of the 1950s and 1960s. Perhaps because of the media attention the Beats received, the underground context of their work became less apparent. The term *Beat* became a more visible rubric, to be replaced by *hippy* as the 1960s wore on. Reinscribing Beat texts within the underground framework in Turkey helps us to take another look at the ways in which those texts foster social change.

THE UNDERGROUND'S ARRIVAL IN TURKEY

The history of the term *underground* in Turkey can be understood only as part of a large-scale shift in Turkish culture that occurred after the 1980 coup. Before this watershed moment in Turkish history, dissent was political, with a Marxist left vying with a nationalist right in often violent clashes. Following the military intervention in 1980 designed to establish order and stability, dissent started to appear in the cultural realm for two key reasons. First, government crackdowns made direct political action far more difficult. More important perhaps, although Turkey and the Ottoman Empire had previously enjoyed cultural exchange with the West, there was a government push to open Turkey to foreign markets that resulted in a wave of cultural imports. The idea of underground resistance, although not unknown previously, became a useful concept that helped to theorize and explain the role that certain texts had to play in challenging the dominant order through cultural, rather than political, critique. Those interested in such works needed a means of thinking about a group of texts that seemed to do something different from what was typically expected from literature and the arts. *Underground* became a term that captured the sense that certain texts lie outside what are perceived to be the standard literary norms for society and thus had the chance to provide an indirect critique of prevailing social expectations.

The shift from the political to the cultural involved the changing role of youth in Turkish culture. Following a more liberal constitution in 1960, youth culture became more politicized in Turkey. Divided into rightist and leftist groups, students engaged in violent clashes that led to the seizure of power by the military in the 1980 coup. With political dissent effectively silenced, Turkey embarked on a more capitalist model economically while retaining traditional values of nation, family, and neighborhood socially. But a tension emerged. The consumerist approach to the economy, which exalted the role of the individual and the freedom to define one's own interests, was in direct conflict with the older model of Turkish collectivism that envisioned an individual's role as a supporter of the Turkish nationalist project. Although many lamented this change, as sociologist Leyla Neyzi, in her article "The Construction of 'Youth' in Public Discourse in Turkey" writes, "the denigrated 'individualism' of young people seems to be about their hesitancy in linking their subjective identities and lifestyles to a single national project. A future-oriented modernist conception of time (the time of the nation) is being replaced by an orientation in the present (the time of the self/body)" (112). The cultural sphere thus became the realm of struggle and dissent, and lifestyle choice replaced political affiliation as the preferred mode of resistance.

The Beats were ideally positioned to contribute to this change. For the most part, they eschewed political engagement in favor of cultural critique and a broad attempt to raise the consciousness of an American population at midcentury. Their motivations can be traced to the containment culture of the 1950s that heavily penalized marginal behavior, as well as to the discrediting of the Marxist left after World War II. Senator Joseph McCarthy's anticommunist campaigns in the early 1950s are perhaps the best-known attack on communism, but the Stalinist purges, the Nazi-Soviet Pact of 1939, the need to support the U.S. war effort in World War II, and the emergence of the Cold War all contributed to the decline of what came to be called the "Old Left" in the United States. Equating communism with deviance, postwar U.S. ideology instead stressed conformity. The Beats, who championed individual freedom and personal expression, found this culture of containment as stifling as dogmatic Marxism. Rather than formulating another political system, the Beats instead opted to respond through work meant to challenge the rigid thinking of the times.

In pre-1980-coup Turkey, however, the Old Left remained viable. As editor İrfan Sancı of Sel Publishing explains, Beat works "had a lesser influence in Turkey because around the same time the political scene developed more" (Sancı interview). Earlier Turkish leftists had little use for the sort of cultural critique the Beats were offering, opting instead for direct political action that often took violent forms. In fact, when the Beats were discussed in Turkey, often it was in attempts to recover them as leftist critics of capitalism, as we shall see in the chapter 5 discussion of Ginsberg's *Howl.* Though the Beats' work had been translated and discussed before the 1990s, their approach was not well suited to a pre-coup Turkey. But after the 1980 coup, their work took on added resonance. As a later Turkish public began to take interest in the cultural as the sphere of critique, the Beats reemerged as perfect models for this "new" type of dissent.

The reception of the Beats as underground literature in Turkey initially involved associating them with another rebellious Western product: rock-and-roll music and the subculture it produced. The Beats first appeared in magazines like *Çalıntı* that were devoted to rock music but would also include other transgressive cultural imports. The October–November 1993 issue of *Çalıntı*, for example, includes original articles by Turkish writers tracing the history, influences, and importance of the Beats as well as translated informative articles from non-Turkish authors, translations of Beat poetry by Gregory Corso, Michael McClure, and Lawrence Ferlinghetti, and several poems by Ginsberg. The issue also includes some prose selections from Burroughs and Kerouac (figure 1.1). This dossier (*dosya*) format would become a staple of Turkish underground publishing. Subsequent issues of such journals as well as more highbrow literary publications like *Kitap-Lık* would routinely include a host of translations along with informative and biographical pieces (often, but not exclusively, in Turkish) that sought to provide a brief overview and introduction of the Beats to Turkish audiences. Even the now venerable underground publisher 6:45, in its appropriately titled publication *Underground Poetix*, typically follows this format today.

Fig. 1.1. The Beats first gained notoriety in Turkey through informative articles and translations of their work in rock-and-roll magazines such as *Çalıntı*, a "monthly magazine of music culture" (*Aylık Müzik Kültür Dergisi*). This image, taken from the poster for the exploitation film *The Beat Generation* (1959), associates the Beats with a subversive challenge to sexual norms. *Courtesy of Suat Bilgi.*

This early reception is important, because it not only introduced Turkish audiences to the Beats but also provided a particular context for their work. To put it bluntly, the Beats were ascribed with the "dark" forces of a rock-and-roll subculture that were seen as a direct assault on authority. As writer and critic Hikmet Temel Akarsu mentions in his *Hürriyet Gösteri* magazine article "Türk Edebiyatı ve Yeni Kara" ("Turkish Literature and the New Dark"; July 2003), which he self-quotes in a later *Varlık* piece,

> In the catastrophe-ridden years of the later capitalist period, the rock music that exerted its authority in the art scene as a negative, dissenting, dark and pessimistic musical genre and avant-garde literature had the same artistic tendencies and addressed the same concerns and worries. We see that the grunge, black metal, power metal, gothic, doom, progressive and symphonic types of rock music as well as the literary products that influence the masses focused on similar themes using similar styles. (18)

Although the Beats themselves were more influenced by the bebop jazz tradition of their day, in Turkey they became associated with this underground scene along with other texts outside the mainstream like science fiction and fantasy works. This association of the rock-and-roll subculture with darkness was reinforced by a series of scandals involving satanic worship and sacrifice that shocked the Turkish public from the late 1990s until the early 2000s. According to Melike Aslı Şahinsoy in her *İstanbul'da Rock Kültürü: Yeraltından Yeryüzüne* (*Rock Culture in Istanbul: From Underground to the Surface*), the media drew explicit links between the dangers of Satanism and the rock subculture that supposedly promulgated it: "In Turkey, the media was using its own standards and criteria to warn parents, and to help them check if their children were Satanists. These criteria, which were mentioned in the evening news, included piercings or tattoos, listening to rock music, wearing silver accessories and most importantly wearing black clothes" (57). The inclusion of the Beats in this rock-and-roll subculture set the tone that would follow—the Beats became anticonformist rebels in direct opposition to mainstream society.

Beat texts did not remain confined within the covers of these magazines for long, however. As presses like Ayrıntı and Stüdyo İmge emerged, the Beats and other countercultural texts were being translated in increasing numbers. Discussing the wider translation trends of the era, Özlem Berk notes in *Translation and Westernization in Turkey: From the 1840s to the 1980s* that the 1980 coup marked a shift in translated texts away from left-wing political works and toward more Western literature. She writes, "In 1979, just one year before the military coup, there were a considerable amount of translations of left-wing political texts. . . . However, none of [them] are found in the translations published in 1982" (221). By contrast, "Since the early 1980s, a wide range of translations of international literature, from prizewinning fiction to popular bestsellers, as well as other translations in the fields of social sciences, history, philosophy, psychology, gender studies and children's literature have been published" (223). This shift signals both the depoliticization of the country as a whole as well as the increasing interest in individualism and identity politics. While Ginsberg's poems "America" and *Howl* were translated as early as 1976, most Beat texts were translated much later. For instance, Kerouac's *On the Road* first arrived in the Turkish language in 1993, and Burroughs's *Naked Lunch* was first translated in 1998.[5] But translations of the Beats are still occurring and on the rise, and given the interest in the underground it seems plausible that this trend will continue.

Nobody is certain where the term *underground* first appeared. It can be found in the rock-and-roll magazines that published the Beats, but as in the United States, it quickly spread to other genres. The literary critic Ömer Türkeş traces the emergence of the term to the 1980s, writing, "After the 80s, we started to hear the word 'underground' often in cinema, music, plastic arts and literature. Many underground novels were translated that introduced us to Bukowski and Genet; even Celine's *Journey to the End of the Night*, one of the legends of the genre, was published" (15). It clearly gets the attention of the Turkish Language Association, a group tasked with collecting foreign borrowings and offering more pure Turkish equivalents. In *Türkçenin Batı Dilleriyle İlişkisi* (*The Relation of the Turkish Language with Western Languages*; 2008), the author Mustafa Sarı provides a list of foreign source words and their recommended Turkish replacements in an appendix. From 1970 to 1980 the term *underground* does not appear, but in the second appendix that updates the list beyond 1980, "*Underground müzik*" (underground music) becomes "*Yer altı müziği*," "*Underground sanat*" (underground art) is replaced by "*Yer altı sanatı*," and "*Underground sinema*" (underground cinema) becomes "*Yer altı sineması*" (281). *Yeraltı* is a fairly direct translation, literally denoting the space "under the ground." At the time of this writing, both *underground* and *yeraltı* (with and without a space) are equally prevalent.

Along with these translations, critics began to take notice of this "new" genre. Writing in the 2005 special dossier titled "Yeraltı Edebiyatı" ("Underground Literature") in *Varlık*, Altay Öktem notes that "in the last three or four years, the interest taken in the genre has also resulted in the formation of a special audience" (3). While isolated translations of such works had appeared before, it was only around the year 2000 when the wider public became aware of this underground genre. Öktem traces this emergence to the work of Ayrıntı Publishing House and its translations of Chuck Palahniuk (particularly *Fight Club*) and Stüdyo İmge's publication of Irvine Welsh's work. As more translations followed, Turkish writers began to pick up the trend (4). The genre is now firmly established, and is used to describe not only Western countercultural imports but also home-grown Turkish works by writers like Hakan Günday, küçük iskender, and Metin Kaçan. While not every Turkish person has heard of the term *underground*, its use seems to be growing—especially given the censorship trials of Palahniuk's *Snuff* and Burroughs's *The Soft Machine* in 2012 (more on this in chapter 4). Bookstores have sections devoted to it, Facebook pages and websites discuss it, and serious literary journals debate its relevance, all of which testify to underground literature's increasing presence in Turkey.

WHO'S READING WHAT, AND WHY

To understand the role of underground literature in Turkey, it is essential to understand the importance of the genre for readers. This is, of course, a difficult task. To gain a better sense of reader demographics and opinions regarding the relevance of underground literature in their lives and thoughts, I worked with Duygu Ergun and Selen Erdoğan on a two-year-long project that culminated in the article "Underground Literature and Its Influence on Youth in Turkey."[6] Based on a series of focus groups conducted at universities across Turkey as well as on the responses from over six hundred questionnaires distributed to both underground literature readers and nonreaders of roughly the same demographic composition and reading tendencies, our study provides valuable information about who is reading underground literature in Turkey, which texts they are reading, and their reasons for their interest in the genre.[7] This data is crucial to fully understand the function and relevance of the Beats in Turkey, and helps to reveal the continued importance of the Beats and their texts in general.

One of the common assumptions about the Beats across the globe is that their readership is dominated by the young. The Beats are typically seen as writers one encounters when in high school or college, only to be forgotten (or revisited nostalgically) as youthful ideas of rebellion fade. Our study did confirm that, in Turkey at least, readers of underground literature are indeed young. Averaging twenty-three to twenty-four years of age, most readers first encountered the genre either in high school (57.9 percent) or in college (22.2 percent) (Mortenson, Ergun, Erdoğan, 90; see appendixes 1 and 2). This average hides a number of older readers, but our study supports the assumption that Beat and underground texts are discovered early.

Another commonplace in both the United States and Turkey is that the Beat Generation is a male-dominated genre. While Beat women writers have rightfully gained prominence in past years, more Beat writers are male, as are the group's most celebrated members—Jack Kerouac, Allen Ginsberg, and William S. Burroughs. This male focus is true of Turkish underground texts as well and has led many to decry the decidedly masculine viewpoints espoused in these texts. While conducting a focus group at Boğaziçi University, for example, one female master's student quipped that the genre mainly attracted males trying to "pick up" young women. Numerous other female focus group participants also noted misogynistic tendencies in the genre, though many nevertheless remained readers of such work, overlooking this male bias. We had thus been led to believe by our preliminary investigations that due to the oftentimes misogynistic content of underground material and the fact that this literary world tends to be inhabited by male characters, the resulting readership would be predominantly male. We discovered, however, that our Turkish readers are *not* predominantly male, as focus groups and initial research suggested.

Of the 302 readers questioned, 46.7 percent were actually female (91). This large female reading base demonstrates that women, too, are finding the genre worthwhile.[8] Given that the work of Beat women writers is, unfortunately, virtually nonexistent in Turkey—only a few poems by Janine Pommy Vega and Diane di Prima have been translated—this gender balance in the readership might be due to the fact that Turkish underground writing does contain several female writers who offer strong female characters and deal specifically with gender issues in Turkey. Turkish female underground authors were read less than their male counterparts, but their numbers of readers were not negligible. Works like Kanat Güner's *Eroin Güncesi*, Sibel Torunoğlu's *Travesti Pinokyo*, and Ayça Seren Ural's *Pogo* garnered lower rates of readership than küçük iskender's poetry, Metin Kaçan's *Ağır Roman*, or Hakan Günday's *Piç*, but their numbers were still significant (appendix 1). Underground literature is a male-dominated genre in terms of authors and themes, but these numbers demonstrate that the genre holds potential for female readers as well, a point worthy of further consideration as womens' issues take on increasing relevance in Turkey.

In addition to a study of the demographic makeup of underground literature readership, we were also interested in discovering the sort of attitudes and opinions associated with underground literature's fan base.

Readers of Beat texts are often considered "seekers." They are looking for new ways to live and new possibilities of thought. It comes as no surprise, then, that underground literature readers are, for the most part, an open group. This open-mindedness makes sense, given the oftentimes provocative and challenging nature of Beat and underground texts. Politically, they tend to fall to the left of center, though there were a significant number of extremely right-leaning respondents (93). Overall, readers are an accepting group, viewing women's rights, foreigners, and minority groups with a willingness to accept different ideas or opinions. For example, most agree that freedom of expression should be preserved under every condition, and do *not* agree with the idea that education is more important for boys than it is for girls (93). Readers of underground literature are a very tolerant group (though not much more so than the nonreaders of our study) and are typically less conservative and less religious. On a scale of one to ten, with ten being the most religious, almost half of readers responded in the zero-to-four category (92). In fact, when asked to specify their religion, 21.9 percent declared "none," more than twice the amount of nonreaders (92). While government statistics claim that over 99 percent of Turkish citizens are Muslim, it is clear that not all are regular practitioners of the religion. Underground literature readers in Turkey seem to be looking for new possibilities of thought, and the genre holds a strong fascination for those seeking answers to life's larger questions.

One thing underground literature in Turkey appears *not* to be doing is changing attitudes about the West. This finding is interesting, since one would assume that reading and appreciating texts from the West would cause a corresponding increase in positive attitudes toward the United States and Europe. Not all underground texts are Western, but readers ranked Western underground literature higher than its domestic counterparts with regard to rebelliousness (*isyankarlık*), literary worth (*edebi değer*), optimistic outlook (*iyimser bakış açısı*), and ability to address social questions (*sosyal meselelere değinme becerisi*). Despite this positive assessment, overall readers were critical of the United States and Europe, more so than their counterparts in the nonreaders group (92).[9] This difference might be explained by Western underground literature's own critique of the United States and Europe; readers clearly agreed with the attack this genre wages on conformity and commercialism.

This critique of the West is even more surprising, since underground literature's readers tend to view Western underground texts more favorably than their Turkish counterparts. When asked to rank foreign versus domestic underground texts in terms of the categories stated above, readers unanimously chose Western texts over Turkish ones. Readers were most familiar with Turkish writers such as küçük iskender, Hakan Günday, and Metin Kaçan, perhaps because of their availability or the fact that these texts could be read in the original Turkish. But U.S. authors such as Palahniuk, Bukowski, and Kerouac were also very popular, and all of the Beats on the list were known to a large portion of the readers group (see appendix 1). Even Ferlinghetti, a rather neglected Beat writer in Turkey, was heard of by approximately one-third of the readers group (103–4). Turkish underground writers garnered a larger share of the audience, but works by the Beats are clearly an important part of the underground phenomenon in Turkey.

Ultimately, readers of underground literature believe that the genre is important for Turkey. Our initial interviews with critics, publishers, and editors of underground literature suggested that the genre holds little potential to influence Turkey, yet our findings suggest something different. Of our readers, 39.4 percent believed that reading underground literature has changed them, and 33.1 percent believe underground literature holds a positive potential for Turkey, a clear indication that these texts are viewed as socially meaningful for a significant portion of their readers (96). Many believed the importance of underground literature lies in its ability to open new perspectives for readers (*hayata yeni bakış açıları sunması*), while others felt that the genre is most important for allowing readers to question perceptions of society and prejudices (*toplumsal algıları ve ön yargıları sorgulatması*; 96). While for some, style was an important consideration, most readers are looking to the genre for social reasons. Clearly, for readers, underground literature does hold potential, on both a personal and a social level.

THE DEBATE OVER THE UNDERGROUND

Underground literature has also caught the attention of the mainstream media. In terms of its Western, imported variant, discussions typically revolve around a single author or text. These pieces are for the most part descriptive, presenting the lives and works of writers like Kerouac, Ginsberg, or Burroughs to readers that are probably unfamiliar with these names. Often such articles appear upon publication of a new translation or the release of a film dealing with such figures. Given that these newspapers and journals are choosing to discuss the topic of underground literature and are addressing new textual products appearing in the cultural sphere, coverage has so far been laudatory. When mainstream media does delve into the issues raised by such Western countercultural imports, the focus tends to be on the rebelliousness of underground literature. The focus here is almost exclusively on Beat Generation texts, though other countercultural products do make an appearance. Beat and countercultural works are seen mainly as engines of social change. The attention so far has tended to rest on the means of this rebelliousness in the U.S. context; few critics discuss the potential such underground products hold for Turkish society at any great length. The bracketing of imported underground products into a strictly Western context allows many topics sensitive to Turkey to be discussed quite openly. Homosexuality and drug use, for instance, are addressed repeatedly, though seldom in relation to Turkish examples. Occasionally critics will venture into the question of literary style, usually to discuss the use of slang. But even here slang typically raises the question of whether such language is transgressive, and the ways in which it is co-opted by the mainstream society and rendered less threatening.

Given that underground literature is a youth phenomenon, it is hardly surprising that much discussion surrounding these texts takes place online, occuring in three distinct forms in both its Western and Turkish variants. The most commercial of these include online journals and publisher's websites. *Koltukname* and *Sabitfikir* are two prime examples of the former. While not exclusively devoted to underground literature, both provide reviews of books and translations, art news, profiles of writers, and discussion of topics relevant to Turkish youth such as the Gezi park demonstrations. Publisher's websites are likewise an important source of information on the issues surrounding underground literature. Sel Publishing's site, for instance, kept readers abreast of the court developments in *The Soft Machine* and *Snuff* censorship trials, and the website of underground publishing mainstay 6:45 promotes a range of products from books to Tshirts to handbags while remaining an important source of information for their fans. As in the West, there are numerous fan sites and Facebook pages devoted to the Beats, but these consist mainly of images, quotes, and other memes—rarely are texts discussed in depth.

The debate over what underground literature means, which texts are included in its canon, and whether it has relevance for Turkey, however, has sparked much discussion in two of Turkey's leading literary magazines: *Varlık* (February 2005) and *Notos* (August-September 2011).[10] Although all involved agree that the underground denotes something lying outside the norm, the nature of this outsider status is the subject of debate. Two overlapping connotations of the term are generally offered. Underground literature is either a label denoting texts generally lying outside normal distribution methods, or it is a type of literature that presents characters, issues, and themes that transgress social norms. Although there is overlap (the underground is antiauthoritarian and often illegal in both approaches) and some critics discuss both positions simultaneously, these two outlooks form the twin considerations that drive debate.

Critics that take up the question of distribution typically attack the label for the inconsistencies it produces. How can you call something "underground" when it enjoys brisk sales and wide distribution? Underground means hidden, and if a text is highly visible then its underground status is undermined. As H. T. Akarsu observes in *Varlık*, "A literary work published by a legal publishing house, with a tax stamp, sold by receipt, and not prosecuted by existing laws, cannot be called Underground literature" (17). Such critics link the idea of the underground to the self-publishing *samizdat* tradition in the Soviet Union. Thus, for many in this camp the term is meaningless because real underground literature exists only in the form of fanzines and self-published work. One of the major ironies of the debate is that despite underground literature's increased media exposure, almost all of the respondents deny its very existence.[11] In their minds, the underground is impossible. Given the widespread expansion of the Internet, the idea that a text exists in a limited number of copies or only in the hands of a few members of a subculture is becoming increasingly rare, and thus for proponents of this position, true underground literature in Turkey simply does not exist today.

This outlook has led many to decry underground literature as simply a marketing gimmick. Perhaps the strongest advocate of this position is the publisher, writer, and provocateur Şenol Erdoğan. Writing in his *Notos* piece, Erdoğan makes clear that there is no such thing as underground literature, claiming that the term "exists as a 'market'-'store'!" ("Yerin Dibi!" 28). It is clear that what Erdoğan and others like him see as true underground work involves a deeper commitment to subversive production and dissemination of texts. Invoking the U.S. underground movement discussed earlier, Erdoğan observes,

> [W]hat happened in America sixty years ago was no different than SAMIZDAT. Small printing houses, what we call "small presses" and of course small publishers, and "self publishing" with their own printing presses and publishers agreed on the idea of producing literature underground. With the help of the whole family and using mimeographs, these people made underground literature by printing their own magazines, booklets and brochures in their homes, basements, work places. (29)

Thus Erdoğan draws a clear distinction between a true underground and the use of the term to sell a product. Erdoğan concludes that "many 'genres' such as Beat, Pulp, Transgressive or Punk may be sold as 'underground' within a market, but this doesn't give anyone the right to talk about Beat literature as underground literature" (28). Erdoğan is not against the Beats by any means. In fact, his publishing house, 6:45, is a major translator and publisher of Beat texts, including the *Beat Kuşağı Antolojisi* (*Beat Generation Anthology*; 2011). What Erdoğan rails against is the miscategorization, as he sees it, of the Beats as something that they are not. Criticizing the desire by publishers to include those tangential to the Beat Generation in their anthologies as a marketing device, Erdoğan laments the inclusion of "rock singers, writers of other, later generations that needed to be inserted, even worse, those with the audacity to include unconnected writers who were friends with the Beats" (*Beat Kuşağı Antolojisi* 8).

Although a critique of what does and does not count as "underground" might appear to be academic hairsplitting, this discussion does raise important questions about the Beats' ability to promulgate social change that should not be ignored. The question is whether a text needs to be considered underground in order to be subversive. The Turkish debate about distribution leads directly into a discussion of the commodification of the Beats and asks to what extent they are complicit in the capitalist system and to what extent do they still have the power to subvert it.[12] Tayfun Polat, magazine editor and deejay, in his article "Alt Üst Oldu" ("Under Became Above" or "Things Are a Mess") in *Notos*, argues that "the fact that the original scroll of *On the Road* by Jack Kerouac has been sold for $2.4 million demonstrates that there is no underground left" (44). This topic is acknowledged in Beat circles but is quickly passed over because of the uncomfortable questions it raises. Perhaps, however, it is time to revisit this issue. As much as we might celebrate the Beats for their challenge to authority both in the United States and abroad, do they still hold the potential for questioning the established order, given their absorption into what has become an acknowledged subculture of dissent?

The Beats have certainly become well-known figures, but that does not mean that their entire corpus has now been rendered mainstream. As Metin Celâl at Parantez Publishing explains in the *Varlık* issue, the rise of some underground works to the surface is inevitable:

> I don't think that a good literary work can stay underground for too long. When you look at the writers we publish at Parantez Publishing, you can say that Henry Miller, Bukowski, and Kerouac are the typical examples of this. Although these authors could be included within the scope of underground literature in terms of their subject matters, language and venues they could find to publish their works when they first started writing, in time they ascended above ground

> from the underground and became world famous authors; they even became classics. (23)

However, as critic and sociologist Hasan Bülent Kahraman notes in his later *Notos* piece, works that are truly underground strive to resist incorporation. He cites the example of the Turkish poet Orhan Veli Kanık, whose work "was underground literature when it was published but, in time, became included in middle school course books" (24). Kahraman's point is well-taken; ask any university student, and perhaps most Turkish people, and they can recite Veli's work verbatim. Nevertheless, not all of Veli's work made it into the canon. Although his "Garip" (a word with Beat resonances, it means both "strange" and "peculiar" as well as "poor" and "forlorn") movement poems have become acceptable in Turkish society, Kahraman notes that "he was not canonized because of his 'Cımbızlı Şiir' and 'Süleyman Efendi' poems or his intention to be a 'fish in a rakı bottle.' Literature didn't indulge in 'this' Orhan Veli" (24). When we examine the commodification of the Beats more closely, we realize that not all of their work has become popular. Kerouac's more stylistic innovations in *Visions of Cody*, Ginsberg's extremely sexual poetry like "Please Master," or a great deal of Burroughs's work with its stylistic difficulties of the cut-up method or disquieting concerns involving violence and sexuality still remain a direct challenge to social and literary norms. Although they are now easily available through online outlets, such texts are typically less important in the commodification process. Thus there appears to be a canon even in the underground, with some works rising to the surface while others remain staunchly subversive.

The debate also raises the question of canonization and what it means for Beat texts. Underground literature is meant to be discovered—it is literature that is passed surreptitiously from one fan to another, usually as part of a scene, or searched out, text by text, as a collector or detective might follow a lead. It is, in the end, a shibboleth. This sort of shared intimacy of being "in the know" can be traced in the words of celebrities like Bob Dylan who, on the back cover of *On the Road*, states that the novel "changed my life like it changed everyone else's"—everyone else hip enough to read it, that is. But as the Beats become more popular and readily available, this clandestine nature of the underground is lost. As Ozan Marakoğlu observes, "Jack Kerouac's *On the Road*, which Ayrıntı Publishing eagerly published under the 'Yeraltı Edebiyatı' ["Underground Literature"] series, instead of being underground, isn't it actually being taught in literature classes in high schools, and regarded as an American, even a world classic?" (48). There is an irony here that such texts need to be well known enough to be noticed and purchased, but still unknown enough to feel like a "discovery." This is even truer in the Turkish context. Despite this clamor about marketing gimmicks and aboveground publication, many Turkish underground texts remain out of print and unavailable. There seems to be a necessary balance between being hidden enough to remain subversive and available enough to allow those interested to find the sort of texts they crave.[13]

This fear of the underground losing its potency through too wide an availability also raises the issue of the Internet's role in disseminating information. While only 4.6 percent of readers in our study claim to have first heard of underground literature on the Internet, numerous fan websites, blogs, and Facebook pages devoted to underground literature and specific authors disseminate news, facts, and opinions to a wide range of readers across Turkey (see appendix 3). In much the same manner as earlier fanzines, these sites provide readers of underground literature with up-to-date information on events, new releases, and goings-on in the genre while also providing a forum for discussion. Facebook pages are even more numerous. Although they seldom delve deeply into the issues that underground literature raises, these sites provide Internet users with a range of images, quotes, memes, and suggestions for further reading that raises the profile of the genre immensely. They also provide discussion threads that allow fans to debate the merits of their chosen authors or to provide additional information that others might find interesting. Discussion is often terse, in keeping with the medium's requirement of brevity, but both personal webpages and Facebook pages provide readers with additional information concerning underground literature outside existing channels of communication.[14]

One major difference between the initial U.S. reception of the Beats (or even their slightly later European one) and their Turkish reception is that access to their message has now become instantaneous. Although Beat translations do not usually appear online, the vast increase in fans' websites, Facebook pages, and publisher's homepages signal an increased interest in the genre. The editors of *Notos*, in preparing their dossier, raise the question of the role of the Internet in the debate surrounding underground literature, asking "Where is underground in the era of blogging?" The answers inevitably critique the role that the underground has to play in an Internet-connected world. Polat quotes the music writer Simon Reynolds and his statement that "the web has extinguished the idea of a true underground" (44). Polat goes on to comment that "in a world where mainstream media struggles to stay alive while blogs take the place of daily newspapers, what exactly does underground mean?" (44). The irony is that by giving everyone a voice, the Internet has denied any particular voice resonance.

Unlike the era of the underground press, when it still took time and energy to produce a paper, the Internet's easy and immediate democratic access to media channels instead produces cacophony. Although this argument begs the question of who gets to determine which voice is important, it is true that in a media-saturated world, the Beats' rebellious message can easily be lost in the crowd. Ultimately, the Internet is a mixed blessing for those who desire the Beats to remain an underground force—it allows those interested to find what they are looking for regardless of national boundaries while undermining the sense that the Beats are a shared secret among devotees.

Does the Internet provide a novel means of rebellion, or is it simply a diversion? As the entire world witnessed in light of the Arab Spring, social media has a role to play in fomenting dissent. Yet for older critics who experienced a more direct political conflict in Turkey's history, cultural change, to invoke Marxist language, is simply the superstructure of the system accommodating minor difference in order for the overall system to remain intact. Many of those I interviewed involved in the debate remained reticent about the possibilities the underground held in Turkey. As the editor Sancı puts it, "The Beat generation is a generation that has been lived and done" (Sancı interview). Yet when I interviewed those involved in the debate over underground literature about the possibility that such texts might have to change the attitudes of its readers, all agreed it held such potential. The Beats and the sort of underground writing they helped to promulgate might change some attitudes, but in a globalized capitalist world, so the argument goes, this change means little. But whether that viewpoint itself is passé remains to be seen.

DARK AND EVIL LITERATURE

The other approach to the underground focuses more closely on the texts themselves, arguing that underground works are transgressive. They are texts that present different lifestyles with different value systems that lie outside traditional cultural norms, characterized mainly by protagonists unwilling or unable to adjust to social dictates. For many in this camp, the transgressions met with in underground literature are characterized by the adjectives *dark* (*kara*) and *evil* (*kötülük*), even though not all critics employ these terms pejoratively. The writer and scholar of Turkish fanzines Altay Öktem, in his *Notos* piece "Yeraltı Edebiyatının Temel Özellikleri ve Edebiyatımızda Yeraltı" ("The Main Characteristics of Underground Literature and the Underground in our Literature"), for example, equates Beat works with "dark" literature (17). Kahraman, in his *Varlık* piece "Kötülük, Yeraltı Edebiyatı ve Yerüstü" ("Evil, Underground Literature and Aboveground"), believes that underground literature is in a unique position to convey evilness, since "Underground Literature springs from an understanding that touches the dark spot of humans" (10). This critique, which is not unlike the sort of reception that the Beats first met with in the United States early during the Cold War, frames underground literature as pessimistic, nihilistic, and, in Turkey, very much a rejection of social expectations to conform to society.

This characterization of underground literature as dark and evil results from it breaking sharply with Turkish social expectations. Ozan Marakoğlu's piece comes at the end of the *Notos* dossier and provides a useful summary of the debate worth quoting at length:

> If distribution companies bring the book that you have in your hands to the shelves of the bookstore, a known publishing house published it, and moreover its sales are not quite bad, then you'll know that it's not under the ground. If you really want to descend under the ground, you need to turn to the stapled photocopy fanzines (if there are any left) that stand in some corner behind the hardcover books. On the other hand, all this excitement about underground literature is not actually that odd in a country like ours. In a country where Burroughs's, Palahniuk's, Marquis de Sade's and many other writers' accepted literary works are banned for reasons such as obscenity, it is utterly natural that every literary work that has obscene words in it and that talks about anti-heroes that are outcasts not involved in the wheels of the system is marginalized, even if only in people's minds, and dragged underground. (49)

This "on the other hand" is really at the crux of the debate. As Marakoğlu notes, underground literature in Turkey is not really underground in the sense of Soviet *samizdat* or 1960s underground press materials. They are indeed widely available and enjoy strong sales. The reason this debate is occurring is that, in Turkey, there still is a very real sense that such work is oppositional. Despite their success, Beat works really do come up against political, legal, and social barriers that have implications for readers. That is why many readers of underground literature, though the books are freely available, still feel uncomfortable reading such texts on the bus or at the café. One of my assistants on this project, Canan Akgöçmen, related her anecdotes about reading underground literature in public while living in the city of Mersin from 2000 to 2003. Canan describes people staring at her on the bus while reading Günday's novel *Piç* (*Bastard*), either because of the novel's provocative title or because the cover depicts a skeletal figure wearing a Turkish banknote set against an ominous sky (figure 1.2). In another instance, she was harassed by a bookseller when purchasing a copy of Irvine Welsh's *Porno.* The translator of Palahniuk's novel *Snuff,* Funda Uncu, underwent even worse harassment when brought to a Bodrum police station to give her testimony concerning the book's censorship trial. Underground literature, at least ten years ago, was difficult to find and carried more of a social stigma. The censorship trials have helped to popularize the genre and galvanize support, but they have also reinforced underground literature's suspect nature in the minds of its detractors. Given the more conservative attitudes in Turkish culture following the 2016 coup attempt, discrimination against the genre may well increase.

Fig. 1.2. The cover of Hakan Günday's *Piç* (*Bastard*) encapsulates what underground literature has come to signify in Turkey—a dark literature that chronicles the lives of the marginal and outcast. Yet the writing at the bottom right-hand corner demonstrates the appeal of such work, announcing that the novel is in its fourteenth printing (*14. Baskı*).

According to many involved in the debate, the reason for such resistance lies in Turkey's more collectivist social structure. Although care must be taken when making generalizations about a culture, Turkish society does tend toward a more communal model of social organization where familial ties, neighborhood interconnections, and narratives concerning national and linguistic identity remain important.[15] Underground literature, however, is populated by highly idiosyncratic characters expressing themselves in ways at odds with social expectations. As Abdullah Yılmaz, editor of the underground publishing house Ayrıntı explains, "In Turkey people are still looking through the eyes of their collective societies. The problem concerns the dissolution of the sense of belonging to the collective; you can only start producing underground literature once the sense of belonging to the collective disappears" (Yılmaz interview). Given its oppositional stance to the demands of a collective society, it is understandable why underground literature is considered dark and even evil.

The challenge underground literature poses to Turkish cultural norms is highlighted in the attempts of the Turkish legal system to silence works they feel pose a threat to the Turkish moral order. In May 2000, for example, Bukowski's short story "The Most Beautiful Girl in Town" was read on *Açık Radyo* (*Open Radio*). This reading resulted in a censorship trial being opened in June 2001, with the prosecution for the Radio and Television Supreme Council stating that the story was against "general morals, social order, and the codes of the Turkish familial life." More recently, Burroughs's *The Soft Machine*, along with Chuck Palahniuk's *Snuff*, underwent another censorship trial. In 2011, Turkey's Committee for the Protection of Minors from Harmful Publications decided that the books were obscene. This legal backlash and the language used in the indictments show that underground literature, which has not seen an obscenity trial in the West for decades, is still perceived as threat to the moral fiber of Turkey, as we shall see in chapter 4's discussion of the censorship trial of Burroughs's *The Soft Machine*.

For underground literature's supporters, however, these works have the advantage of providing a way out of cultural binaries by offering novel viewpoints. The poet Süreyya Evren, writing in *Varlık*, recognizes the merits of the Beats in recording the lives of those outside the system, but laments the reductive view that underground literature is purely a literature that captures the lives of the "marginal." Evren sees his work, by contrast, as an exploration of "the road not taken" rather than a sociological exploration of a group lying outside the mainstream (20–21). Küçük iskender, again in *Varlık*, appears to agree, arguing that "it is important to be able to leave, to refuse, to formulate the fractures of perception, to interpret the criminal /

the evil / the amoral / the irrational and to have the courage to bear with all of these; this 'to be able to' is actually the main theme of the underground" (21). The point here is that for these two Turkish underground writers, the purpose of the genre is not simply to record characters and moments spent "outside" dominant culture but also to explore the possibilities being outside might hold for conventional literature, current language, and contemporary ways of thinking. For the critic Ömer Türkeş, the power of underground literature is its ability to level distinctions in society and thus open up debate on topics that were previously consigned an inferior status: "What gives underground literature its privilege is its normlessness that knows no boundaries; values like right / wrong, good / bad, beautiful / ugly, supreme / low are listed not as binary oppositions that do not intersect, but as the natural states of the human condition" (15). Underground literature is important not just because it produces "strange" characters outside society's norms but because the genre provides new modes of thinking.

THE TURKISH UNDERGROUND RESPONDS

What draws readers to most Turkish-produced underground literature, however, is its description of lifestyles that lie far beyond the norms of society. Turkish underground works are, in the main, either autobiographical or thinly veiled fictional accounts of their authors' struggles to live their lives in an underground world of sex, drugs, and other illegal and immoral activities. They are stories of truly marginalized people and less the celebration of deviant behavior. Though they encounter numerous problems in the attempt, most Turkish underground narratives embrace the decision to live outside society's strictures. There is, however, ambivalence about the choice—although characters celebrate the freedom to live life as they please, many remain unhappy with this marginal existence but do not know how to integrate themselves back into mainstream society. Thus Turkish underground literature is in a sense Beat as in "beaten down" but without the "beatific" sense of garnering a purer knowledge or understanding because of it. Unlike Beat texts that portray such marginalized suffering as ultimately redemptive, the majority of Turkish underground texts present lives that are characterized by struggle. The power of these texts lies in their social critique, and not in turning the suffering of their characters into mystical understanding or countercultural revolution.

Despite its singularity, underground literature is not without its antecedents in Turkish literary culture. The one group most often discussed in this regard is the "Garip," or "Strange," movement. Founded by three friends in

Ankara—Orhan Veli Kanık, Oktay Rifat, and Melih Cevdet Anday—these writers first gained notoriety in 1941 through a slim collection of poems that included a manifesto written by Orhan Veli. In an era that considered literature a tool for nation building and the writer a spokesman for the people, the "Strangers" instead offered poetry that probed the unconscious and the unsaid. According to Talat Halman in his magisterial work *A Millennium of Turkish Literature*, these "Strange" writers, like the Beats, turned away from the poetry of their forebears to craft a new poetics focused on life in the streets. Halman observes, "The Garip (Strange) Group, as the Kanık-Rifat-Anday triad is referred to, endeavored to write not only *about* the common man, but also *for* him. In order to communicate with him, they employed the rhythms and idioms of colloquial speech, including slang" (134–35). This desire to break free from the trappings of the past in order to explore new thoughts and new modes of writing catapulted the Garip movement to national prominence, and they remain a fundamental inspiration for underground literature in contemporary Turkey.[16]

The work of novelist Hakan Günday helps to clarify the understanding of underground texts in Turkey. Much like writers such as Kerouac who chafed at the term *Beat Generation*, Günday dismisses the underground label. Yet his works are marketed as such by his Doğan Kitap Press, are sold in the underground section of bookstores, and are almost obligatory in discussions of underground literature in Turkey. Günday presents deviant characters who go beyond the sort of outsiders normally encountered in the Beat genre. In fact, they are best characterized as sociopaths—they lack pity and remorse, and they engage in violence indiscriminately. Evren Karataş, discussing the novels *Kinyas ve Kayra* (2000), *Piç* (2003), and *Zargana* (2002) in his article "Underground Literature in Turkey and the Traces of Underground Literature in Hakan Günday's Novels," provides a list of characteristics of Günday's characters that read as an apt description of Turkish underground literature as a whole: discord with life, idealizing death, preferring loneliness, not being able to become socialized, protesting against institutions and moral principles, addicted, violent, and against civilization. In *Zargana* (literally "garfish" or "sea needle"), the story of a young runaway raped by four Algerians in Berlin, the titular character searches for an identity outside even his allotted species: "Zargana, who believed he was not human, was depositing tens of thousands of Deutsche Marks to various bank accounts every week so that he could touch and hear the lifestyle he dreamed of, in other words to reunite with his own species, whose name he did not know but of whose existence he was certain" (104). Ultimately, he is able to come to terms with his identity and reintegrate into society. The novel ends with Zargana leaving Berlin with his girlfriend, the implication being that he will now embark upon a more "normal" life.

Günday's work is interesting because despite this obvious appeal to underground themes such as social deviancy, many critics exclude his work from the underground canon. Given the extensive marketing of his work and its high sales volume, for those who believe the underground should be well hidden and hard to find, Günday is clearly aboveground. The highly fictionalized nature of his work also draws attention, demonstrating that underground in Turkey remains closely associated with personal documentary and confession rather than literary imagination.[17] Finally, the fact that Günday's characters typically reintegrate into Turkish society is a sign that they are not really offering a social critique. They are instead indulging in underground themes but not to call attention to the plight of those trapped by social expectations. Rather, they offer readers a chance to enjoy an exhilarating ride into a subterranean world but with the ultimate assurance that stability and sanity will return at the novel's close. Turkish underground writing typically requires a more pessimistic view.

Truly underground works perform a social function by providing first-hand, realistic accounts of the lives of those forced to suffer at the hands of an unaccepting society. Purposefully transgressive, they call attention to social ills and to those people outside the mainstream who are, in a sense, forced underground to survive on their own terms. Given the pressure to fit into Turkish society, this focus on the deviant is understandable, as it forces the reader to at least confront the problems of those unable or unwilling to accept social tenets. The work of Mehmet Kartal, who published six novels in the 1990s before dying of pneumonia in 2001, is exemplary in this regard. As a writer who was incarcerated multiple times in both penal and mental institutions, Kartal provided readers within an insider's knowledge of the underworld. In the process, he exposed social hypocrisy, the state's lack of concern for child criminals and orphans, and the horrible conditions in the penal system.

The underground's desire to chronicle the socially occluded can clearly be seen in another key underground writer in Turkey, Metin Kaçan. His celebrated novel *Ağır Roman* (translated as *Cholera Street* and made into a film of the same name; 1995) chronicles the backstreets of Istanbul's Beyoğlu district where poverty, filth, crime, violence, and drugs are a way of life. Providing realistic accounts of the lives of those forced to live outside the mainstream, Kaçan forces readers to confront Turkey's social ills. In the language of the streets, the novel explores the lives of those stuck between the temptations of the big city and the fading morals of the Anatolian village:

> The age of electronics exploded in Cholera in all its fury. As the television was considered "the tool of the devil," peasant women and the wives of religious zealots watched it with fear after they had covered their heads and wiped their houses clean. While they watched the TV calmly with a sigh of relief when there was a female reporter on the screen, they ran away to the kitchen or the room next door when they saw men on it. When their husbands were not home, they secretly watched male reporters through the half-open door and rubbed themselves against the edges of the sofa. (58)

The women of "Cholera Street" are attracted by the new possibilities offered by the city but cannot break free from social expectations in order to fully enjoy themselves. The young narrator struggles to survive in this world but ultimately commits suicide (as did the author himself). *Ağır Roman* provides readers with an insider's knowledge that characterizes works like Ginsberg's *Howl* or Burroughs's *Naked Lunch*. For many in Turkey, this gritty portrayal of lives normally left unseen is the real payoff of underground literature, in both Turkish and Beat varieties. By providing characters outside the mainstream, underground works can finally bring to light issues that are normally muted in the culture.

The importance of raising taboo social questions in the Turkish underground is also clearly seen in texts written by the genre's women authors. The works of Sibel Torunoğlu, Kanat Güner, and Ayça Seren Ural share with their Beat counterparts a desire to present new possibilities for women by challenging both gender expectations and the status quo that supports them. These authors have earned the countercultural title of "underground" in Turkey by presenting protagonists that break free from social expectations. However, given gender issues inherent in Turkey, these texts also reveal the difficulties women face when challenging a masculine-dominated society. Turkish underground women writers demonstrate a freedom from social constraint, but their work also reveals the tenacious gender expectations operating in Turkey. Despite historical and cultural differences, both Turkish underground and Beat women writers share a critique of social norms as well as aesthetic strategies in their attempt to portray strong female characters living their lives on their own terms.

A comparison between Beat women writers and Turkish women underground writers is compelling because both groups respond in similar ways to similar social conditions. The work of Nancy M. Grace and Ronna C. Johnson has been particularly useful in understanding the sort of rebellion formulated by Beat women writers. These critics view Beat women writers as representing an intermediary stage between the silent acquiescence of the 1950s and the more radical feminism of the 1960s and 1970s. In their introduction to *Girls Who Wore Black*, Johnson and Grace explain, "Although it is formally diverse, most writing by women Beats is what second-wave feminists termed woman centered: it takes (mostly white, mostly middle class) women as its point of departure. It focuses on women's lives and existential concerns in postwar bohemia; on challenging stereotypes of white women's passivity and sexual frigidity in the fifties; on the liberation of women's sexuality and self-expression" (22–23). Beat womens' writing focuses on the difficulties of being a woman in a male-dominated society. But it does so through a portrayal of personal issues and their expression, rather than through appeals to a large-scale social activism. As Johnson will go on to discuss in relation to Joyce Johnson's *Come and Join the Dance*, such texts make "no claim to address directly the emancipation of women; its corrective discourses are written in a Beat key rather than with the rhetoric that would be familiar from later women's movements" ("And Then She Went" 70). Though they are distanced in both time and space, Turkish women underground writers are not offering a re-theorization of women's role in society either. They raise a voice of protest as women, like their Beat predecessors, but do so individually and not as part of a larger feminist movement.

The women's movement in Turkey is, in many ways, experiencing the sort of second-wave feminism that was prevalent in the West during the late 1950s and early 1960s. As Zuhal Yeşilyurt Gündüz explains, the struggles of women to achieve equality in Turkey can be divided into three phases. The first began in the Ottoman Empire, with a series of laws in 1839 during the Tanzimat, or "Reform," period. The second occurred with Mustafa Kemal Atatürk, who granted women certain rights as part of his attempt to modernize Turkey along Western lines. But it was not until the 1980 coup that women themselves began to initiate reforms aimed at "questioning the authoritarian regime, bringing 'private' topics like violence against women to the political agenda, and finding solutions to women's problems" (115). Much of the post-1980 discussion revolved around domestic abuse and "honor killings," as well as the right of women to control their own bodies, especially in terms of sexual freedom. Gündüz observes, "In Turkey the symbolization of women continues. Women are treated as a mechanism for the protection of the cultural borders of the community. Therefore they are the guards and the social and biological carriers of tradition, society and collective identity" (124). Much like the rhetoric of the U.S. postwar years when women were viewed as responsible for maintaining a strong domestic sphere in the face of a perceived Soviet threat, Turkish women are seen as an essential part of a familial structure that is integral for the continuation of the Turkish state. Recent events in Turkey, such as the statements of President Recep Tayyip Erdoğan equating abortion with genocide and admonishing all Turkish women to have at least three children, demonstrate that the struggle for gender equality is far from accomplished.

Just as the works of Beat women were meant to offer a counternarrative to postwar gender expectations, Torunoğlu, Güner, and Ural likewise challenge social constraint in their work. The marginalized, "underground" lifestyle portrayed in these works presents an escape from Turkish social norms that the characters feel are constraining their freedom, mobility, and exploration of self. All three of these novels thus offer a counterpoint in individual expression, with characters choosing to live life on their own terms. Sibel Torunoğlu's *Travesti Pinokyo* (*Transvestite Pinocchio*) presents the lives of transvestite sex workers in Istanbul's rugged Dolapdere neighborhood. In her book Torunoğlu discusses, in an unconventional style, the very real physical and psychological problems such residents face, like violence, rape, and abuse. Kanat Güner's *Eroin Güncesi* (*Heroin Diary*), as its title implies, describes the narrator's struggle with her addiction. While it provides a sympathetic treatment of the addict, it also involves the narrator's attempts to free herself from the social norms of the culture and discover her own sense of self. Ayça Seren Ural's *Pogo* (the title referring to the "pogo" style of dancing associated with punk rock) is perhaps the more upbeat of this genre. Like Diane di Prima's *Memoirs of a Beatnik*, Ural expands on her real-life adventures to produce a text that exceeds strict autobiography. The novel presents a world where two females fend for themselves, oftentimes resorting to theft and robbery to pursue their desires. Like Beat women writers who felt constricted by a society that expected them to perform the duties of wife and mother, these writers likewise rebel against social obligations.

While Beat women writers fought against the standards of a constraining 1950s society, these Turkish writers were also frustrated with the lack of freedom they had come to expect from their middle-class upbringings. In the wake of a liberalization following the 1980 coup, the rhetoric of individualism created expectations that were not always met. Discussing her group of friends, the narrator of *Heroin Diary* comments that "all of us appeared to be children of good families, but in reality, it was our families who put us in this dead end. They rejected the idea of raising children who could fit into social norms. They gave us some freedom, but we couldn't use such freedom in this society, and when we felt different we became distanced from society and could not go back. As time went on, we became imbalanced" (33). The main reason for the narrator's resorting to heroin is her frustration with her parents and with society as a whole. Her family led her to believe new opportunities were possible, but in actuality, Turkish society was as constraining as ever before. This rejection of a middle-class life is a recurrent theme in the work of many women Beat writers as well. The supposed joy and security of family life actually represents a trap, and its rejection the beginning of a search for true freedom.

Pogo takes this rebellion even further. Echoing the punk mentality that inspired the author's desire to go "on the road," Ural's novel chronicles two female protagonists and their all-out quest for adventure. The protagonist Değer is able to rob and steal without qualms because her victims are part of a larger system that she feels is unjust. The narrator is frustrated with an imbalanced world of violence and consumerism, claiming, "This bullshit called society life is full of crime, tyranny, killing, massacre and never-ending ambitions, so why would we care about this world?" (32). She thus aligns herself with the masses of disgruntled youth who feel that society has betrayed them. With an increasing population and the destruction of the natural environment, Değer explains,

> In the end, the rebellious children of the metropole emerged . . . we decided to destroy their values, in popular language, their "trends," with a slap. Neither the Left nor any other movement that looks at the world with blinders on can end the empire of money. For this reason resistance became individual, and will get more individual. If I rob a grocery store, if I break someone's nose when I lose my cool, and if I feel no regret it's only because of my hatred against this stench. (32)

Given the narrator's frustration and anger, "dropping out" is seen not as negative rejection but rather as an attack on a society whose values have become polluted and debased.

The general conceit in Turkey is that such underground texts are peopled with disturbed characters who are not able to properly adjust to society. But looking at these Turkish women underground writers presents a more complicated picture. Like their Beat women counterparts, they are doubly oppressed: they fight both social and gender norms. But the adjective *dark*, which is often used to describe such literature in Turkey, really only applies to Güner's *Heroin Diary*.[18] The narrator falls into increasing drug use and fantasizes about getting clean. The text closes with a note from the friend she helped kill asking her to write about all that has happened. With the book finished, it appears as though her motive for living ends as well: "To dream is as hard as drinking cleaning fluid! I have nothing left to write. . . .

Yes, it's over. Curtain!" (116). In real life, Güner committed suicide by purposely overdosing in a bathroom after a reading. But this bleak situation is by no means representative of the genre.

Ural's novel, for instance, is far more upbeat. The novel ends happily with Değer's reunion with her boyfriend, Kunt. Despite her travails, love finds a way, and she enjoys her adventures without a negative repercussion. Though the novel occasionally lapses into the incredulous, it sends a message of two women empowered by their friendship and willingness to enter into spheres normally coded masculine, even if success is ultimately measured in terms of relationships. While gender is an issue in the novel, Değer and her traveling partner, Rüzgar, let nothing hold them back in their very Beat quest for adventure and self-discovery. Ural's personal life is likewise successful. She works as a street vendor in Istanbul, and went on to publish two more novels as well as to win thirty thousand Turkish liras in 2012 on the Turkish television show *Who Wants to be a Millionaire?*

Torunoğlu's work, while not as upbeat as Ural's, also presents a message of redemption. *Transvestite Pinocchio* depicts a world mired in violence and sadness, and Torunoğlu herself was institutionalized several times against her will. But the love shared between the characters, and the power of imagination to transcend difficult social realities, lends the book a feeling of hope. The characters form bonds that allow them to thrive in their milieu, despite its many obstacles. This feeling of camaraderie and mutual support is palpable and lends the novel an uplifting feeling despite the negative forces that surround the characters. These three Turkish women authors present marginalized lives as an escape from social strictures. The lack of an extensive subcultural network in Turkey like that which Beat women enjoyed makes their struggles perhaps more difficult, but in all three of these novels the support that characters get from each other allows them to persevere.

Comparisons between Beat women writers and women of the Turkish underground are difficult, due not only to cultural differences but also to shifts in possibilities and expectations for women occasioned by the nearly half century that separates these texts. Moreover, as Johnson and Grace have demonstrated, women Beat writings are not homogenous. While they shared gender concerns, these authors often took different paths in their work. Turkish women underground writers are no exception. Nevertheless, all of these works share a desire to challenge social expectations to explore possibilities different from those offered by mainstream society. While no text can escape its cultural moment, these chronicles of characters struggling to live their lives in ways unacceptable to many in the mainstream posed a challenge not just to social norms but to gender expectations as well.

Establishing the exact nature of the relationship between Beat and Turkish underground texts is extremely difficult. Some writers, like küçük iskender, make direct reference to the Beats, and thus the connection is quite clear. In his "Türkiye" ("Turkey"), for example, iskender draws on Ginsberg's "America" for both his line and his theme. "Türkiye" works through long breath-lines to chronicle the various social ills that plague Turkey. Beat references also appear throughout Şenol Erdoğan's work, which is self-consciously addressing the Beat canon, and even in Günday's *Kinyas and Kayra*, where one character describes himself in a shared diary by comparing himself to Dean Moriarty in Kerouac's *On the Road.* Ural mentions Kerouac as well, and her two protagonists who travel on the road clearly invoke Kerouac's novel. But ultimately, Turkish underground writers on the whole are even farther removed from society than their Beat counterparts. As Halime Öcal Çoğulu concludes in her study of the genre, "In short, in America, Underground Literature is a literature that is outside the system, but inside life. However, in Turkish literature, it is clear that [underground literature's] social mission is not that well-defined and that it remains a much more individual struggle and effort in the society" (75). Because the United States has more of a history of individual rebellion, deviation from the norm forces one to become an outcast, but that decision still leaves the individual with a position in society and often a rather large network of like-minded "misfits" with whom to associate. Thus, the Beats, although undeniably alienated from society, "beaten" down by it, were nevertheless tapping into a larger postwar current of dissent that would eventually manifest itself in the 1960s countercultural movement. Turkish underground writing is far more isolated.

The Beats are also not as pessimistic as Turkish examples of the underground. Writing in *Varlık*, editor, writer, and academic Feridun Andaç highlights this distinction between underground as "evil" and as a portrayal of another lifestyle that might hold the possibility for hope:

> When I discovered Jack Kerouac, I also got curious about his life too. I found the book *An Illustrated Biography / Jack Kerouac* by David Sandison in between heavy metal CDs in an unusual bookstore in Vancouver. . . . [In it] you felt that the concept of "Underground" was not decay, that it was the reflection of an outlook that expressed the malaise a human being felt . . . in an environment of societal cracking. (14)

The assumption in Turkey is that underground literature must be depressing and despairing, since it chronicles life on the margins of society. Yet when Andaç encounters Kerouac's life and work, he realizes that it is more of a social critique than a record of despondency. This is not to claim that Turkish underground writers are somehow more authentic or rebellious than their Beat predecessors. Beat texts, especially in the early postwar period, were a direct challenge to authority in much the same way that Turkish writing poses a threat to commonly held Turkish norms. But the sort of cultural revolution the Beats helped to inaugurate has proven adept at transforming those very texts from oppositional to classic. In a country like the United States, where teenagers are expected to rebel and undergraduates to discover themselves, Beat texts become a legitimized zone of experimentation. Only time will tell if such a change will occur in Turkey, but at least for now, underground literature does offer characters who directly confront the mainstream and, given the country's current cultural climate, will likely remain controversial for the foreseeable future.

Comparing Beat writers with their Turkish counterparts demonstrates the ability of the spirit of Beat critique to transcend both temporal moment and cultural distance. Turkish underground authors likewise explore a marginalized space that shares many similarities with their U.S. counterparts. By "dropping out" of mainstream society to embrace alternative lifestyles, both groups renegotiated the roles allotted them, even if that attempt was sometimes fraught with difficulty. The result is a body of writing that chronicles a similar feeling of oppression and offers a comparable message of determination in the face of social constraint. This shared attempt demonstrates the universality of the countercultural struggle. The desire to explore new modes of living and writing in order to discover a more authentic version of the self clearly knows no boundaries, even if cultural difference ensures that writings which challenge society will never look exactly alike.

CONCLUSION

It is easy to overlook a name. As time goes forward, terms such as *Beat* or *Beat Generation* seem to become self-evident, commonplaces that no longer need interrogation or discussion. But debates over classificatory rubrics are a positive means of raising awareness of how a group of writers or texts function in society. Love them or hate them, such terms are both necessary and here to stay. Groups of texts and writers need some way of being collected and organized, and even though terms like *Beat* never do full justice to the specifics of the case under discussion, they are essential. Without them, there would be no means of understanding larger trends and currents, and thus no way to begin talking about a group of texts or writers and the function they are serving in the literary community and beyond. The constellation of associations built up around words like *Beat* means that whenever they are used (or even avoided), they send a message. Given that inevitability, it makes sense to reexamine our ideas of "Beat" and the meanings attached to the term.

The Turkish reception of the Beats through the prism of the underground label has meant that *Beat* is often understood in Herbert Huncke's sense of the term as "beaten" or "tired" rather than in Jack Kerouac's conception of beat as jazz ecstasy or spiritual enlightenment. Of course, there is no reason why this state of affairs must remain unchanged. As the Beats and their work gain more attention, there is an opportunity for new readers to look at the movement with new eyes. The underground literature rubric predisposes readers to see the "darkness" in the Beats, and if they remain under this banner, then the current reading will probably maintain its hold. After all, it is difficult not to focus on the transgressive aspects of a book that one receives clandestinely. But if readers begin to encounter these texts in different settings such as the classroom or hear about them in more staid contexts, then other readings are possible. The place, time, and condition of reading does indeed matter.

Beat texts do seem to be moving out from the underground and into more accepted venues. No longer relegated to obscure publishing houses and underground fanzines, in Turkey it seems as though the Beats are now taking their place as legitimate literary classics. Yet given the more oppressive cultural climate following the 2016 coup attempt, there is the distinct possibility that the Beats might again become marginalized and suspect. Should they suffer further repression and censorship, they might find themselves again facing the stigmas that characterize underground literature in Turkey. In an ironic twist, the fear that underground literature has become too popular might be set to rest, as subversive countercultural literature once again finds itself relegated to the edges of society. While that outcome might reinstate the subcultural clout of the Beats and the underground, it would also mean that access to literature meant to stimulate thought and provoke critique would be more difficult.

Beat influence on Turkish underground writing is circuitous, ending in literary work that while sharing a desire to challenge social expectations, is not always immediately recognizable as "Beat." But perhaps that result is understandable and indeed desirable. Given Turkey's current state, the more pessimistic viewpoint of Turkish underground writing might seem warranted. What the Beats offer is inspiration. Beat is an attitude, and if it is going to remain useful when it travels, it must be malleable. Turkish underground writers draw on this inspiration to craft work that critiques the particular problems and issues in contemporary Turkish society. Their work is Beat in spirit if not always in tone.

Tracing the reception of a term like *Beat* in a different cultural setting like Turkey offers a fresh perspective on the possibilities of the classificatory rubrics we employ. It is not that another culture's viewpoint must be accepted; only that such a disjunct creates the space to challenge assumptions and enliven thinking. We are never going to arrive at a final understanding of a word like *Beat* (or any such term, for that matter) because the use of such terms is always in flux. *Beat* will always shed some connotations and absorb others as readers find new uses and perspectives for the texts that make up the Beat canon. But in that process of continual redefinition exists the possibility to continually question what we mean and what we are hoping to achieve when we say the word *Beat*.

2. BUILDING COMMUNITY OUTSIDE THE MAINSTREAM
UNDERGROUND POETIX AND THE TURKISH ALTERNATIVE PRESS

"I'm so lonely." This simple confession became one of the cult sayings of Kaan and Mete, two late-night radio show hosts whose program *Losers' Club* (*Kaybedenler Kulübu*) became an underground hit on Kent FM during the 1990s. The pair, who spent the show drinking, smoking, and asking their female listeners "Have we had sex before?" garnered more widespread fame when a film was made of their exploits. *Losers' Club* (Dir. Tolga Örnek; 2011) was fond of juxtaposing time-lapse photography of ferries, traffic, and people traversing the city of Istanbul with the slow, meditative leisure of two guys talking "*geyik muhabbeti*" (literally "stag chat") or improvised speech bereft of purpose or direction. Despite their desire to remain obscure "losers" more interested in each other's conversation and exploring where it takes them, Kaan and Mete reach an ever-increasing audience. The actual radio show leapt from obscurity to number one in the ratings over its short run, and the film chronicles this rise through jump cuts to listeners enraptured by the hosts' banter. "Brit" sitting alone drinking wine, "Devrim" ("Revolution") sculpting in his studio, "Kuşbeyin" ("Birdbrain") listening intensely on the floor while candles flicker, and a girl in a head scarf, "Ayşe," sitting alone by the radio so nobody else can hear: all are images that attempt to capture visually the hold the show had on its radio listeners. Juxtaposed with a frenetic Istanbul, the film presents Kaan and Mete's fan base as an isolated community who are nevertheless able to share intimate parts of their own lives through the disembodied space of the airwaves.

The success of *Losers' Club*, both as a film and as a radio program, testifies to a Turkish desire for some forum where the "real" issues, those excluded from public discourse, can be discussed openly and positively. Kaan and Mete delve into topics normally considered too taboo to be discussed in Turkish society: sexuality, religion, polygamy, loneliness, death, and the desire to distance oneself from commitment. The film and the hosts that inspired it do sometimes border on the puerile, such as when a young female caller is dismissed after the hosts find out she is a virgin, turning instead to the topic of "the most popular sexual positions of the twentieth century." As listeners, critics, and even the film itself notes, the treatment of women as interchangeable sexual commodities is a problem. But overall, the film depicts Kaan and Mete's discussions as important for opening up dialogue concerning controversial topics. Atilla Dorsay, a columnist for *Sabah* newspaper, argues that while such radio shows may seem mundane in the West, in Turkey, Kaan and Mete should be considered pioneers: "It is one of the earliest examples of a type of radio show that we have very little of." *Losers' Club* listeners formed a virtual community in the space of telephone line and radio airwave. Listening to their hosts and callers like themselves describe similar problems provided a way to alleviate loneliness, and helped them to realize that they were not the only "losers" out there, not the only ones "beaten" by social demands.

This chapter explores another such attempt to create a forum where like-minded individuals can find camaraderie, support, and, oftentimes, their own voice: the magazine *Underground Poetix* (2008–present). As its name implies, this Turkish publication is heavily influenced by an earlier U.S. countercultural tradition. Edited by Şenol Erdoğan and Kaan Çaydamlı and published by underground mainstay 6:45, *Underground Poetix* sees itself as heir to a 1960s publishing practice that sought to challenge society by voicing concerns that could not find vent elsewhere in the culture. Thus this chapter begins with an examination of the underground or "alternative" press in the United States, as well as the Beats' relationship to this new form of media. In the postwar context, the underground press established publications for those who could not speak their minds in preexisting publishing forums. This alternative press was the voice of the counterculture, expressing dissenting opinion at a time when mainstream publications were deemed mere mouthpieces for the establishment. *Underground Poetix* operates in much the same vein. Drawing on Western countercultural traditions but amending them for present needs, the journal offers a radical critique of Turkish society through an appeal to Western imported cultural products such as the Beats. Intensely provocative in both style and content, *Underground Poetix* is a unique publication designed to inform, stimulate, and provoke its readers. The magazine also invites its subscribers to submit their own work, and the ways in which these poems highlight, reinforce, and sometimes reinterpret the publication's overall thrust provide insight into how Western counterculture is redeployed in the Turkish context. Like *Losers' Club*, the publication *Underground Poetix* attempts to give voice to a silenced minority and so build solidarity outside mainstream Turkish society.

AN ALTERNATIVE TO THE MAINSTREAM

The U.S. underground or alternative press, as these names imply, constituted a system of informal publishing venues designed to circumvent the established media outlets and to "get the word out" to a like-minded readership. Beat and countercultural writers had a difficult time placing their challenging works in traditional publishing venues. For reasons of both theme and style, such oppositional works needed their own avenues for dissemination. Ideologically opposed to the mainstream media, the underground was a place where writers and intellectuals could openly oppose the status quo. For many, publication in the mass media was not only impossible but also undesirable, given their ideological opposition to the established culture of the time. The underground press was where such oppositional works could find a voice and, hopefully, an audience who could understand and appreciate the countercultural stance the dissenters promulgated.

Often referred to as the "mimeograph revolution" due to changes in technology that made publishing cheaper and quicker, 1960s underground publications could inform their countercultural communities and disseminate new writing directly and immediately. As Steven Clay and Rodney Phillips explain in their introduction to *A Secret Location on the Lower East Side*, "Direct access to mimeograph machines, letterpress, and inexpensive offset made these publishing ventures possible, putting the means of production in the hands of the poet" (14). The importance of such publications consisted not so much in their ability to convert new followers but rather to build and strengthen solidarity among their constituents. The underground press fostered interconnectivity, and in the process allowed both writers and readers to gain strength through shared conviction. Underground presses and alternative publishing venues probably did little to convert more conservative citizens to their viewpoint, but they were adept at informing their underground communities about topics important to them and building solidarity among the brethren.

The underground press was in direct opposition to the mainstream culture of the time. In an often-reprinted statement, William S. Burroughs outlined the purpose of the underground press as follows: "In Western societies, where a democratic facade is still maintained like an old film back drop, the real power rests in the hands of those who manipulate the mass mind through mass media. An effective counter to this control is posed by the underground press and in consequence the underground press is subject to continual attack on spurious pretexts" (Preface 44). Burroughs's quote, written as a preface to the anthology of the British underground newspaper *International Times* (1966–73), was a mainstay in underground publications of the time, becoming something of a mantra and even making it into German underground publications like *päng* (1970–76) and *Zero* (1971–73) in translation. Mass media had become a mere mouthpiece for establishment views, and the only way to break this stranglehold on media outlets was to offer an "alternative" press that ran counter to prevailing discourse, challenging the supposed objectivity presented in mainstream publications with a vision of the world as the counterculture saw it. Burroughs's statement demonstrates that the underground press defined itself through opposition, challenging dominant views with clandestine publications that raised issues normal media outlets refused to address.

The stakes in this struggle were real. John Sinclair, a poet and an activist involved in the publication of Detroit's underground newspaper *Fifth Estate* (1965–present) was sentenced to ten years in jail in 1969 for the possession of marijuana (and released shortly after a 1971 rally that included John Lennon, Stevie Wonder, and Allen Ginsberg). Sinclair printed another statement that laid out the goals of the underground movement and became a rallying cry for its supporters. "The Alternative Press," dated "Marquette Prison 11-7-69," was published in the form of single piece of paper folded to make a letter, with the inscription "Free John Sinclair" at the bottom:

> The alternative
> press. Presses. Free Poems, oh yes,
> a free press
> of our own. Or to put it one more way,
> "What we demand is the unity
> of politics and art, the unity of content
> & form, the unity of revolutionary political content
> and the highest possible perfection
> of artistic form"

. . .
And we will press that alternative
in the face of whatever it is
would not have us free—we will press it,
and press it,
until our lives themselves
become the poem. (Sinclair)

Sinclair's declaration encapsulates the thrust of underground publishing by one of its own practitioners. The form of the poem itself (a broadside folded into a letter) highlights the principle of art being in the service of direct action. The document was intended to be mailed, perhaps repeatedly, to spread the word about the writer's political predicament and to stress the importance of the underground movement. Sinclair's poem demands this melding of "politics and art." In the end, life itself "becomes a poem," as readers are admonished not just to consume literature but also to embody it in their daily lives. The alternative press is essential in galvanizing such support by spreading the news ignored by mainstream media in order to help its readers realize their goal of a better and more open society.

The concept of the underground or alternative press covered a wide range of publication types and styles. Sinclair seems to be referring to literary publishing in his poem, but those involved in the underground did not believe in clear demarcations. Perhaps the most recognizable form of the underground press today is the countercultural newspaper. Publications such as the *Berkeley Barb* (1965–80), the *East Village Other* (1965–72), the *Los Angeles Free Press* (1964–78), and the earliest example, the *Village Voice* (1955–present), were designed to circulate among a countercultural community in a specific (usually urban) location. These publications looked like any other newspaper in circulation, but when one delved into their idiosyncratic layout and analyzed their content, the antiestablishment tone became apparent. The *Berkeley Barb* provides a typical example. This newspaper, reporting on all that was happening in the Bay Area "scene," provided readers with accounts of the Human Be-In that took place in Golden Gate Park; complaints about the University of California educational system; advertisements for head shops, local theaters, and upcoming rock concerts; and editorials and personal ads. The *Barb*, as the paper was called, also disseminated local information, such as where to catch a Yippie Bus to the Chicago Demonstration or how to sign up for welfare payments. Coverage of drug busts and local drug news was extensive and included articles on how to make an Afghani "chillum" to smoke hashish. The paper also covered the latest happenings in the gay, black power, and feminist circles. As the paper itself proudly declared, the *Barb* offered "All the News *They Fear* to Print." The disparate needs of local communities and readers meant that some underground publications were more political while others focused on specific "scenes" such as the university or the psychedelic communities. But whatever a subcultural community needed, underground presses such as the *Barb* tried to provide.[1]

The underground press likewise challenged stylistic expectations of a newspaper or periodical. The 1960s were a decade that witnessed a technological revolution. New printing technologies along with the explosion of color television heralded a more visually focused media culture. Writing in the November/December 1967 issue of *Print*, Janet Vrchota attempts to make sense of these new techniques in her article "The Underground Press." She describes such publications as "a journalistic form characterized by a blithe disregard and scorn for every hallowed precept about what a newspaper is supposed to be, do, contain and look like" (11). She then goes on to detail the new way the underground press used images: "Graphics—whether photographs or drawings—are not considered convenient but essentially unnecessary appendages to text pieces, but rather are viewed as integral elements in the total 'statement'" (14). Rejecting the staid form of journalism that offered the reader an objective account of an event, the underground press chose to present an array of material that, while coherently antiestablishment, nevertheless reveled in the joy of the countercultural experience and allowed the reader (and the viewer) to draw his or her own conclusions. Little was held sacred. Submissions were rarely edited, and typographic errors, spelling mistakes, and puns (both intentional and unintentional) proliferated. Editors were not afraid to retain profanity, and many underground publications included a good deal of nudity. Direct attacks on political and religious figures were common, and other countercultural figures would come up for critique and ridicule as well. As alternative publications self-consciously promoted life outside the mainstream, they often became outrageous, but at the same time more interesting and provocative.

Countercultural newspapers, however, were not the only type of underground publications. Literary journals and periodicals likewise proliferated during the postwar period. These "little magazines" shared much with earlier modernist small-press publications like the *Dial* (1840–1929) and *Blast* (1914–15). As Jerome Rothenberg points out, underground publications look back to the "first (golden) age of 'little' magazines and presses," established by figures such as Gertrude Stein, Ezra Pound, Mina Loy, and William

Carlos Williams, that were "noncommercial" and "often poet-run" (9–10). Postwar alternative literary journals, published irregularly as material became available and always on a shoestring budget, provided writers with an outlet for work that challenged literary and social norms. The publishing arc of Kansas-based *Grist* (1964–67) is paradigmatic. Starting out as a stapled newsletter, *Grist* featured student poetry that would probably not have found publication elsewhere. As the journal progressed, production became slicker, and *Grist* printed works by more established countercultural figures like Michael McClure, d. a. levy, Charles Bukowski, and Allen Ginsberg. The journal took a stand, publishing Ginsberg's critique of the United States and its war in Vietnam with "Wichita Vortex Sutra," a poem Ginsberg composed spontaneously as he traveled through the Midwest, juxtaposing American scenery with media coverage of the war. *Grist* also offered its readers provocative cartoon illustrations and photographs. Like many such underground literary periodicals, *Grist*'s contents were eclectic. Robert Creeley, David Antin, Robert Bly, and Hunter S. Thompson could all be found within its pages. The independence enjoyed by such alternative periodicals meant that editors and writers were now able to foreground countercultural themes and issues.

THE UNDERGROUND PRESS AND THE BEATS

Beat writing was often highly provocative, and thus it comes as no surprise that these writers relied on the underground press extensively to get their countercultural message out to readers. Journals such as *Neurotica* (1948–51), *Semina* (1955–64), *Evergreen Review* (1957–73), *Yūgen* (1958–62), *Kulchur* (1960–66), *City Lights* (1952–55), *Chicago Review* (1946–present), *Beatitude* (regularly from 1959 to 1960; intermittently to 1996), the *Floating Bear* (1961–71), *Angel Hair Sleeps with a Boy in My Head* (1966–69), and *Big Table* (1959–60) used the Beats as part of a direct challenge to their social milieu. *Evergreen Review*, certainly the most commercially successful of these, was also the most influential. In his introduction to the *Evergreen Review Reader: 1957–1966*, Ken Jordan discusses the journal's reliance on both Beat writing and the European avant-garde, claiming the journal was "unique in bringing these two strands of postwar writing—two columns of attack forces in the effort to transform the culture—together under one set of covers. While not the first magazine to publish the Beats, *Evergreen* was certainly among the first, and it was definitely the most important" (n.p.). Its second issue, titled "San Francisco Scene," included the Beat writers Jack Kerouac, Ginsberg, Gary Snyder, Lawrence Ferlinghetti, McClure, and Philip Whalen, and its seizure by customs officials for obscenity raised these authors' profiles even further. But *Evergreen Review* was not the only journal that faced censorship battles. *Big Table*, launched when a Beat issue of *Chicago Review* was suppressed by the University of Chicago administration, helped to draw attention to Beats such as Kerouac, Gregory Corso, Burroughs, and others in several of its early issues. In addition, small presses like Totem, Corinth Books, New Directions, Grove, and the important City Lights provided early outlets for Beat work. This alternative press scene allowed transgressive Beat writings to be heard, and was instrumental in building a community around Beat works.

Underground publications were very reader-oriented. Not only did they often print letters and other material sent in by readers, but possession of such journals was akin to a personal statement. Journals were part of a shared sense of belonging to a subcultural community. Texts took on a new life as well. When encountered between the pages of these underground publications, Beat works became more than just literature for private consumption. A full-page poem of Ginsberg's "Hiway Poesy LA-Albuquerque-Texas-Wichita," complete with colorful illustrations, or a broadside with a provocative title like "Bomb" by Corso, becomes more of a declaration when tacked to a wall or a door.[2] As James D. Sullivan observes in his study *On the Walls and in the Streets*, the materiality of such texts points to their function as objects that do cultural work: "Those tangible and visible qualities of design and publication carry the traces of the artifact's use, and thus make poetry as a cultural practice, rather than simply as a series of texts" (3). The amazing artwork of a newspaper like San Francisco's *Oracle* (1966–68), for instance, was clearly meant for more than casual perusal. It sent a signal to others that the owner was part of the underground psychedelic community. The context of reception, then, is just as important as the content of the material in producing meaning.

These "little magazines" also allowed writers to form supportive communities for their work. Gilbert Sorrentino, who was directly involved in *Yūgen*, *Kulchur*, and *Neon* (1956–60) argues in his contribution to the collection *The Little Magazine in America* that these early Beat periodicals functioned *inter*dependently to solidify their opposition stance. He observes that the

> bulk of this writing was done by a rather small group of writers, so that many little magazines drew on essentially the same authors as contributors. There slowly evolved a kind of network of magazines acting as a general clearinghouse for new methods, techniques, and ideas of literary composition and criticism. (300)

Following the advice given him by William Carlos Williams, Sorrentino saw these collaborations not as anthologies of new writing but as a chance for a group of like-minded individuals to stake out a position. This desire for camaraderie and mutual support was helped tremendously by the speed in which such alternative publications could be produced and disseminated. The spread of alternative press publishing allowed writers to get material out quickly and receive timely responses from their readerships. Discussing her years editing the literary newsletter the *Floating Bear*, Diane di Prima relates of Charles Olson that "one of the things he talked about was how valuable the *Bear* had been to him in its early years because of the fact that he could get new work out that fast" (x). This impulse for an immediate form of publishing likewise informed Alexander Trocchi's "Sigma Portfolio" project, a collection of bulletins from writers like McClure, psychotherapists such as R. D. Laing, and filmmakers like Stan Brakhage meant to provide writers with quick access to a public. Given that these writers were fighting an elitist and entrenched literary community as well as a stifling postwar conformist society, their banding together made sense, lending their publications more force than if they were published independently and allowing their writing to respond to changing developments immediately.[3]

Ultimately, underground newspapers and alternative literary journals bled into one another. Both were engaged in an attack on postwar American values, and strict genre demarcations were just another barrier to overcome. The title of Ed Sanders's journal, *Fuck You: A Magazine of the Arts* (1962–65), encapsulates this erasure of the line between high and low culture. Proclaiming "Total Assault on the Culture" in its editorial page, *Fuck You* is both a literary and an irreverent critique of cultural norms.[4] The underground literary journal was often political, while many of the underground newspapers routinely carried poetry. *Nola Express* (1967–72) was a political newspaper that published the names and addresses of the New Orleans draft board but also became well known for running Charles Bukowski's column "Notes of a Dirty Old Man." And Harold Norse's Beat-centered *Bastard Angel* (1972–74) combined the eccentric drawings, photographs, and collages typical of the underground newspaper with the literary magazine. In the end, the terms *underground* and *alternative press* were popular because they expressed the emergence of a new type of publishing that was concerned less with what a publication should be than with the goal of providing its readers with interesting, entertaining, timely, and provocative work that challenged all conceptions of mainstream U.S. society.[5]

Beat-inspired publishing continues today. While not exactly underground, these publications keep the Beat spirit alive into the new millennium.

These later magazines, however, face different conditions of reception. The U.K.-based *Beat Scene* (1988–present) for example, addresses a problem similar to that faced by the Beats in the early 1950s—literary obscurity. But by 2000, the problem was not so much the rebellious nature of the Beat challenge to literary and cultural norms but rather the postmodern saturation of media. As editor Kevin Ring explains,

> *Beat Scene* began in 1988 and has continued to promote, investigate, and profile the Beat Generation and all those associated with it. Fifteen years later we are still here determined to follow through on those original ideals, giving coverage to the books, the music, the poetry, etc. of the Beats that mainstream media mostly ignore, that is unless they happen to be fashion flavour of that week and can help shift a few pairs of chinos. We interview the poets, review the obscure books, profile the big names, Heavens, we've even interviewed some of them too. Otherwise we fear much of this would slip by largely unnoticed, missed if you happen to live in Cleethorpes or Selkirk or Croydon and other places off the media radar map—that is everywhere besides London it seems. Even then Beat news from the USA mostly evades all radar. *Beat Scene* tries to put that right. (3)

Beat Scene looks back on the Beat moment from a remove. Although it does run some original writing by the Beats and contains tributes and memoirs from those who remember these authors or the scene, as Ring explains, it is more about "promoting" the Beat Generation to a new audience beyond its original moment of reception. *Beat Scene*, like many other such later magazines devoted to the Beats, has a different task than earlier Beat publications. In a hypermediated world where access to everything is virtually unlimited, such publications seek to keep the Beat message alive by not only documenting and chronicling the Beats and those who were with them but also likewise "selling" this project as important to a new generation with even more cultural options from which to choose.

Nor is this reclamation conducted only in the popular arena. *Moody Street Irregulars* (1978–92), edited by Joy Walsh and Michael Basinski, announced in its inaugural issue that it would "include announcements, queries, articles, controversy, and notes of special interest to Kerouac scholars and those, for love of Jack, who are involved in the mind-bending experience of Kerouac" (2). The journal, its first issues printed on cheap paper and proclaiming its cost at "1 buck," quickly increased in quality, length, and advertising as subsequent issues came out. *Moody Street Irregulars*, as its editors announced, has a more scholarly bent, carrying reprinted articles from journals such as

American Literature and *boundary 2*, and including announcements by the University of Texas at Austin's Humanities Research Center concerning the availability of Kerouac's materials for perusal. The journal is a veritable who's who of Beat scholarship. Many well-known Beat scholars such as Jaap van der Bent, Ronna C. Johnson, Gregory Stephenson, Jennie Skerl, and Gerald Nicosia contributed to the journal at earlier stages of their careers. The journal also published some original work by Kerouac and related Beats, as well as interviews and poems by others, along with drawings, illustrations, and photographs that became more professional as the journal progressed. *Moody Street Irregulars* was also surprisingly international, with many foreign contributors represented. It attempted to promote the Beat message from *within* academia in order to help carve out space for the Beats in a generally hostile scholarly environment.

The rise of an Internet culture across the globe has only intensified the competition for readers' attention. There has been an increase in the Beats' global presence due in large part to the proliferation of Facebook pages and websites devoted to their lives and writings. The Allen Ginsberg Project, Jack Kerouac: American Novelist and Poet, Literary Kicks, and other sites provide images, links, bibliographies, and news updates to Beat enthusiasts. Perhaps the most popular is the online journal *Beatdom*. While many sites are fairly short-lived and other magazines such as *Beat Scene* have begun to establish an Internet presence, *Beatdom* has been active online since its founding in 2007. As editor David S. Wills declares in his mission statement, "*Beatdom* is the world's most popular literary journal dedicated to the study of the Beat Generation. We are dedicated to improving the state of modern literature by publishing poetry and fiction inspired by the Beats, while also providing the highest quality essays on original Beat literature" (Wills). The Internet is a useful vehicle for delivering a wide range of texts to a wide range of people. The website RealityStudio, which focuses mainly on Burroughs, provides not only a forum for Burroughs enthusiasts but also includes archives of Sanders's *Fuck You: A Magazine of the Arts*, *Kulchur*, and the German little magazine *Rhinozeros* (1960–65), all accessible at the stroke of a key. Yet the Internet also means that the Beat message must contend with a plethora of other voices of resistance. With so much information at one's fingertips, it is easy to quickly jump to another site or link. Nevertheless, the Internet has been a crucial engine driving the dissemination of the Beats and their works, providing countless people across the globe information concerning Beat lives and even access to quotes, photographs, and texts that would otherwise be too expensive or time-consuming to acquire by other means.

Given the rise of an Internet culture across the globe, it is easy to overlook the importance that the underground press, in all its forms, played in establishing a collegial interconnectedness and disseminating Beat writings to an ever-increasing audience. In fact, it might not be too hyperbolic to claim that this often overlooked aspect of the Beats was a crucial reason for their success. The underground press was an important means of building a community of not only like-minded writers but like-minded readers as well. By establishing a strong underground following, the alternative press, in all its forms, set the stage for a wider breakthrough of Beat writing that was to come, a flowering that continues today with other nontraditional publishing ventures meant to capture the Beat spirit.

UNDERGROUND POETIX

While the original radio show *Losers' Club* was meant to foster a sense of shared belonging among its disaffected listeners, the film version articulates the desire to share the burdens of loneliness through an appeal to the written word. To heighten the connection between those dissatisfied with contemporary Turkish society and an underground literary practice that critiques that very discontent, much of the film incorporates an existing literary scene. This admixture of the imagined past, the "real" past of the radio show, and the current literary present is extremely fluid. Şenol Erdoğan, one of the real-life editors of the publishing house 6:45, appears in the film as Kaan's assistant at the publishing house of the same name, which he runs as his day job apart from the show. The real-life Kaan Çaydamlı, who indeed is the owner of 6:45, makes only a cameo appearance, but his character often accompanies Şenol and his partner Mete to the real-life nightclub Kargo, in Kadiköy's famous *Barlar Sokağı* (Street of Bars). Run by Tayfun Polat, who himself has contributed to the underground literature debate, Kargo plays host to deejays, film screenings, and other alternative events, and such references would not be lost on Turkish viewers involved in the underground literary or music scenes. This crossover from film to reality and back again reinforces the film's alternative credentials by aligning it with an underground reading public and provides the publishing house 6:45 with additional exposure and countercultural clout.

Given that 6:45 is an important source for translations of Beat texts in Turkey, it comes as no surprise that these countercultural figures appear repeatedly in the film. The connection between 6:45 and the Beats is made explicit at the outset, with a photo of Ginsberg appearing on the opening credits, and those of Burroughs and Bukowski adorning the walls of the publishing house. Though not all textual references in the film are countercultural, those to the Beats satisfy viewers who know 6:45's dedication to publishing such transgressive material. Direct reference to Kerouac, for instance, does not appear, but the film includes several voice-over meditations by Kaan on the nature of the road during shots of him traveling to a cemetery on his motorcycle. The character Birdbrain (*Kuşbeyin*), an older caller who listens meditatively in a room full of candles, is a clear reference to Ginsberg's poem of the same name that became the title of Hakan Arslan's 1991 translation of a selection of the poet's work (more on this in chapter 5). Birdbrain is the only male caller the pair actually meet, and during their visit to his home he draws a comparison between the photograph of Norwegian jazz saxophonist Jan Garbarek and that of the Turkish poet and flutist Neyzen Tevfik hanging on his walls, claiming that "they blow the same breath in two different parts of the world." As the film critic Alper Turgut argues in his review, "You can enter [the film] from the Beat Generation and come out from underground literature. . . . [E]ven when you do not hear your own voice you can be everybody's voice." Shared knowledge of Beat and countercultural writing unites both film characters and viewers at home.

The other textual image repeatedly referenced in the film is the cover of 6:45's flagship publication, *Underground Poetix* (2008–present). This magazine is, in many ways, the publishing house's signature product. Although 6:45 has produced numerous translations of not only Beat texts but also works of fantasy, science fiction, and the Gothic, it is *Underground Poetix* that provides its editors with a forum for voicing their opinions and serves as a vehicle for quickly disseminating texts they believe are important for the Turkish countercultural community. The publishers have been savvy in their marketing strategy. They maintain a well-developed website, offer a range of products such as handbags, notebooks, posters, and T-shirts, and are regulars at the Istanbul book fair. They have also launched several side projects, such as their *Panpa* (*Bro*; 2012–present), a slicker periodical aimed at a wider youth market, as well as *Peyniraltı Edebiyatı* (*Whey Literature*; 2013–present), a monthly literary journal. Though these products are clearly meant to produce revenue, it does not seem as though monetary gain is the driving force behind 6:45. Like their cinematic counterparts, Erdoğan and Çaydamlı are more interested in building community and getting the word out. Their *Underground Poetix* magazine remains their mouthpiece. It offers a cocktail of rebellion, providing Turkish readers with access to countercultural themes and texts that would be difficult to find translated and discussed elsewhere.

A TURKISH FANZINE

Underground Poetix is best thought of as a fanzine. Cheap to produce and easy to disseminate, these photocopied pamphlets swept through Turkish youth culture in the 1990s. A portmanteau coined from the words *fan* or *fanatic* and *magazine*, fanzines were meant to represent the voice of a minor or subcultural group denied access to existing media channels. For a middle-class generation struggling to find its voice, the fanzine offered an opportunity to mock and ridicule an expanding consumer culture. Borrowing from the West while simultaneously critiquing it, the 1990s fanzine scene in Turkey was the belated offspring of several underground traditions. Stylistically, Turkish fanzines borrowed readily from a punk scene that had emerged in 1970s Britain among working-class youth fed up with high unemployment and low wages chronicled most famously by Birmingham Centre theorists Dick Hebdige in *Subculture: The Meaning of Style* and Stuart Hall and Tony Jefferson in their *Resistance through Rituals*. But fanzines, both in Turkey and earlier in the West, were indebted to a countercultural 1960s mimeograph revolution characterized by a profusion of small press publications. Like these earlier movements, Turkish fanzines sought to connect users and thus build a community in the days before widespread Internet use made instant connection possible. These ephemeral, do-it-yourself products were meant to get the word out, informing fellow fans about events and news while establishing a shared voice of social critique and dissatisfaction. Antiauthoritarian and, in Turkey, usually illegal, fanzines were the mouthpieces for subcultural youth groups focused on music and poetry that challenged the Turkish status quo in the 1990s.

A comparison between an early fanzine and an issue of *Underground Poetix* reveals similarities in both layout and theme. According to Murat Altun, in his master's thesis "The Photocopied 1990s: Youth, Culture, and Fanzines," *Mondo Trasho* (May 1991–1993?) was the first fanzine in Turkey (83). Done in the punk style, the cover of *Mondo Trasho*'s first issue presents an interesting hybrid of styles and themes (figure 2.1). Pasted over a picture of David Lynch's iconic "Henry" (Jack Nance) from *Eraserhead* is a series of titles printed in punk cut-outs. In a mockery of capitalism, a fake trademark sign appears in the upper right-hand corner. Turkish battles English for supremacy, with the word *Underground* left in English but incorporated into the Turkish declaration "*Underground'un süperstarlarından*," or "from the superstars of the underground." Jack Kerouac makes an important appearance with a translation of his review of F. W. Murnau's classic *Nosferatu*, while countercultural figures like the subversive French writer Jean Genet and media guru Marshall

Fig. 2.1. The 1990s Turkish fanzine scene drew heavily on Western counterculture to challenge the status quo with an anything-goes punk style.

McLuhan stand next to Andy Warhol's film icon Edie and John Waters's transvestite star "divine" (announced in French-derived Turkish as an "*ajan provakatör*" or "*agent provocateur*"). *Mondo Trasho*, its title itself a nod to earlier American 1960s low-budget cultural products meant to shock and outrage, presents a punk-inspired anything-goes attitude that levels East and West, high and low, to challenge and provoke through appropriation and mockery.

Compare this early fanzine with *Underground Poetix*'s second issue (figure 2.2). This cover, which adorns the walls of Kaan's office in the film *Losers' Club*, presents a veritable smorgasbord of revolt. At this point, the journal still includes "Kadıköy" in its title, a nod to their local roots in the Asian district of Istanbul (they will drop this in subsequent issues). Underneath the title is the false announcement of the publication date as "2040" and the issue number as "#99." Punk-style cut-outs announce themes ranging from "Burroughs" to "Turkish Punk Poetry" and the "Kreuzberg'ın Sokak Kopeklerı" ("Street Dogs of Kreuzberg"). The issue traverses national boundaries, going from "Chicago '68," a reference to the countercultural events at the Democratic National Convention attended by Burroughs, Ginsberg, and Genet, to the West Germany terrorist organization "Baader Meinhof (R.A.F.)" and the "Psiko Cografya" ("Psycho-Geography") of France's Situationist International. A defiant, tattooed woman, complete with punk-style studded wristband, stares out disdainfully at the viewer. The interior makes good on the promises connoted by the cover, delivering these and other articles on Che Guevara, Turkish porno films, photographs of seminaked women, articles on the Beat connection to jazz and punk, and even one titled "Anti-Caliphate." Over time, the journal became better produced, and shifted into a more subdued aesthetic. Issue thirteen captures the new look, with a photograph of Burroughs and David Bowie taken by Terry O'Neill in 1974 (and hand-colored by Bowie) above a white band below which contains an ironically placed barcode and the publisher's name (figure 2.3). Despite this slicker look, content remains the same. *Underground Poetix* continues to deliver all themes countercultural, in all variants and varieties, to its readers.

Fig. 2.2. *Underground Poetix* follows in the footsteps of an earlier Turkish fanzine tradition, offering its readers a range of countercultural texts in a publishing style meant to shock and entice.

Fig. 2.3. Later issues of *Underground Poetix* provide the same countercultural content in a new, slicker package. Here David Bowie poses with William S. Burroughs to create a cover that is both hip and transgressive.

But *Underground Poetix*, while following in the fanzine tradition, is an anachronism. It self-consciously styles itself on earlier fanzines and countercultural publications, but exists in an Internet generation that has rendered its hard-copy dissemination more of a stance than a statement. Noted commentator Altay Öktem, who has published several anthologies of Turkish fanzines, claims, "In a way, fanzines were subcultures' medium of communication. . . . People who were interested in underground literature, who lived the underground life style generally followed these fanzines rather than literary publishing or popular publishing" (Öktem, interview).[6] Fanzines originally functioned as *samizdat*, but with the rise of the Internet, such hard-copy communication became unnecessary. Thus 6:45's choice of the fanzine genre for its magazine format speaks to a desire to capture the spirit of a historical moment that has long since passed, due to either the countercultural prestige fanzines enjoyed or nostalgia for a hard-copy past, or both.

Moreover, like its cousins *Çalıntı* and *Stüdyo Imge* discussed in the first chapter, *Underground Poetix* follows in the fanzine mode but is distinguished not only by its increased production values but also by its governmental legitimacy. Most fanzines were strictly illegal. Every Turkish publication must pass the censor, and *Underground Poetix* is no exception. But part of the appeal of fanzines, and the cornerstone of their underground status, is that most were sold *behind* the counters and from the *back* of book and newspaper stalls rather than in mainstream bookshops. Not only did this reinforce the subcultural status of their readers, but it also meant that fanzines could push boundaries that other journals were afraid to approach. As we shall see, *Underground Poetix* pushes against both legal and social barriers as well, but it does so with the knowledge that it has to eventually pass the censors to be published. Earlier Turkish fanzines were under no such constraint.

Underground Poetix self-consciously draws on Western counterculture in its open stance against the establishment. The title itself is a nod to both the underground tradition discussed earlier (which characteristically remains written in English) and to the alternative "Comix" scene of the late 1960s, characterized by mavericks like Robert Crumb. The editorial front material goes on to make this link explicit. On the publication page of issue 2, the editors announce the journal as an "independent 'Counter-Culture' Project published every three months" (*3 ayda bir neşredilen bağımsız "Karşı-Kültür" Projesi*).[7] *Counterculture* used in quotes here directly relates to the 1960s underground, while *project* is a term that gestures toward the open and collective, rather than the edited journal or magazine. Further solidifying this connection to U.S. countercultural modes, the editors write "Total Freedom" and "Free Press," again aligning the journal with the underground tradition.

These countercultural phrases, and others like them, appear repeatedly in other issues (in both English and Turkish translation), making it clear that *Underground Poetix* sees itself as heir to the countercultural tradition.

The influence of the American countercultural moment on the magazine's editors is especially pronounced when it comes to attacks on linguistic censorship. Like its underground counterparts in the West, *Underground Poetix* takes an anything-goes attitude toward its editorial policy. Not only do the editors not alter submissions, there are also frequent misspellings and grammatical inconsistencies in their own pieces. Disdain for traditional grammar and spelling was a hallmark of the American counterculture and is indeed a recurrent theme in the underground press as a whole. Another journal in the underground tradition, the *Radical Therapist*, was devoted to rethinking practices in the field of mental health care. Like many contemporaneous publications, it declared that its articles were unedited and uncensored: "articles—with their split infinitives and sometimes peculiar punctuation—appear here exactly as they were submitted to, and published in, *The Radical Therapist.* No effort was made to edit for consistent style. Each voice remains original" (Agel xiv).[8] Allowances are made for profanity as well. Words normally excluded from "polite" society and mainstream publications find vent in the underground press, with Ed Sanders's magazine *Fuck You: A Magazine of the Arts* being the most egregious example. These challenges to linguistic norms are meant not only to shock and outrage accepted morals but also to force a society to question the assumptions they make about the very words they speak. This commitment to linguistic freedom is thus in keeping with a general challenge to social expectations evidenced in the counterculture as a whole.

In the Turkish context, this disdain for the "rules" of society expresses itself in a direct rejection of the Turkish Language Association (*Türk Dil Kurumu*; TDK). This organization was founded in 1932 as part of the new Turkish Republic's attempt at language reform (*dil devrimi*) designed to replace the Arabic alphabet with the Latin and to "eliminate the Arabic and Persian grammatical features and the many thousands of Arabic and Persian borrowings" from the language (G. Lewis 2). Early Kemalists tried to consolidate and censor what they believed was an elitist language that lay outside their new version of a democratic Turkey, while Islamicists countered that the reform was meant to cut the people off from the language of the Qur'an. *Underground Poetix* takes a third position, weighing in on the side of linguistic freedom. The journal and its contributors are clearly against religious fundamentalism, but they often employ older, more archaic Ottoman words as a challenge to Kemalist reforms. The editors declare from the outset in the front matter of issue 6 that "[a]ny rule of the linguistic society is not valid for this piece." The point is made even clearer in issue 2: "Fuck tdk." The heyday of the society ended in 1950 (G. Lewis 153). Concerns over linguistic hegemony, when they do appear, now center on the influx of English and the rise of the Internet. But the society still exists and continues to decide on linguistic matters. While Western counterculture was fond of challenging an older generation's established rules of grammar, syntax, and notions of linguistic propriety, in the Turkish context, language holds an even more pivotal forum for challenging authority.

With the rise of the Internet in the mid-2000s, the Turkish fanzine became a thing of the past. The Internet has erased the underground nature of the small-press publication. Whereas before these underground publications functioned as a shibboleth among fans signaling subcultural membership, many feel that the Internet has made everything too open and easily accessible. Increased access to countercultural materials has been paid for with the loss of the aura and uniqueness that used to surround such clandestine texts. Öktem summarizes what many in the subcultures believe:

> I mean, that spirit is completely dead now. That spirit transformed itself on the internet because we cannot find the spirit of the 1990s fanzines on the internet. That's because when it comes to the internet that spirit changes, willingly or unwillingly. Though the contents are quite similar, an internet site does not have that texture, and cannot reflect that kind of subculture or underground culture. . . . The internet reflects colder and more technological aspects. (Öktem, interview)

The fanzines were addressed to the fanatic, the seeker, the one who sought out all things pertaining to their subcultural interest. This relationship between a publication and its readers can still be true of the Internet. But online publishing also means a cheapening of material as it becomes just another document or webpage to glance at, not something to hold, touch, and collect. Also signaled, perhaps, is a loss of the element of chance or mistake that epitomized a do-it-yourself production culture. *Underground Poetix* attempts to recapture the magic of the fanzine experience by giving its readers a physical object to hold, distribute, and cherish.

A REBELLIOUS COCKTAIL

To facilitate the challenge that the Beats pose, each issue of *Underground Poetix* consists of various types of pieces that attempt to provide readers with information and original texts from countercultures both past and present.

Although Turkish writers do sometimes make an appearance, the bulk of the material deals with Western sources. By far the majority of each issue is devoted to author profiles, interviews, and informative pieces. The Beats figure prominently in each. Kerouac, Ginsberg, and Burroughs are continually profiled, and their interviews and transcripts translated in almost every issue of the magazine. Other writers such as Corso, Gary Snyder, and Lawrence Ferlinghetti also make appearances, and much attention is paid to the countercultural writers Richard Brautigan and Tuli Kupferberg. But *Underground Poetix* is nothing if not eclectic. The magazine presents an array of rebellious and innovative figures, and while this broad range ensures that all readers will find something to enjoy, it also helps mobilize a disparate constellation of figures into a united front of rebellion.[9]

Such eclecticism of rebellion also occurs in the informative pieces the journal runs. Here again Beat topics such as the Gallery 6 reading in San Francisco and the figure of the road predominate, but *Underground Poetix* also delves into early American counterculture with articles on the Students for a Democratic Society (SDS), the Diggers, the Black Panthers, the Weather Underground, and other revolutionary movements. Music, too, receives much attention, with pieces focusing mainly on bands that challenge the status quo, such as various punk groups, Sonic Youth, and Godspeed You Black Emperor. The journal also tends to be interested in the disruptive potential of the European avant-garde, with informative articles on Guy DeBord and the Lettrist Situationist International, Dada, and Futurism. The journal delves into a host of disparate, though relevant, topics such as stencil culture, how to meditate, and "Satanism in Islam" ("İslam'da Satanizm"). As is often the case with underground publications, the quality of the journal improves with every issue. Articles become better researched, the format and layout more sophisticated, and the print and graphics more professional. But *Underground Poetix*'s eclectic mix of themes, authors, and subjects, along with its emphasis on the countercultural Beats, always stays the same.

In addition to informative content, *Underground Poetix* provides its readers with access to a variety of original poetry and prose. The bulk of material comes in the form of translated Western texts, mainly by Beats like Kerouac, Ginsberg, and Burroughs (with Charles Bukowski also well represented). Though they sometimes vary in quality, these translations supplement the press's countercultural list with poems and excerpts that would be difficult and costly to acquire in the original and nearly impossible to find elsewhere in Turkish translation. But underground Turkish authors like those discussed in the first chapter are represented as well, along with original reader poetry that will be discussed later in this chapter. Figures like the popular novelist Hakan Günday and the gay poet küçük iskender appear, and the editors promote work from 6:45's own list of writers such as Mehmet A. Öztekin's *Veronica Pompa İstiyor: Bir Kadıköy Western'i* (*Veronica Wants the Pump: A Kadıköy Western*; 2011). Despite the presence of Turkish writers, the journal's primary function is to provide access to foreign countercultural texts, especially those of the Beats.

But this last title, and the litany of male names covered in the journal, are telling. *Underground Poetix* is mainly addressed to a young, male audience who wants to be titillated as well as informed. Öztekin's work, with its sexually suggestive title, chronicles the exploits of a vigilante as he attempts to track down the madam of a gang of prostitutes. Along the way, the unnamed protagonist attempts to save these women by beating them, while reserving his sexual desire for the elusive Veronica. The illustrations are provocative, and an endorsement on the back cover declares "I got really hard" (*iyice sertleşmiştim*). The journal is also fond of including naked women in suggestive poses in almost every issue. This has led to a backlash—Turkish women's rights groups complained that the first four issues were sexist (Erdoğan, interview). In response to these complaints, the editors began to incorporate more feminist and LGBT pieces, such as the Riot Grrrl manifesto and space devoted to Kathy Acker, Camille Paglia, Lydia Lunch, and Lady Gaga. Still, this misogynistic tendency is disturbing, and reinforces the often problematic nature of Beat gender politics. Increased attention has been paid in the West to those women and to minority Beat writers marginalized from the Beat canon. Although *Underground Poetix* does include some work and portraits of African American Beats like Bob Kaufman and Ted Joans, with the exception of a translated interview with Carolyn Cassady, few Beat women have found their way into the journal's pages. Such treatment reinforces the idea of the Beats as a boy's club with women nothing more than the object of sexual attention.

Such gender questions are important, since *Underground Poetix* sees itself as a promoter of the Beats. Erdoğan's championing of the Beats is not just about posing a challenge to a Turkey that he believes needs immediate changes. Erdoğan is also on a crusade to educate his audience about what "Beat" means. In our interview, Erdoğan laments, "William, Jack, Allen . . . In Turkey, people idiotically put them all on a par. More than anything, we want to break that myth. In Turkey, readers are not able to consider [these writers] as individuals" (Erdoğan, interview). *Underground Poetix* sees its role as not only the disseminator of Beat texts that could impact the future state of Turkey. The editors also believe that they are doing the

Beats' literary legacy a valuable service by clearing up myths and providing more detailed, accurate information that will help put Burroughs, Kerouac, and Ginsberg's contributions into the appropriate contexts. In his introduction to 6:45's *Beat Generation Anthology*, Erdoğan lambastes those who lump the Beats in with an array of other American countercultural figures: "half-witted anthology editors become merchants by inserting even hippy generation gurus into Beat literature and publishers encourage them" (*Beat Kuşağı Antolojisi* 8). What starts off as a defense of *The Soft Machine* becomes an insistent tirade against what Erdoğan sees as an ever-increasing desire to expand the Beat canon for purely commercial reasons. The *Anthology*, along with *Underground Poetix*, seeks to set the record straight by providing Turkish readers access to primary texts by these different Beat authors as well as other pieces that seek to explain and elucidate who each Beat was and the sort of role they played in the movement. The press sees itself as both educational and revolutionary.

The "belatedness" of *Underground Poetix* means that the magazine is in a unique position among international Beat publications. Time has in some ways tempered the Beats and their message, turning them from iconoclastic rebels to classic countercultural forebears. In the 1950s, the Beats were the "only game in town." By the late 1960s, identity politics resulted in a host of social challenges such as women's groups, black power, and gay rights. Today, countercultural options have expanded further still. Yet for a Turkey in the midst of social upheavals, the Beats are still very much an active component in countercultural struggle. In the West, the moment of direct countercultural struggle, in its broadest sense, has passed. While there is little doubt that problems like social inequality and ecological uncertainty still remain, the Beats have been consigned to a more nostalgic status as early exponents of a cultural change that seems anachronistic in the West today. The Beats are now part of a corpus of classic countercultural American literature, and while they still inspire consciousness expansion, drug experimentation, and the college road trip, the idea that their works will spark another cultural revolution seems past. This might likewise be true of Turkey, but for Erdoğan and others like him who promote the Beats, they still have the possibility to provide a direct social challenge. *Underground Poetix* is a hybrid. Like newer journals, it looks back to the Beats from a privileged temporal vantage point. But like older Beat journals, it positions the Beats as direct challenges to the status quo.

Yet unlike western journals that can rely on a built-in audience for Beat works, in Turkey, 6:45 needs to build a readership. While the Beats do indeed enjoy heightened media exposure, they still lack the sort of presence that they enjoy in a Western context where they have been on the scene for some time. This means that the Beats arrive as part of a "package" of rebellion that includes other figures. Erdoğan wants readers both to acknowledge the Beats and their message and to harness that understanding in mounting a challenge to Turkey's current social climate. To achieve this end, he must first educate his readers as to who the Beats are and provide a context for their work. Of course the two go hand in hand. To learn about the Beats is to learn about their struggle to free themselves from the social expectations of the early Cold War. This blank slate is useful, since the reader can come to the Beats without preconceived notions about their message or their morals. But it also requires a more robust salesmanship. In the West and particularly in the United States, where the Beats are easily received as part of a tradition of dissent, their concepts and purpose are perhaps more readily absorbable, though certainly not all readers are willing to embrace the Beat ethos. In the Turkish situation, *Underground Poetix* and other promoters of the Beats need to make a stronger "pitch" as to their relevancy, especially given their outsider status. As Turkey lacks the same sort of tradition of a resistant cultural poetics, the editors cannot simply rely on the Beats' status as countercultural forebears (though they do attempt this at times). The Beats are pitched as a new way to live, a new way to think, and a new way to write.

RESPONSE OF TURKISH READERS

Underground Poetix does more than just provide access to the Beats—by including writing produced by readers, it also offers a space for individuals whose thoughts, ideas, and feelings lie outside the Turkish norm to express themselves in a nonjudgmental forum. Given the oftentimes draconian state of Turkish society, the airing of these concerns are not only frowned upon but would also be considered immoral and perhaps even illegal if aired in more widespread public forums. By publishing the writings of its readers, *Underground Poetix* allows a cadre of like-minded individuals scattered across Turkey an opportunity to indirectly communicate with one another in an open manner. This section reads the poetic contributions of *Underground Poetix* readers in order to see what sort of textual community these reader-writers have created through their contributions.

A look at readers' work reveals how they refigure Beat and countercultural themes, texts, and writers to express dissatisfaction with their current Turkish society. While not all reader response pieces invoke the writers and texts presented in the magazine directly, the anything-goes style of the majority of contributions has direct Beat antecedents, and the desire for personal expression evidenced in these responses is very much in the Beat vein. *Underground Poetix* thus provides an interesting insight into the thoughts, feelings, and concerns of Turkish Beat fans. Given the journal's editorial policy (or lack of one) of allowing anyone to say anything unencumbered by revision, grammatical or otherwise, these poems lend insight into how the readers process the magazine's contents, what they see as the role of underground literature in Turkey, and their own issues and biases that they bring to their work.

Underground Poetix's readership is not large. While the journal can be found at numerous bookshops throughout Istanbul, the journal draws on a subscriber fan base of roughly six hundred members for support. The bulk of *Underground Poetix*'s readers (80 percent) come from Turkey's principal cities—Istanbul, Ankara, and Izmir. But there are a significant number of readers in the Black Sea region (15 percent), with the remainder scattered throughout Turkey (Erdoğan, interview).[10] Erdoğan explains that there are two main groups of readers: "The first one is the high school seniors and college crew. You know, teenagers or a little older. Other than that, we think that the average age is quite high . . . above thirty is a high age for magazine readership in Turkey" (Erdoğan, interview). For many of these readers, the chance to publish their own work is *Underground Poetix*'s primary draw. As Erdoğan notes, it is very difficult in Turkey for authors, especially unpublished ones, to find venues for their work. *Underground Poetix*, with its open editorial and submission policies, provides a forum for those trying to see their work in print.

But what these writers lack in numbers they make up for in intensity. Few other publications cover such a range of controversial themes and viewpoints in Turkey. By far the most numerous type of reader writing are works that offer a direct confession of personal loves, fears, problems, and traumas. That readers are willing to voice concerns usually withheld from public discussion in Turkey demonstrates that they are finding a comfortable, accepting forum to voice their problems. Although these poems are oftentimes confusing and unpolished, their naiveté is precisely the point. They reinforce the notion of poetry as a space to help work through problems; poetry as process rather than as literary craft. This is one of the main reasons for the Beats' appeal—their willingness to spontaneously express their innermost feelings and beliefs acts as both a spur and a license for younger writers to write in an uninhibited manner. Beat writers offer a model of writing that legitimizes the description of personal experience, and it should come as no surprise that much of this work resembles Beat writing, with Kerouac and Burroughs mentioned by name in a number of reader poems. No topic, theme, or style is taboo, and readers know from the journal's front matter that their work will appear exactly as they write it. The goal is to create a space for people to express themselves fully.

Maria Damon's concept of the "micropoetic" explains what is at stake in such nontraditional writing practices. In her usage, "micropoetries" comes to stand for writing that lies outside the mainstream, or "macro," field of poetics. Slam poetry, fanzines, prison writing, and other extraliterary production challenge standard notions of highbrow poetry with work that fails to follow the rules. As Damon explains,

> Micropoetries are traces of the poetic within the everyday, unworked-over—raw material left raw instead of being cooked into artistically self-conscious collage, pastiche, retelling, or other incorporative literary genre. Micropoetries are conversely also the banal that raises its spectrally perverse dread-head in the field of the "poetic": the clunker, the cringe-worthy line, the obstinate appearance of the groaner in a field of niceness. (*Postliterary* 194)

In other words, "bad" poetry. The reader-produced writing in *Underground Poetix* is best described in precisely such terms. The goal of these works is self-expression, not literary fame, and thus the majority of this work focuses on capturing the thoughts and feelings of the writer in a style that often strikes the reader as odd or unpracticed. Yet it is precisely this "unworked" quality that lends the writings in *Underground Poetix* their force and power. As Damon goes on to explain, "But the term micropoetics also points to, conversely, the appearance of what would otherwise be doggerel in contexts that render it dignified, moving, appropriate: the child's poem read at her father's funeral" (194). The context of the writing's reception is important.

This desire to connect or at least commiserate with the writings of others demonstrates the communal nature of the micropoetic writing found in *Underground Poetix*. The journal offers its audience the opportunity to voice their feelings and frustrations in a forum where they will be listened to and respected. Damon traces this possibility for the communal to the notion of an inherent respect for the voice of another: "there's a tonal quality of close attention and respect that compels our audience, our careful respect for these resonant and audient performances. To listen to someone who's really listening, to begin to hear people listening, is the beginning of collaborative intellectual communities" ("Post-Literary Poetry" 144). Damon sees in this idea of respect the possibility for poetry to move beyond a private concern and into a public sphere where it can offer a far greater impact. *Underground*

Poetix is an instance of such a public project. By offering readers access to the writings of others in their underground community, the magazine creates an arena where any issue or concern can be raised without fear of reprisal.

Full expression in *Underground Poetix* often results in highly personal poems that can appear sentimental and overwrought. Jan Ender Can's "Son" ("End"), for example, describes what appears to be a romantic breakup in the form of a dream description. In the very first line, the poet relates that he will "explain everything starting from zero" (*her şeyi sıfırdan başlayarak anlatacağım*) (177). Can then goes on to narrate an encounter in a park, where he sees a heart beating within another heart sitting on the bench. As he goes to touch the heart, a voice that had been guiding him throughout his journey stabs him in his own heart. As he falls, he sees a woman walking away, and he gazes upward to see himself as the man who guided and stabbed him. At the end of the poem, loneliness asks the speaker to turn off the light (*yalnızlık, / ışığı söndürmemi söyledi*), and he then realizes that love is "flying in the black night" (*aşk, / siyah gecenin içinde uçan*) and that "death on the other hand appears with white" (*ölümse beyazla görülürdü*) (177). By invoking classic images of traumatic love such as stabbed hearts and black birds, the poet is able to convey his emotional traumas in language that, while somewhat clichéd, nevertheless captures a real inner turmoil. When I showed such *Underground Poetix* poems to my upper-division class at Koç University, the result was snicker and derision at what they felt to be banal work. But Damon's concept of the micropoetic teaches us that nonestablished poets have insights to offer even if their work is not seen as traditionally literate or does not follow the rules for good poetry. Can's work demonstrates an attempt to express the very underground themes of isolation and heartache, and we are asked to commiserate with the writer as he unburdens his soul to us.

Can's poem speaks to universal feelings, but many writers in *Underground Poetix* voice more specific concerns. Büşra Kurtar, in her poem "Üryan geldim" ("I Came Naked"), presents a speaker who describes a difficult family trauma involving the problems of her mother. Although it is not stated explicitly, the poem suggests that her father physically abuses her mother. As the poem progresses, her mother dies and her father becomes unable to walk (*Baba bir daha yürüyemeyecek*), and the speaker concludes by declaring herself a transvestite (*Ben de bir travestiyim*) (146). While it is unclear whether this claim should be taken literarily as the source of her sexual choice or simply a metaphor for her troubled situation between an abused mother and a problematic father, in any case the poem chronicles the speaker's response to a difficult family situation. The title thus comes to signify not so much physical nakedness (*çıplak*, or "nude," in Turkish) but rather the exposed or vulnerable state of the speaker. Given the importance placed on family in Turkey, raising the neglected topic of spousal abuse is provocative. While care must be taken not to simply conflate the speaker with the author, in either case, "I Came Naked" questions the underlying assumptions of familial relations as the supposed backbone of a strong Turkish nation.

Personal expression and social critique combine in a number of works by readers. Melda Köser, in her poem "Then mama says nö!" uses a satirical stance to criticize both homophobia on the one hand and what she sees as the shortcomings of a celebrated global consumer culture on the other. The poem is addressed to "küçük bey," a term used in Turkey by servants to show respect to the children of their employers. But "mama's" lesson questions negative Turkish attitudes toward homosexuality. She lists possible combinations unthought of by her young charge:

> Women love men and men also love men.
> Men love gentlemen [*efendilerini*] and women.
> Women love their bosses and women.
> (*kadınlar adamları ve adamlar da adamları severler*
> *adamlar efendilerini ve kadınları severler*
> *Kadınlar, patronlarını ve kadınları severler*) (11)

The poem then shifts, contrasting a list of deplorable circumstances sanctioned by society with the supposed "unnaturalness" of the couplings just described. "Perfect women with silicone lips" (*Silikondan dudaklarıyla ideal bayanlar*), "Nobody becomes Black by listening to a little blues" (*Aslında tüm dediğim, biraz bluesdan kimse zenci olmaz*), and "Everybody should accept that if Hitler hadn't become a dictator, he would have been a style counselor" (*Ve herkes Kabul etmeli ki hitler bir dictator olmasaydı, başarılı bir stil danışmanı olurdu*) all express a sardonic view of global image culture (11). The relationship to the West in the poem is likewise vexed. The speaker castigates "Uncle Sam" (*sam amca*) while keeping her title in English (though "no" is spelled with an umlaut, "nö"). But Köser makes it clear that in a world filled with contradictions, same-sex relationships should be the least of "küçük bey's" concerns (11).

Religion comes under attack in a number of reader poems. While Beat writing typically embraces either a more inclusive Buddhist practice as in the work of Snyder or Philip Whalen, or a broad-based spiritualism as in Ginsberg and Kerouac, in the Turkish context, religion is often equated with repression. Mustafa Kemal openly attacked Islam, dissolving Dervish lodges and undermining the power of what he saw as a backward Islamic tendency in the country. Tayyip Recep Erdoğan's Justice and Development (AK) Party, with its ever restrictive policies meant to align the country more closely with traditional religious beliefs and practices, has reignited the fears of many that Turkey will become an Islamic-based country. The high percentage of religious adherents in Turkey and AK Party's continual shift toward the right make religion an obvious target for readers frustrated with the status quo.

A good example of such frustration is found in Çetin Yılmaz's untitled poem. Yılmaz begins provocatively, subsuming a monotheistic God under the rubric of "Gods" and then denying the existence of all of them: "In the name of one of the nonprotecting, nonforgiving (actually nonexisting) Gods" (*Esirgemeyen / ve / bağışlamayan / -aslında varolmayan- / tanrılardan birinin adıyla*) (75). The poem, however, continues on to mimic the Qur'an itself. Exhorting the reader to "Recite" (*Oku*), here Yılmaz references the well-known sura 96, where the word of God commands "Recite! Your Lord is the Most Bountiful One, who by / the pen taught man what he did know" (Qur'an 96:3–4). The sura is concerned with those who disobey the Lord, claiming, "Let him desist, or We will drag him by the forelock, / his lying, sinful forelock" (Qur'an 96:15–16). Yılmaz's poem, which does exactly what the sura forbids by denying God and mocking his word, is meant to question the worship of God and provoke a response. The speaker views himself as a heretic in both this world and the other, replacing a sura titled "Clots of Blood" with a "Chaos Sura of Destruction" that calls for "paint[ing] the Medina red with Molotov cocktails" (*yıkımın kaos suresini // kızıla boya / Medine'nin gerdanlığını / molotoflarınla*) (75). The speaker ultimately sees himself as outside God's purview resisting the call to submit, and thus ends up a "bastard" (*piç*), willfully denying the presence of the Lord (75).[11]

This religious critique often bleeds into a governmental critique of the AK Party and its policies. Medsen Kerubi's "BENIM ADIM SİK-K-ME BAŞ" ("MY NAME IS 'FUCK HEAD'") presents a litany of complaints, each delivered in a separate line of his long poem. The title itself is a provocative comment on the head scarf issue in Turkey. The wearing of head scarves in government offices and public facilities was banned under the Kemalist regime, and the AK Party's revocation of the ban met stiff resistance from those who believed that it would open the doors to an Islamic Turkey. Kerubi's odd title is a play on a derogatory term for women who wear head scarves—"sıkma baş." In Turkish, "sıkmak" means "to squeeze," and thus the phrase can be translated literarily as those who "squeeze" their heads into head scarves (*turban* in Turkish), but figuratively as a narrowing, or squeezing, of thought. By transposing an "i" with the original "ı," Kerubi has turned *squeezed* into *fucked* (170–72).[12] The phrase is shocking and derogatory, and expresses condemnation of the AK Party's support of such outward markers of Islam. As with many other contributors, the writing is often incoherent and makes no attempt to sustain an image or theme. Kerubi invokes the Beats, claiming "BEAT CRASHED—JAZZ DIED—A NEW CENTURY. THIN WHITE LINE" (BEAT ÇÖKTÜ—CAZ ÖLDU—YENİ 1 YÜZ YIL. İNCE BEYAZ ÇİZGİ; *Beat* left in English, *a* rendered as "1") (170). Not only is the meaning of this line unclear, but it is difficult to know whether this is an observation, lament, or celebration. Kerubi does make his feelings known in other lines, however. Distancing himself from the religion endorsed by the government, Kerubi asks, "WELL THEN (mr.) PRESIDENT: IS GOD IN THE MOSQUE? / EVEN IF HE'S THERE / I'D NEVER THINK HE'D EXPECT TO FIND AN ADDICT LIKE ME!" (PEK-A-LA [bay] BAŞKAN: TANRI CAMİ-DE-Mİ? / O-RADA OLS, AAA-BİLE, / BENİM GİBİ BİR KEŞ-İ BEKLEDEĞİNİ HİÇ SANMIYORUM!) (170). Kerubi conflates several critiques into one, comparing Erdoğan and his religious stance to the speaker's own underground status as a user of illegal drugs (a topic raised by other writers as well). The poem is purposefully meant to shock and outrage an array of Turkish institutions and authority figures.

But Erdoğan's AK Party is not the only political group to come under fire in the magazine. In a series of short poems, Bahadır Dilbaz comments on Turkey's vexed "Kurdish issue." Locked in a struggle with the Kurdistan Workers' Party (Kürt İşçi Partisi or PKK) throughout the 1990s, the previous Kemalist government responded with a series of repressive measures meant to stifle Kurdish solidarity. In addition to travel restrictions, there was also a ban on the Kurdish language. In the poem "I cannot smile you" ("gülemiyorum seni" [*sic*]), Dilbaz's speaker states, "I know that I cannot speak Turkish / my name cannot be said in Kurdish . . . if my words do not come out of my lips / forgive me / for things that I said to you / my lies / my countries I cannot know / my clothes / America I couldn't learn / Europe I couldn't go / because I cannot wear I cannot smile you" (unpaginated).[13] The incorrect grammar of the poem is not a mistake. As the speaker mentions in the first line, s/he is not a native speaker of Turkish, and thus suffers as do all who must live their lives in a foreign tongue. But the speaker is not allowed to speak Kurdish either. Dilbaz draws attention to the plight of Kurds caught between their desire to retain their language and heritage, and their economic need to fit into an often unwelcoming Turkish society. The speaker is ashamed of their condition, their Turkish, even their clothes.

There is no escape, since as the speaker claims in another two lines that are again rendered in broken Turkish, "America I couldn't learn / Europe I couldn't go." The speaker is socially marginalized as a Kurd, much like the treatment of minority groups in the United States and other parts of the West. Other such groups are addressed as well. Dilbaz's next poem, "kırmızı mevsimi" ("red season"), is probably referring to the persistent persecution of the Alevi religious group in Turkey, while in issue 10 (2011) Kerim Akbaş recalls the sufferings of leftists, Kurds, and Roma at the hands of police. But while the Beats sought to recover minority experience as a more authentic response to a materialistic postwar U.S. society, no such recuperation occurs here. Dilbaz uses his poem simply to raise awareness of the plight of Kurds at the hands of systematic government repression.

CONCLUSION

The Turkish underground publishing scene has a lot in common with Beat and countercultural journals. As we have seen throughout this chapter, *Underground Poetix* borrows heavily from the heady days of the 1950s and 1960s in the United States and Europe. But to claim that underground publishing in Turkey is simply a copy of the West would be wrong. Not only does the magazine take up specifically Turkish concerns, but it does so by establishing its own framework and style. The Beats continue to have a role in fostering oppositional communities abroad, but those communities, while oftentimes drawing on a Beat or countercultural spirit, look very different from their Beat antecedents.

The Beats' primary contribution is to provide an inspirational model that condones the expression of very personal feelings in an idiosyncratic style no matter how far outside the norm this might lead. This is perhaps one of the greatest legacies of the counterculture as a whole. By mimicking the lax editorial policies of their countercultural forebears, *Underground Poetix* fosters an anything-goes spirit that allows both editors and contributors to challenge the limits of what can be said and how it can be expressed. In contemporary Western Beat journals such as the *Kerouac Rag* that include creative reader submissions, the style is often being influenced by earlier Beat writing. Perhaps because Turkish readers are getting a lot of their Beats in translation, stylistic concerns seem less relevant. In our study, for example, we found that most Turkish readers read in translation.[14] Stylistic concerns do come through, and reader submissions to *Underground Poetix* certainly have a more open style, but the forms employed are never directly attributable to particular Beat or countercultural writers.

Beat and countercultural works also raise provocative issues that have become touchstones for Turkey's underground community. Perhaps because of Turkey's belatedness on the countercultural scene, these imported texts can still have an impact on Turkish social issues. Current Western journals devoted to the Beats appear more celebratory, or seek to uncover texts and information about Beat writing and lives. *RealityStudio: A William S. Burroughs Community*, one of the premier online sites for the discussion of Burroughs's work, is almost academic in its posting of links to archives and difficult-to-find material. Discussions on its site are very learned, often encompassing publication histories, contextual concepts, and biographical data on Burroughs. *Underground Poetix*, by contrast, still operates very much in the provocative spirit of the 1950s and 1960s, building solidarity around issues that help to define their alternative, subcultural communities. While issues of social and governmental oppression, alternative lifestyle choices, and the desire for personal expression are consistent with Beat and countercultural themes, the ways in which these topics are discussed become refracted through specifically Turkish situations. The Beats inspire, provide themes, and exhort, but ultimately Turkish writers are more interested in exploring their own issues and concerns, in their own way.

The Beat underground journal is, in many ways, a thing of the past. But the impact of the Beats still resonates in the present, thanks to new forms of social media capable of spreading the Beat message across space and time. Members of each new generation of young adults discover the Beats and become inspired to emulate some of the lifestyle choices the Beats undertook in their desire to stretch the limit of their understanding. A look at the Beats' global reception reveals that their work can still offer a chance for social critique. That moment may have passed in the United States and perhaps the West in general, but in countries such as Turkey, the Beat challenge to personal limitations and individual expression remains alive. And as long as that desire for change remains, there is still a place for the underground press, even if it does not always remain hidden.

3. "WHAT'S YOUR ROAD, MAN?"
JACK KEROUAC'S *ON THE ROAD* IN TURKEY

In 2001 the Turkcell Company introduced its "Free Girl" (*Özgür Kız*) advertisement campaign for its new prepaid cell phone cards. In a series of related commercials, a nationwide audience followed the adventures of the "free girl" Nil and her love interest Yiğit.[1] Their love story begins when the two pass each other on their way into a Turkcell store. Both hit the road separately, each with their backpacks, with Nil sporting a Western-style cowboy hat. The two make their way across a desert plain that looks like the American West but whose road signs for the cities Tatvan and Bitlis indicate that they are actually in the Kurdish area of eastern Turkey. Their travels involve seemingly endless treks through arid countryside, as well as hitching rides on motorbikes, trucks, and even tractors full of Anatolian villagers. The tension increases—will they meet again? At one point, Yiğit is riding in the back of a truck while Nil is in the cab with the driver and his wife, offering the smiling old woman Turkcell phone cards while the woman gives her an embroidered piece of white cloth. In a later commercial, they are together, camping, running, and holding hands. Yiğit now wears the cowboy hat, and Nil is often seen carousing in shorts and a bra. But their freedom is short-lived. In a quick trip to get more cell phone minutes, Nil leaves, and when her note to Yiğit is lost, he takes off, and the couple are unable to find each other.

The third commercial begins with the lines "whatever will be will be." The Turkish pop star Tarkan makes an unexpected appearance, traveling through desert heat and winter snow, calling Nil to sing her his "song of freedom" with the lines "Freedom is inside / it is in your heart." Reinforcing this notion of *kısmet*, or the idea that love will find a way, Tarkan arranges their reunion at his concert. With everyone in black and white, Tarkan throws the cowboy hat to Nil as it becomes colorized, whereupon she sees Yiğit, who likewise flowers into color as they reunite. The rest of the advertisements turn even stranger, as Yiğit is kidnapped by the Russian mafia and Nil, in keeping with the notion of gender reversal, must save him. The leader of the mob, Nuri Alço, was an actor made famous by his roles as a notorious rapist in earlier Yeşilcam films of the 1970s and 1980s. In a series of scenes increasingly implausible, Alço is killed and Yiğit saved. Exiting the building, Nil says, "I can't believe Nuri Alço is dead; it's like the end of an era." Nil is referring to a cultural shift of course, but with the threat of this well-known rapist metaphorically exorcised, Nil and Yiğit are free to resume their travels. Despite Turkey's limited rail network, the penultimate scene finds them nestled together in a railroad boxcar, traveling with another recognizable figure from Turkish film, the lovable shoe-shine man Cilalı İbo. In the last commercial, Nil enters a university classroom, getting everybody, including the aged professor, to dance to the tune of "We're University Students."

In a post-1980-coup Turkish society that many feel is changing from a more communal model where support comes from family, friends, and neighbors to a world where the individual is responsible for their own well-being, the cell phone seems to provide a bridge between the two, a tether for adventures outside the designated social field. As Nilüfer Göle argues in her contribution to *Rethinking Modernity and National Identity in Turkey*, "In opposition to the modern West, where the basic presupposition is that absolute truth is a matter not of the collective but of the individual conscience, in Islam this urge is met by submitting oneself to God and letting the community (*cemaat*) serve as one's guide through life" (91). The rise of consumerism that followed the 1980 coup, however, challenged this communal model. Although Turkish youth expected a corresponding increase in personal freedom along with economic opportunity, social ties remained strong. Turkcell offered to bridge this gap by offering its customers mobility that was still tethered to community through the fragile airwaves. Critics and viewers alike, however, scoffed at the possibilities of such a promise. In his article "Özgür Kız ve Postmodernlik" ("Free Girl and Postmodernism"), Esat Arslan comments that "Free Girl is an advertisement campaign that both represents and changes youth who are modern, intellectual and socially fulfilled enough to consider life as a game. It has an important place in Turkish history. It demonstrates how the ideal of freedom becomes distorted in the postmodern era and its success comes from that fact" (Özgür Kız"). Another observer, writing in Turkey's online "sour dictionary" (*ekşi sözluk*), commented, "She is a utopic character. Because my country cannot raise free individuals, she can only live in commercials." Nevertheless, Turkcell's Free Girl campaign was an attempt to present a new model for Turkey, and to sell a product in the meantime. The popularity it enjoyed demonstrates the attraction of the lifestyle it offered.

While the Free Girl ad campaign may appear as just another means of profiting from youthful desire, the dynamics of the interactions between the various characters and the response it received in Turkish culture raise the issue of what freedom means in Turkey and the extent to which it can be realized. This chapter examines this cultural discussion to provide a context for the reception of a Beat text equally concerned with freedom, mobility, and even love—Jack Kerouac's *On the Road.* Kerouac's novel is a classic work of countercultural literature that resonates with a variety of specifically American themes. Reading it in the context of its reception in Turkey provides a better understanding of how "American-ness" is constructed, and where and why such formulations might break down. Through reader responses to the novel, interviews with translators and publishers, media analysis, and comparisons with the closest genre to the American road novel in Turkey, Turkish cinema, I hope to provide a useful counterpoint to the understanding of the novel in both U.S. and Turkish contexts. The ways in which a text about two friends traveling across the North American continent is received by Turkish readers says a lot about the cultural assumptions prevalent in society, and how such a countercultural text from such a different culture may or may not be able to alter or amend those conceptions. *On the Road*, a text that presents extreme characters and situations, tends to provoke strong reactions in its readers and is thus the perfect vehicle for such an inquiry.

The publication of Kerouac's novel in 1957 marked a pivotal moment in the American counterculture. The novel celebrated an America that Kerouac and his fellow Beat Generation writers believed was becoming lost: an America of open spaces and freedom of movement best represented by the myth of the West, a country that was the antithesis of an encroaching conformity occasioned by middle-class values. Kerouac's work made an indelible mark on American culture that continues today. But when Kerouac's novel travels halfway around the world to Turkey, it meets a new culture with different assumptions. Can such a displacement still allow for the sort of oppositional stance the novel takes to society? An analysis of the reception of Kerouac's novel in Turkey reveals that Beat rebellion is not timeless and universal but rather relies on a particular postwar U.S. context for its articulation. Though Turkish readers understand and enjoy *On the Road*'s message of leaving the social order behind to explore the freedom of the open road, they are likely to read Kerouac's work more as representing a spiritual journey than as an actual taking to the road in a rejection of society. Beat texts like Kerouac's *On the Road* still have the power to foment change but in ways particular to present temporal and cultural concerns.

THE FREEDOM OF THE OPEN ROAD

Although the Free Girl advertisement never makes the connection explicit, one of the implicit assumptions is that the cell phone is always there in case of emergency. Nil and Yiğit are still tied to others, even in their lonely travels, by the presence of this device and the fact that Nil is always near a Turkcell store. Of course the irony here is that the cell phone creates an extremely tenuous connection. Without a charged battery and the cards to refill minutes, the phone is useless, a situation that causes the couple's breakup in the first place. But as in all commercials, everything works out in the end, and the phone is instrumental in Nil's saving Yiğit. The notion of freedom is a marketing gimmick designed to give youth the impression that a cell phone equals a new form of lifestyle, despite actual social conditions. As Oya Dinçer Durmuş writes, "Free girl travels from one corner of the country to another, and enjoys freedom with her cell phone. In this way, she gives the message that 'people can get a taste of freedom via having a cell phone.' The obvious target here is youth, who want products that make them feel good" ("Popüler Kültürün"). Turkcell is thus offering a particular conception of freedom. Rather than promoting an abandonment of society through travel, users are offered choice instead—they can go where they want, when they want, because they never really have to leave others behind. The ad campaign plays on the desire for both individual freedom and communal support.

While a television commercial functions differently than a literary novel, both are cultural objects designed to send a message, and a comparison of the Free Girl advertisement and *On the Road* reveals two very different notions of freedom. Beat freedom, by contrast, is a lot more tenuous. *On the Road*'s critique begins with the very American celebration of the lone individual, standing outside mainstream society, whose marginality poses a challenge to the dominant order. Based on the real-life exploits of Kerouac's friend and road companion Neal Cassady, Dean Moriarty embodies the rebellious image of an individual unable and unwilling to fit into "normal" society. Growing up without a mother and with an alcoholic father, Dean inhabited the margins of society at an early age. Dean describes an episode when he accompanied his father and his father's friend on an excursion to sell home-made flyswatters during the Depression: "mostly for charity the nickels were given us, two bums and a boy, apple pies in the sky, and my old man in those days was always singing 'Hallelujah, I'm a bum, bum again'" (188). Later, after staying drunk for "five days and five nights," the two adults argue, and as Dean explains, "my old man was arrested and I had to plead at court to the judge to let him go cause he was my pa and I had no mother" (188–89). Despite the obvious neglect he suffered as a child, Kerouac focuses on Dean's resilience in the face of such adversity. Dean becomes adept at not just surviving on his own but also thriving, and though he eventually lands in reform school for his habit of stealing cars for joyrides, in the end Dean's unorthodox upbringing is celebrated.

Because of his troubled past, Dean stands apart from mainstream U.S. society, and is thus able to offer a remedy to the stultifying culture that surrounds Kerouac's stand-in, Sal Paradise. Sal observes that "Dean's intelligence was every bit as formal and shining and complete, without the tedious intellectualness. And his 'criminality' was not something that sulked and sneered; it was a wild yea-saying overburst of American joy" (9–10). According to Sal, all his "intellectual" friends critique society with their "bookish or political or psychoanalytic" reasons, but Dean celebrates the desires that capitalism excites but typically stifles with his "wild yea-saying overbursts" (9–10). Unlike his fellow Americans, Dean does not delay gratification. He consumes—food, liquor, drugs, cars, whatever he can get his hands on. Dean represents individualism taken to the extreme: a complete abandonment to desire as it responds to the ever-changing conditions of the passing moment. Of course, this constant pursuit of desire has its consequences. Dean destroys several cars and two marriages, and often leaves his children and his friends (including Sal) stranded as a new pursuit engulfs him. Nevertheless, such rugged individualism and insistence on self-reliance and freedom to pursue one's own interests are presented as desirable throughout the novel, and Dean becomes a compelling force that propels Sal into action.

Kerouac reads Dean's life as more than simply the inability for some individuals to fit into society. Dean represents a wholesale critique of the society that shaped him. As Alan Nadel argues in *Containment Culture*, the postwar years in America were marked by the notion of conformity. He writes, "It was a period, as many prominent studies have indicated, when 'conformity' became a positive value in and of itself" (4). Driven by fears of the atomic bomb, this culture sought to "contain" deviant behavior in a bid to produce a homogenous society thought to be capable of fighting off communist threats. Dean's idiosyncratic behavior posed a direct challenge to such an order. Rejecting career, marriage, and a stable home, Dean provides Kerouac with a model for social transgression.

A glance at the novel's U.S. reception reveals the power of *On the Road*'s critique. Although it garnered some positive reviews, in general Kerouac's novel was initially the subject of attack, both in terms of its signature style and its rebellious content. This was not the first time Kerouac had been reviewed by the critics. It was, however, the first time that one of his novels had attracted so much attention. Though he had published *The Town and the City* several years before, it was *On the Road* that "made the best-seller list for five weeks late in 1957" and launched Kerouac's overnight success (Charters, *Kerouac* 288). On the day of its publication, critic Gilbert Millstein praised it as "an authentic work of art" and "a major novel" (Nicosia 556). Not all critics, however, were as receptive as Millstein; many rejected Kerouac's novel, and *On the Road* soon became a hotly contested work. Although critiques of the novel often focused on its innovative style, what garnered most attention was *On the Road*'s depiction of marginalized characters and controversial topics. Three days after Millstein's review, an article by *Times* critic David Dempsey marked a turning point in public opinion against Kerouac, claiming that while the novel was "entertaining" it was nevertheless a depraved work full of "freaks" (556). *Time* magazine followed suit, attacking the novel as degenerate and hedonistic while calling Kerouac the "Hippie Homer" writing about a "disjointed segment of society acting out its own neurotic necessity" (Charters, *Kerouac* 290). This sense of Kerouac and the Beat Generation as an affront to an otherwise content nation is a theme that is encountered in many other media settings. As one critic of the novel put it, *On the Road* was the "quintessence of 'everything that is bad and horrible about this otherwise wonderful age we live in'" (Tytell 159). While Sal is certainly challenging the status quo, it is the character of Dean Moriarty who most strikingly epitomizes this shocking new Beat lifestyle.

Kerouac attempts to recuperate Dean as an American archetype. For the narrator Sal, Dean epitomizes the lonely cowboy, alone on the prairie, a symbol of self-reliance, and his joyous outlook "was Western, the west wind, an ode from the Plains, something new, long prophesied" (9–10). Dean thus represents the West and the freedom that it has come to signify in American culture. Yet while Dean might hark back to the image of the Western cowboy, he is also part street hustler and urban hipster, adept at surviving in cities like New York and San Francisco on his wits, cunning, and charm. Dean comes to epitomize a Beatness that is at the heart of Kerouac's book. Writers like Kerouac and his friend and poet Allen Ginsberg celebrated those beaten by society, including drug addicts, petty criminals, and peripatetic hoboes. Kerouac and Ginsberg defined *Beat* in two ways—as the basic rhythmic unit of the ecstatic jazz performances that occur throughout the book and as a celebration of those individuals unable to conform to a rigid postwar society. Dean exemplifies this term, both in his love of jazz and his mystic celebration of its performances, as well as in the sense of being beaten by society. Dean is an outcast, a motherless child recently released from prison whose search for his alcoholic father Kerouac equates with the exploration of America itself.

To this definition Kerouac adds a third component—religious ecstasy. In a pivotal moment of the text, while Dean is being harangued by a group of women for his inability to maintain a job and support a family, Sal arrives at the realization that Dean is a "Holy Goof," a man who by dint of his inability to fit into society has become its most sanguine critic and savior. Sal turns Dean into a saint and martyr, claiming, "He was BEAT—the root, the soul of Beatific. What was he knowing? He tried all in his power to tell me what was knowing, and they envied that about me, my position at his side" (177). It is precisely Dean's outsider status that helps elevate him to the level of saint in Sal's eyes. Like Jesus of the Beatitudes, he is beaten down and ridiculed by an undeserving society, his message deliverable only to true believers like Sal. Dean's message is one of redemption, and one that Sal believes America needs to hear—a challenge to the fear and conformity of the era.

THE TURKISH CONTEXT

On the Road is well known in Turkey, though among Beats Kerouac arrived a bit late on the Turkish underground scene. While Ginsberg's work was translated as early as 1976, *On the Road* appeared in Turkish translation only in 1993. In fact, *On the Road* was not even the first of Kerouac's works to be translated—that distinction goes to Nevzat Erkmen's translation of *The Dharma Bums*, which appeared in 1982.[2] Despite its late start, *On the Road* is a major U.S. text in the underground canon in Turkey. According to our study, *On the Road* was read by 16.2 percent of our respondents, compared with William S. Burroughs's *Naked Lunch* at 5.6 percent and Ginsberg's *Howl* at 5.3 percent (see appendix 1; Mortenson, Ergun, and Erdoğan 103–4). While there might be some overlap, 13.6 percent of respondents reported seeing the film version of *On the Road* (dir. Walter Salles, 2012; 103–4). These numbers are still behind those of the ever-popular Chuck Palahniuk's *Fight Club* and Turkish underground favorites like Metin Kaçan's *Ağır Roman*, Oğuz Atay's *Tutunamayanlar*, and Hakan Günday's *Piç*, but they are significant (103–4). Kerouac's famous novel approaches the popularity of Bukowski, whose work almost half of respondents have read (or watched film versions), the undisputed leader of American underground writers in Turkey (103–4). Readership of Kerouac's other novels are slim by comparison, with *The Subterraneans* (*Yeraltı Sakinleri*) receiving 11.9 percent, *The Dharma Bums* (*Zen Kaçıkları*) 5.6 percent, and *Big Sur* (*Big Sur*) a mere 2 percent (103–4). *On the Road* is clearly an important underground text and *the* Kerouac work to read in Turkey.

A large part of *On the Road*'s visibility is attributable to the generally positive media coverage Kerouac and his works have received in Turkey. Most of these pieces are informative articles that provide Turkish readers with introductions to the man and his work. Given the autobiographical nature of much of Kerouac's corpus, it is unsurprising that many articles provide extensive biographical data, with Kerouac's relationship to the real-life Dean Moriarty, Neal Cassady, receiving special attention along with Kerouac's French Canadian background. Discussions of *On the Road* and Kerouac's other novels receive descriptive but extensive coverage, with writers hailing the text as a masterpiece but opting to discuss plot points and to contextualize the work within a postwar U.S. framework rather than offering critical comment on the text or its applicability to the Turkish situation. *On the Road* is lauded as an important text in the countercultural canon, but the implications of that critique for present-day Turkey remain largely unexplored.[3]

Despite *On the Road*'s popularity, the celebration of the individual rejecting society meets resistance as it travels to Turkey. In an interview with Can Kantarcı, *On the Road*'s Turkish translator, I asked to what extent was the idea of the road culturally dependent and to what extent was it universal. Kantarcı's response highlighted the place of individuality in Kerouac's novel: "Indeed, culture makes a difference. One could see that although the travelers in *On the Road* are doing lots of trips together, they are, most of the times, on their own. The individuality in the novel is palpable throughout. Turkish culture is kind of more communal. It depends more on solidarity" (Kantarcı, interview).[4] Though care must be taken so as not to, in the words of Edward Said, "invent collective identities for large numbers of individuals who are actually quite diverse," nevertheless the differences between U.S. and Turkish outlooks need to be taken into consideration (xxviii). The United States is typically seen as being more individualistic. Geert Hofstede, in his important work *Culture's Consequences: Comparing Values, Behaviors, Institutions, and Organizations across Nations* (2001), compared the thinking and actions of members of fifty nations to try to understand the effects of national culture on the value systems of individuals. Both the U.S. and Turkey were part of the study, and the index values that Hofstede found for individualism and collectivism demonstrate that the two countries evidence pronounced differences in national outlooks. Hofstede found that the United States ranks first on the individualism index. Turkey is twenty-eighth of fifty (215). In the United States, the emphasis is on independence and the development of self-contained, separate selves. Of course this value does not mean that family and social ties are nonexistent in the United States. But these ties are often ancillary to a focus on the self.

The importance ascribed to the individual, however, is not universal. In many countries self is subordinated to society. Collectivist societies, in opposition to the United States, stress *inter*dependence rather than independence, and thus selves tend to be defined not autonomously but rather through familial, social, and cultural relationships. With its insistence on shared religion, familial relations, traditional neighborhoods, and national solidarity, Turkey tends toward the collectivist.[5] In Orhan Pamuk's *Istanbul: Memories and the City*, for example, the Nobel Prize winner draws a distinction between the *hüzün* of Istanbul and the sort of melancholy espoused by some in the West. For Pamuk, *hüzün* is a sort of honorable, collective resignation to the vicissitudes of life. Pamuk contrasts Western notions of melancholy based on individual solitude in Robert Burton's *The Anatomy of Melancholy* with the Islamic thinker El Kindi's belief that *hüzün* was antithetical to the community: "The central preoccupation, as with all classic Islamic thinkers, was the *cemaat*, or community of believers. He judged *hüzün* by the values of the *cemaat* and suggested remedies that returns us to it; essentially, he saw *hüzün* as an experience at odds with the communal purpose" (92). Pamuk argues, "The *hüzün* of Istanbul suggests nothing of an individual standing against society; on the contrary, it suggests an erosion of the will to stand against the values and mores of the community and encourages us to be content with little, honoring the virtues of harmony, uniformity, humility" (104). The will of the community eclipses the desire of the individual.[6]

The collective nature of Turkish society is important, since it shapes the way that Kerouac's novel is understood in the Turkish context. When I asked Kantarcı, "Are there any aspects of the Beats that are particularly difficult for Turkish audiences?" he responded that "again I would say that the 'extreme' individuality depicted in the works of Beat Literature may be too much at times" (Kantarcı, interview). Admittedly Kantarcı's is only one voice among many, but his immersion in both cultures (having spent several years at the University of Missouri–Columbia) makes his viewpoint interesting. *On the Road* was shocking when it was published in the United States in 1957, and its depiction of a carefree life on the road remains shocking today. But in a Turkish context where collectivism demands that social considerations be given a weight equal to that of personal desires, Kerouac's novel becomes even more revolutionary.

Because of this insistence on collectivism, in the Turkish context Dean's actions are often seen as bizarre or counterproductive rather than liberating. This notion was made abundantly clear to me when I taught the novel outside U.S. borders. In a senior seminar titled American Culture in the Postwar, I partnered with U.S. colleague Dr. Matt Theado at Gardner-Webb University, a private institution in North Carolina, to establish an online discussion regarding the text. In this class, as well as in other courses in Turkey where I taught Kerouac's novel, most of the students agreed that in Turkey, where more emphasis is placed on family relations and social commitment, it would be difficult to live the sort of life Dean portrays. At Koç, a private university modeled on U.S.-style higher education, the middle- and upper-class students who are underground literature's primary readership read Dean as an interesting character but one who was fundamentally "other." As the Turkish student Başak Akdoğan explained,

> Basically, we give a lot of importance to being a "community" and other people's thoughts about how we live and shape our lives are highly significant in our culture. . . . Being a community, a "family," a collectivist culture, et cetera, all of these cultural issues are, this way or that way, related to religion. You can't hit the road, do drugs, have sex, et cetera whenever you want. Maybe I shouldn't use *can't*,—of course we can do that stuff—but to have a place in the society or not to be an outcast in Turkey, religious and other culture-related issues have to be taken into account to survive in this "community."

Akdoğan claims that religion underlies this insistence on collectivity, and it is true that most Turkish citizens consider themselves Muslims even if they do not practice the religion regularly. Regardless of the root cause, it is undeniable that ties to the family and to the local community play an instrumental role in the lives of many Turkish people. Turkey is a country where attendance at weddings, funerals, sickbeds, birthdays, and other family gatherings, even for more distant relatives, is often obligatory. Ties to the community are equally strong. The Turkish notion of *mahalle*, or neighborhood, encompasses a sense of shared space where close ties between neighbors, businesses, and social groups established over long periods create a significant social network. Though perhaps waning in the larger cities, even connection to the village of one's birth is still important, and many newly arrived immigrants to the city will find jobs, housing, and perhaps even spouses through connections to a particular region or even village.[7]

Given this cultural situation, it is easy to see why Dean would appear out of place in the Turkish context. Bereft of family, Dean has no ties to those around him. He does have wives and children, though he easily leaves them behind at a moment's notice. Dean searches for his father, whom he never finds, and is excited to reconnect with his cousin, who, during the course of their brief conversation, disowns him. Dean's communal ties are equally tenuous. His childhood neighborhood consists of the bars and cheap hotels of his father's drunken milieu, and though he does have a circle of friends in Denver, Dean is happier being on the road, in constant motion and always looking for new women to love and new people to "dig." It is indeed an irony in Kerouac's novel that Dean actually desires the communality of collectivist societies, though his insistence on personal freedom inevitably means that such moments of intersubjectivity tend to be fleeting.[8] Dean's tendency to retain his personal freedom at all costs struck many Turkish students as bizarre. While they could certainly understand him as a character in a novel, he was difficult to translate into the real world.

Not that Dean always made complete sense to the U.S. students on the forum either. Many found his behavior baffling or immoral. Both groups expressed incredulity at the hazards Sal and Dean were willing to run in their road experiences, such as hitchhiking and living off small sums of money. Yet American students still find the novel not only believable but perhaps even a model to emulate, and are often willing to overlook Dean's faults to embrace his message. As Josh Padgett, an American student on the forum, commented, "America, even though it is called 'the land of the free,' is subject to social expectations just as much as every other country. This book, however, ended up inspiring people to break these norms and to go out and do these things." In my ten years of experience teaching the novel in the U.S. classroom, I was surprised to see just how often the novel galvanized some students (and often those uninterested in other readings) into undertaking road trips in the spirit of Sal and Dean. Koç students, for the most part, found *On the Road* intellectually interesting but ultimately untranslatable into action.

THE DESIRE AND THE ABILITY TO MOVE

Dean's rebelliousness resides not just in his individuality but also in his state of constant motion. Such mobility is destabilizing, since it challenges the assumption of containment culture that citizens should be loyal and dependable. While men in their "grey flannel suits" hold a steady job at a company so that they can make mortgage payments and support their wives and children, Dean insists on living a life free of encumbrances that might limit his movement. He works, marries, has children, and makes car payments, but these claims on his time and freedom to travel are quickly abandoned whenever he feels the desire to, as Sal puts it, "perform our one and noble function of the time, *move*" (121, italics in original). Of course mobility has a long tradition in U.S. history and in its literature. From early European immigrants looking for a place to build a new life (for religious or economic reasons, or both), to a belief in manifest destiny that catapulted later Americans across the continent in search of land and wealth, to twentieth-century urban migrations for work, Americans have been on the road since before the founding of their country. *On the Road* also follows in a long tradition of U.S. works such as Mark Twain's *Huckleberry Finn* and Herman Melville's *Moby Dick* that chronicle the changes that occur as characters are subjected to a destination-less travel experience. The postwar period was no exception. Fueled by an economic boom that brought cars, suburban homes, and Eisenhower's highway system, travel was taken up by more citizens than ever before.

Sal and Dean's epic cross-country journeys, however, go beyond the need to commute to work or the occasional weekend outing. These trips are a quest for movement itself, a desire to move for the sake of moving. Throughout the novel Sal emphasizes the journey, not the destination, in keeping with the novel's title. *On the Road* celebrates the spaces between destinations and the act of being in transit. This sense of the book's title is captured by the Turkish translation *Yolda*. The German translation, *Unterwegs*, likewise conveys the emphasis on motion, as do many of the other foreign titles the book has been translated under. The difference here is not so much linguistic as cultural. While the literal idea of being "on the road" might be translatable, in many ways the cultural meanings attributed to this state of being remain embedded in an American context.

Dean is literally a product of the quest for a better life, a latter-day migration that takes place in a car rather than in a boat or a wagon train. Sal repeatedly remarks on Dean's battered suitcase, always packed and always under the bed, ready at a moment's notice. Sal even comments that "Dean is the perfect guy for the road because he actually was born on the road, when his parents were passing through Salt Lake City in 1926, in a jalopy, on their way to Los Angeles" (3). Such mobility defines Dean and is a driving force behind Sal's own trips and discoveries. At the end of the novel, Sal dreamily reflects on "America when the sun goes down and I sit on the old broken-down river pier watching the long, long skies over New Jersey and sense all that raw land that rolls in one unbelievable huge bulge over to the West Coast, and all that road going" (281). Despite Sal's leaving Dean, battered and mumbling, at the side of the street while he drives off with another friend, he nevertheless eulogizes the road. The novel ends with this homage to Dean and the moments "on the road" that he helped Sal to experience. After all, as Sal states earlier in the novel, "the road is life" (192).

Mobility has been an integral part of Turkish history as well. Turkish ancestors were originally a nomadic people who covered quite a bit of ground to arrive in present-day Asia Minor. Their origins can be traced to the sixth century A.D., where they began as only one of many nomadic tribes north of China who would intermingle and begin an inexorable migration west and south.[9] Turkish history is replete with peripatetic movement. Early Turkish ancestors were known predominantly as fierce horsemen who could cover long distances to engage in battle. Later, at the height of an empire that included much of North Africa, the Balkans, and parts of the Arabian peninsula, famous writers like Evliya Çelebi (1611–82) traveled throughout the realm to record the variety of peoples and customs contained within the Ottoman Empire. Even today, a scaled-back Turkey is larger than most European countries, and a bus trip from Istanbul in the northwest to Doğubeyazıt on the eastern border with Iran can easily take twenty-four hours to complete. All of this travel, migration, and movement resulted in an extremely ethnically diverse population. In keeping with the popular depiction of Turkey as a crossroads between East and West, today's Turkey represents an amalgamation of peoples, cultures, and languages from around the world.

Despite the cosmopolitan nature of Turkish society, there are limitations to the idea of unfettered travel throughout the country's borders. Due to internal conflicts beginning in the early 1920s with Kurdish resistance to Turkish policies, travel to the East was severely limited, and whenever violence and tension arise, checkpoints increase (Zürcher 178). Few Turks have visited the eastern regions of their own country other than for family reasons, preferring instead the sunny Mediterranean coasts. Mentioning to a Turkish citizen in Istanbul that you are traveling east to cities like Kars, Van, Diyarbakır, or Urfa will normally elicit a guarded admonition to be safe. With the present threat of the Islamic State (ISIS) just south of the Turkish border and the crackdown on Kurdish politicians following the 2016 coup attempt, tensions in the area are only likely to increase. Although tourist travel is increasing and attitudes about the East changing, cross-country road trips in Turkey are dissimilar to those undertaken by Sal and Dean, a fact that bears remembering when considering how a book like *On the Road* is received.

While the American idea of being on the road is clearly understandable in Turkey, many critics, translators, and readers argue that because of conditions in Turkey, such movement is read more as an inner search than as a physical one. Mehmet Ada Öztekin, known best for his dramatic series for Turkish television, when interviewed about the underground film *Uluma* (*Howl*; 2008) he made with 6:45 editors Şenol Erdoğan and Kaan Çaydamlı, said,

> If you want to talk about Beatniks then inevitably you have to include the term "road." Because the road is what created the Beatniks. Sometimes with a car, sometimes on foot, sometimes in the rain, sometimes in the cold, they had always been on the road, they traveled around America from one end to the other, searching for themselves on the road. (Uludere, "Interview")

Although the film is meant to chronicle the reading of 6:45's translation of *Howl* (more on this in chapter 5), images of Erdoğan and Çaydamlı's travels "on the road" and dialogues concerning Kerouac on the way to the reading precede the event. According to Çaydamlı in our interview, despite this understanding of the road's importance to the Beats, Turkey presents a different situation: "First, the concept of being on the road is different geographically. America is a huge continent; it takes weeks to go from one place to another but here it takes two days. Because of that, being on the road is perhaps understood as a more spiritual journey in the Turkish context" (Çaydamlı, interview). *On the Road*'s translator, Kantarcı, also concurs, stating, "There have been other instances of road trips, naturally; however, the thing that constitutes the crux of *On the Road*, to map out your country / your people / yourself while traveling is not something that has been done extensively or widely" (Kantarcı, interview). While the type of road trip that Sal and Dean undertake is clearly possible in Turkey, for reasons both cultural and geographical, the sort of search that *On the Road* conducts remains specific to the American context.

The difficulty translators have in reading Kerouac's fascination with the hoboes and bums he meets on the road also highlights the complexity of the novel's reception in Turkey. *On the Road* is replete with these figures—the Shrouded Stranger, the Ghost of the Susquehanna, Hyman Solomon, Dean's Father—who come to represent a lost America filled with the freedom from social obligation that the novel champions. Kerouac celebrates Dean because he was "actually born on the road," but in Turkey such a pronouncement would hardly be cause for celebration. This sort of itinerancy is associated more often with the *çingene* (Roma), a marginalized group in Turkey seen as irresponsible and undereducated beggars, trash pickers, and musicians. While these are stereotypes, they are the public faces of the Roma for many (in Europe as well) and are certainly not celebrated as the possessors of a more "authentic" form of Turkish life or the harbingers of social revolt.

There really is no Turkish equivalent for those willfully dropping out of society to wander the country that are so celebrated in Kerouac's novel. As Çaydamlı explains, "[In our culture] one can be homeless at best, or a wino. We don't have an exact equivalent" (Çaydamlı, interview). The hobo has to be explained in Turkey. Zeynep Demirsü, in one of the few critical articles on the novel, argues, "Maybe a term used constantly in *On The Road* and left without translation in the Turkish version since it implies something more than idleness or vagrancy may illuminate us: Hobo" (32). After expressing some reservations with Kerouac's novel in terms of its treatment of women, Demirsü goes on to discuss what she sees as the important figure of the hobo by providing a brief history of the concept in the United States. While Erol Bakan claims the term resembles the older Ottoman word *sergüzeşt*, meaning "adventure" (and might call to the Turkish mind Samipaşazade Sezai's 1888 novel of the same name), Kantarcı does not even translate it in *Yolda*, preferring to add a footnote explaining, "In America this name is given to people who travel by illegally boarding trains. They have no permanent place to stay, no money, and look like beggars. They find work here and there. But there are people who consciously *prefer* [*tercih edenlerde bulunmaktadır*] this lifestyle" (italics mine; Kerouac, *Yolda: Orijinal Rulo*). Güzin Özkan and Ferruh Armutçuoğlu, in their first translation of *On the Road* in 1993, use the term *hobo* italicized in English only once, immediately redefine it as *berduş*, or vagabond, and then continue with the Turkish term throughout (Kerouac, *Yolda* 24).[10] In Turkey the road is the means to get from village to city and back again. While events certainly occur on it, it is the destination that matters more than the travel.

THE TURKISH ROAD

Turkish literature is replete with narratives of travel, but such journeys seldom focus on the road itself. The most famous of these accounts, Evliya Çelebi's ten-volume *Seyahâtnâme*, or *Book of Travels*, chronicles his perambulations across the Ottoman Empire. Evliya traveled with the sanction of religious imams and under the protection of the sultan. His account is concerned with recording the places and people he met, and praising God's glory, rather than with his own self-discoveries. The closest Turkish literature gets to the sort of open-ended travel experiences discussed in *On the Road* is in the Turkish "car narrative." In her article on the subject, Turkish literary critic Jale Parla traces this subgenre from Recaizade Ekrem's account of a man's love for his carriage in the Tanzimat, or Reform, period of the late Ottoman empire, through the Marxist poet Nazım Hikmet's fascination with machines and motors, to Adalet Ağaoğlu's *Fikrimin İnce Gülü* (*The Slender Rose of My Thought*) in which a Turkish guest worker in Germany returns home in what he thinks will be triumph to his village in a new Mercedes Benz.[11] The emphasis, however, is on the machine rather than the movement. Parla concludes that the trope of the car "is related, first and foremost, to that inexhaustible subject of Turkish writing, the effects of Westernization and modernization" (535). This is an important contrast to Kerouac's novel. It is not the car that is celebrated in *On the Road* but its ability to provide speed and movement that drives the narrative and the realizations of the characters ever onward.[12]

While the image of the road does occur in Turkish literature, it receives its most extensive treatment in Turkish film. The closest Turkey gets to the American-style road trip is in cinema. Turkish film gestures to the road trip, but contrary to Kerouac's insistence that "the road is life," in Turkish cinema what appears to be stressed is the destination rather than the journey. The reason for travel is likewise different. Whereas Sal and Dean move just to move, Turkish protagonists tend to travel to resolve a familial conflict or other problem. Along the way, these films raise contemporary political and social issues, though they are oftentimes secondary to the conflict that necessitated travel in the first place.

Winner of the Palme d'Or at Cannes, Yılmaz Güney's *Yol* (1982), for example, chronicles the homeward journeys of a group of prisoners taking a week-long leave. The emphasis is not so much on their travels, however, as it is on the familial difficulties they encounter upon their respective returns home. One prisoner must trek through a dangerous mountain pass to perform an honor killing, another searches reluctantly for a wife, while a third is bound to take the wife of his brother, who has died during a nighttime raid along the Syrian border. All the prisoners travel eastward, allowing the film to comment on Turkey's volatile political situation with regard to Kurdish separatists. Written while the director was in jail, it also provides "a radical critique not only of the oppressive Turkish state, but also of the feudal traditions prevailing in rural Turkey" (Suner 6). Along the way *Yol* also delivers majestic scenes of life on the Anatolian steppe. But the journeys themselves are not the focus of the picture. While the prisoners do bond with each other and experience the sort of hardships that bind road companions like Dean and Sal, the main thrust is not the experiences along the route but rather the difficult choices that lie ahead in their respective home villages. Thus the title *Yol*, which means "road" or "way" in Turkish, while an obvious reference to the trips home, mainly comes to signify the difficult life choices that the convicts are forced to make.

Güneşe Yolculuk (dir. Yeşim Ustaoğlu; 1999), translated as *Journey to the Sun*, likewise emphasizes destination over movement. After being mistaken for a Kurd, the life of protagonist Mehmet takes a turn for the worse, and when his Kurdish friend Berzan dies, he decides to deliver the man's body to the village of his birth on the Iraqi border. On the way, a variety of encounters demonstrate the difficulty of the trip as well as highlight various aspects of Turkish national pride. Children selling subversive papers almost land him in trouble, an episode that demonstrates the dangers of travel to the East, especially in areas known to be Kurdish strongholds. But he also meets with kindnesses and generally counts on the support of his fellow Turks, Kurds among them. The focus, however, is still on life in Istanbul. The village represents a sort of primal claim to Anatolian heritage, a connection with the land and its people that draws a sharp contrast to the urbanity of Istanbul. By the end of the film, this connection is proven tenuous. The village is submerged and its inhabitants displaced, a not-so-veiled reference to Turkish dam-building aspirations that threaten many such villages (some, like Hasankeyf, centuries old) in the East. But the protagonist is still able to launch Berzan's coffin on the water, sending his friend back to his home village. While villages may be ruined, social relationships remain intact.

Another award-winning film by an internationally recognized director, Nuri Bilge Ceylan's *Uzak* (2002), plays on this dichotomy between village and city. A more contemporary film, *Uzak* spends less time portraying Turkey's internal political strife, instead focusing on current economic realities, the differences between urban and rural life, and the limits of social obligations. While not exactly a road trip, *Uzak* begins with a long shot of an Anatolian valley, as a lone traveler makes his way to Istanbul in search of work when the factory in his town is closed. Yusuf stays in the house of his cousin Mahmut, who is dealing with a failed marriage and is reluctant to help him, though he feels the burden of familial obligations to do so. The plot revolves around this situation as Yusuf searches in vain for the employment necessary to support his family back home while his host Mahmut, a successful photographer, becomes more and more frustrated with his presence. In fact, the one short road trip that occurs in the film ends in frustration as the two protagonists fail to achieve the sort of camaraderie that defines the genre. The title, which means "distant" in Turkish, hints at this contrast. The road, as in all these films, does not become a focus in itself but rather forms the tenuous thread that measures the gap between village and urban life, and the commitments that bind them.

AN OPTIMISTIC DEAN

While Sal celebrates Dean's willingness to constantly move, Sal himself is tethered to the figure of his aunt, who is always ready with a meal, a check, or a place to stay. Dean's secret is that he has no such reserve. Bereft of family, career, and permanent home, Dean is "free" to wander the country in search of his "kicks." Exchanging the horse for a car and the open prairie for the open road, Dean represents the modern-day cowboy, a lonesome figure always passing through but never staying long. Such transience results in an increased focus on the passing moment. Ultimately, Dean's appeal resides in his spontaneous nature that allows him to experience a richer world than those around him. Defending his friend in an argument, Sal states, "[B]ut now he's alive and I'll bet you want to know what he does next and that's because he's got the secret that we're all busting to find" (178). This "secret" is simply that Dean acts spontaneously. Free of the anxieties and fears that trouble a middle-class life, Dean is able to give himself completely to each passing moment.

Dean's message is made even more powerful through contrast. Comparing their lives to those of the passengers in the car they are sharing, Dean explains to Sal,

> they're counting the miles, they're thinking about where to sleep tonight, how much money for gas, the weather, how they'll get there—and all the time they'll get there anyway. . . . But they need to worry and betray time with urgencies false and otherwise . . . their souls really won't be at peace unless they latch on to an established and proven worry. (189–90)

These passengers use "worries" to mitigate the uncertainty that the future holds. Through creating a specific anxiety over "money," "gas," or "weather," the average citizen is able to forget the larger troubles that the future might bring. Dean, by contrast, does not attempt to abstract himself out of the moment by focusing on the details that might occur. Instead, he revels in the instant. Responding to the conditions of the present rather than the fears of the future, to Sal, Dean appears more "alive," a man worthy of emulating since he points the way out of the stultifying postwar society entrapping them all.[13]

Such spontaneity was not confined to Kerouac's novel but was an integral part of the postwar zeitgeist in U.S. arts and letters. From the abstract expressionist painting of artists like Jackson Pollock to bebop jazz musicians and even into the mediums of sculpture and dance, spontaneity offered a means of critiquing the cultural expectations of the period. In a postwar world where citizens were supposed to think and act in conformity with accepted notions, spontaneity meant liberation and individual expression. As Daniel Belgrad observes in *The Culture of Spontaneity*, "the social significance of spontaneity can be appreciated only if this aesthetic practice is understood as a crucial site of cultural work: that is, as a set of activities and texts engaged in the struggle over meanings and values within American society" (1). Spontaneity, by definition, is not a codified movement but rather an open stance toward the world meant to foster possibilities and to challenge dominant thinking. In a country filled with "a combination of wartime and Cold War xenophobia (a fear of 'un-Americanism') and pride in America's material prosperity ('The American Way of Life')," this culture of spontaneity allowed for a third space where such assumptions could be critiqued (1). Dean's insistence that every moment be lived to the fullest and that no restriction be placed on his mobility is as much social critique as personal creed. He points to a new way of living, free of a postwar containment culture that stressed commitments to work, home, and country. Kerouac's novel, while certainly one of the most influential texts of the period, was not alone in its critique of this homogenized American culture. Rather, it was one voice among many calling for a reevaluation of what it meant to be an American in a time of escalating Cold War anxieties and conflicts.

Dean thus comes to exemplify a countercultural notion of freedom pushed to the limits of self-expression, but it is important to recognize that this agency evolves from a specific outlook that has its cultural counterpoint in the tradition of American optimism. What allows Dean to run so many hazards is that he does not see this behavior as being dangerous. Ultimately, Dean is optimistic about its outcome—he trusts that everything will work out, and even if it does not, he has already reconciled himself to the consequences of his actions. Thus even in one of Dean's darker moments, recently evicted by his wife and suffering numerous health complaints, Dean is still able to remark, "And yet—and yet, I've never felt better and finer and happier with the world . . . and I know, I *know* everything will be alright" (169). The United States, unlike its allies and adversaries, was virtually unscathed after the Second World War. The period just after the war became a time of economic abundance that is remembered nostalgically even today, a time when the GI Bill and easy credit made education, homes, and cars available to a wider range of Americans than ever before. Giddy from victory and the fruits it seemed to confer, Americans looked to the future with optimism.[14] Dean seems to have taken this feeling to its logical extreme, to believe unreservedly in the grace and bounty that many believed were their due.

Dean's wholehearted belief in giving oneself over to the passing moment is conveyed by numerous direct quotes throughout *On the Road.* No other character besides Sal is allowed to speak so frequently. In one of his many soliloquies, Dean explains to Sal, "Everything is fine, God exists, we know time. . . . As we roll along this way I am positive beyond doubt that everything will be taken care of for us. . . . I know the people, I know what they do" (108–9). Dean's announcement is a curious blend of fate and agency. On the one hand, "Everything will be taken care of" suggests that there is some force that dictates the future. Yet Dean does not simply abandon himself to the moment. Rather, he actively engages the moment on its own terms—his actions work because they are right for that particular moment. Though situations change, he "knows the people," how things work, and is confident that he will choose the appropriate course of action. Such optimism is contagious. In another of his excited moods, Dean explains to Sal, "[W]e all must admit that everything is fine and there's no need in the world to worry" (121). Sal agrees and goes on to give an example translated into his own terms: "The purity of the road. The white line in the middle of the highway unrolled and hugged our left front tire as if glued to our groove" (121). The car is almost driving itself, the tire and the road fusing into a "groove" that will guide it effortlessly. Spontaneity creates a symbiosis with the world that is a strange mixture of both engaging and letting go. But for it to work, there must be an assumption that one is up to the task. Otherwise freedom quickly devolves into fear.

The corollary to this optimistic outlook is that even if things do not work out so smoothly, everything will still be fine in the end. Despite Sal's worries over Marylou, who has promised to leave Dean and become his lover once they get to San Francisco, Sal is infected with Dean's enthusiasm enough to claim, "But why think about that when all the golden land's ahead of you and all kinds of unforeseen events wait lurking to surprise you and make you glad you're alive to see?" (122). Dean's lesson is that while things may not work out to your liking, they nevertheless resolve themselves in some fashion, and that too is miraculous and wonderful. In the end, America becomes the proverbial land of plenty to both: "He and I suddenly saw the whole country like an oyster for us to open; and the pearl was there, the pearl was there" (124). Sal is speaking metaphorically of course, but the novel does play on images of acquisition that dominated the postwar period as the United States shifted from an industrial to a consumer society. Though their consumption is neither conspicuous nor excessive, Sal and Dean nevertheless continually consume throughout *On the Road*, a testament to the belief that America was a land of limitless supply and growth.

THE UNPREDICTABLE FUTURE

On the Road's Turkish reception reveals that Kerouac's novel is firmly rooted in an American optimism that is by no means universal and timeless. Dislodging Kerouac from his U.S. moorings and placing him in a Turkish context demonstrates just how important cultural context is when trying to understand meaning. In a country already known for economic and political instability, my Turkish students argued, why tempt fate with such reckless behavior? As another Turkish student, Gizem Özkan, explains,

> However, when we consider today's Turkey because of overpopulation and poverty, a regular university graduate might not find the job Sal finds temporarily in the book. We are burdened with debt mostly and should constantly think about the future in every step we take, not necessarily to achieve a good quality of life, but to prevent becoming poor. . . . To sum up what I am trying to say is because of a nonfunctioning social state, our future is never guaranteed and this might lead us to obtain a more precarious point of view as a society. Secondly, I might probably be right by saying terrorism in Turkey is much more than terrorism in United States. Because of Turkey's geopolitical location and unhealthy relationships with its neighbor countries, nearly every day someone is dying because of terrorist attacks. . . . Think about it, hitchhiking in a country with these environmental issues. I'm not saying we live in a constant fear of death but spontaneity could easily cost your life especially if you're living in the eastern part.

Gizem was not the only student to point out the problems that have plagued Turkey over the years. Inflation, currency devaluation, and unemployment have created a culture filled with anxiety over the economic situation, a country where one thinks less about "a good quality of life" and more about simply not "becoming poor." Today's Turkey is experiencing one of its strongest periods of growth ever, but the 2016 coup attempt has already created fears that the economic situation could change overnight. Economic instability exists in the United States, of course, and Özkan is voicing concerns relevant to any graduating university student. The reception of *On the Road* has a temporal as well as geographical component, and given the interconnectedness of today's globalized world the novel's optimism might strike both Turkish and U.S. students as a bit naïve. But the history of economic volatility in Turkey is certainly a major factor in the way *On the Road* is received in the country.

The same can be said for the issue of political instability. One of the reasons that the Free Girl campaign appeared so ridiculous to many was that the commercial's depictions of these eastern travels were nothing less than incredulous. For the past several decades, eastern Turkey has become associated with violence and political unrest, due in part to a history of domestic violence and honor killings in the region, as well as clashes between Kurdish resistance groups and the Turkish government. The "eastern part" of Turkey, a long-time Kurdish stronghold, was for many years inaccessible to most Turks due to such fighting. The commercial was aired at a time when the armed conflict between government forces and the Kurdistan Workers' Party (PKK) was at an ebb, and travel in the region became easier. In August 1999, Abdullah Öcalan, the leader of the Kurdish resistance, was brought to trial, which resulted in a ceasefire. Violence in the region decreased for several years, and the organization itself was reestablished only in 2005. Still, the memory of violence in the area remains strong, and the idea that two lone travelers could explore the region armed with little more than a cell phone made the advertisement seem absurd to many of its viewers. Today one would be equally cautious of the problems in Syria and Iraq, as well as the growing ISIS threat throughout Turkey and the threat of Kurdish resistance in the East.[15]

In such a volatile climate, the idea of fate or chance takes on a much different significance. If the future is dependent on antagonistic forces beyond one's control, then the sort of spontaneous behavior that the Beats championed is more difficult to achieve. In Turkey there is an idea that something will occur "if it fits" or "if God wills it" (connoted by the often-heard phrase *İnşallah*) rather than if spontaneous action meets with favorable conditions. This belief finds its most poignant expression in the term *kısmet*. This word is translated (when it is translated at all) as "destiny" or "fortune," but there is an underlying sense that what will happen in the future is outside of one's own control, and thus one should always proceed cautiously. *Kısmet* is an optimistic belief in the future, but one that does not suppose that the end result depends on the speaker. It is usually said ex post facto, after the good thing comes, by way of explanation. Believing in a positive outcome too strongly is seen as jeopardizing that desire, so wishes are often expressed as requests to be fulfilled (if at all) by an outside force. Dean, by contrast, always retains a sense of agency—his actions influence how the moment will unfold. Beat spontaneity is based on a faith in the moment, on the idea that if someone approaches each instant with openness and perception their actions will fit the requirements of the moment such that desirable results will occur. But to those who face a more uncertain future, Dean simply appears reckless.

Dean's recklessness is not simply that he pays no attention to the future but rather that he courts disaster with the assumption that things will work out fine. *Nazar* or *mavi göz*, the ubiquitous blue eye adorning countless cars, homes, and boats in Turkey, is a symbol meant to ward off the desiring gaze of another. But this "evil eye" is not so much a talisman that protects the owner and their property from the acquisitiveness of others as it is a modest devaluation of their possessions in an attempt to not stand out in the crowd. Thus Turkish mothers will often call their child "ugly baby" not because of its physical appearance but because they do not want to appear too delighted in the possession of what other women might themselves desire. *Kısmet* and the *mavi göz* represent more of a letting go of personal agency, conveying a wish that does not want to call attention to itself. Needless to say, such statements are sweeping in their scope, and it would be easy to find contradicting examples. Yet Dean is clearly in the American mode. Although his spontaneous behavior does not attempt to fully control the situation, it sets events in motion, providing the catalyst that allows the elements of the moment to interact. The outcome may not be certain, but Dean is confident that the results will be positive. Though he knows better than to attempt to control the situation, Dean believes in his ability to turn it to his advantage. In Turkey such a wish would appear presumptuous.

Torn between his desire for experience and the stability of home life, Sal is a far more understandable character for Turkish readers. In contrast to Dean's heady mix of itinerant-ness, optimism, and risk-taking, Sal is more staid. While he certainly "shambles after" Dean, Sal is equally drawn back to the stability of religion, family, and marriage (7). Sal repeatedly uses both his Catholicism and his newly found interest in Buddhism as a filter for the revelations and visions he experiences on the road. And not only is his aunt (in real life, his mother) waiting for him with a hot meal and a warm bed, but the novel ends with Sal falling in love with another woman and thinking about settling down. In fact, by the final pages Dean becomes a mere memory, a wistful thought of a life that has already passed beyond him. Sal becomes the voice of reason in the novel—Dean is the enticing aberration.

KEROUAC LOOKS EAST

Sal's anxieties about the mobility and independence championed by Dean in the novel are mapped onto an imaginary dream space of the East filled with danger and intrigue. This should come as no surprise, since the city of Istanbul is a placeholder for the mysterious throughout the Beat canon. Working with Burroughs, the man who would become the character of Old Bull Lee in *On the Road*, Kerouac coauthored the noir-inspired novel *And the Hippos Were Boiled in Their Tanks* (written in 1945). In the novel, Burroughs introduces the character of Phillip Tourian, "seventeen years old, half Turkish and half American," whose father, "born of uncertain parentage in Istanbul," was a "sort of underworld broker dealing in dope, women, and stolen goods" (53). Phillip's father clearly represents the East as imagined by Burroughs, for him a utopian space of loose morality and quasi-legal transactions. Burroughs, like many Orientalists before him, fashions the East in terms of the licentiousness of the harem, a dreamed place of fulfilled desires that serves as counterpoint to the restraints of their present Western society. Later, when Kerouac introduces Old Bull Lee in *On the Road*, he describes him "in Istanbul threading his way through crowds of opium addicts and rug-sellers, looking for the facts," though Burroughs never actually traveled to the country (130). Turkey is the inversion of the United States, a land of intrigue and mystery.[16]

Kerouac's East appears in a dream that provides a counterpoint to the freedom of the rest of the novel. Describing a decision that he was trying to remember but could not recall, Sal states that it was caught up with his dream of the Shrouded Traveler, "a strange Arabian figure that was pursing me across the desert; that I tried to avoid; that finally overtook me just before I reached the Protective City" (112).[17] Sal's orientalist fantasy inverts the insistence on movement that the rest of the novel displays, sundering the connection between mobility and individual freedom that Dean represents. The road becomes a space filled with danger, a vast absence haunted by the "strange Arabian figure." The "Protective City" is that urban space where security is found, a caravanserai where a traveler can find respite from the rigors of travel. Sal may claim that the "road is life," but it is only behind city walls where he envisions security in his dream.

Sal, however, does not make it to the city. Instead, he interprets the Arabian figure as the death that chases humankind across the "desert of life" as we struggle to attain "heaven" (112). The fact that Sal is overtaken points to a Freudian death drive, an attempt to experience, as Sal states, "some lost bliss that was probably experienced in the womb and can only be reproduced (though we hate to admit it) in death" (112). Dean, with his characteristic emphasis on lived life, rejects this desire. Sal relates his dream to Dean, who "would have nothing to do with it, and I agreed with him then" (112). This "then" is telling, since by the end of the novel Sal parts ways with his comrade to live a more sedentary life. Though he endorses Dean's individualism and remains nostalgic for the sort of lifestyle Dean engenders, Sal is more ambivalent about the sort of breakdown in identity that spontaneous life on the road entails. The Shrouded Traveler maps Sal's unconscious fears onto the spaces of the East, presenting the reader with a glimpse into the anxieties such endless movement fosters.[18]

Despite Kerouac's insistence on travel, his narrator is often disturbed by such uninhibited movement. By all accounts, the real Dean Moriarty was an excellent driver. Charles Bukowski, in his *Notes of a Dirty Old Man*, describes Neal Cassady as a virtuoso behind the wheel, deftly maneuvering in and out of traffic on a rain-slick road, a description that Tom Wolfe will echo in his account of Cassady's command of Ken Kesey and the Merry Prankster's day-glo-painted bus in *The Electric Acid Kool-Aid Test.* Sal, by contrast, is afraid to drive, and while he admires Dean's ability to seamlessly become almost a part of the automobile, Dean's carefree movement frightens him. Driving to Chicago, Sal climbs into the backseat, afraid to watch as Dean weaves the car in and out of traffic at high velocities with reckless glee, a "mad Ahab at the wheel" (213). Thus Sal is both excited and unnerved when he hears that Dean is following him to Denver to drive him and another friend to Mexico, stating, "Suddenly I had a vision of Dean, a burning shuddering frightful Angel . . . pursuing me like the Shrouded Traveler on the plain, bearing down on me" (230).

The reason Sal equates Dean with the Shrouded Traveler that haunts his dreams is that Dean is an ambiguous force in Sal's life. Dean becomes both "Angel" and Devil, a force of liberation as well as one of destruction. Sal describes Dean in apocalyptic terms, and ultimately it is difficult to tell whether Dean's arrival is welcome or feared. Sal states, "I saw his old jalopy chariot with thousands of sparking flames shooting out from it; I saw the path it burned across the road . . . destroying bridges, drying rivers. It came like wrath to the West" (236). The reason *On the Road* is open to so many divergent readings is that Dean represents Sal's desires, in all of their complexities and inconsistencies. Sal desires the energy and uncertainty that Dean brings to his life while, at the same time, fearing the possibility for destruction that Dean represents. The "madness" of Dean brings liberation from a stifling society bent on rationality, but also the possible usurpation of limits that leads to destruction. Both are represented by the automobile itself—a machine whose ability to facilitate movement can instantaneously become a conveyance of death.

The images of the East that haunt *On the Road* demonstrate the anxiety that lingers just below the surface of its celebratory language. Again drawing on the myth of the East as a place for the strange and unsettling, Sal describes a night spent in a Detroit movie house filled with "Beat Negroes," "white bums," "whores," and "young longhaired hipsters" (222). Out of funds, Sal and Dean sleep through innumerable showings of a double feature, one film about a "Singing Cowboy Eddie Dean" and the other "a picture about Istanbul" (222). By the end of the night, Sal claims that "we were permeated completely with the strange Gray Myth of the West and the weird dark Myth of the East" (222). Both myths leave Sal unsatisfied, and he wakes up feeling horrible, little better than the garbage that the usher sweeps up as the movies finish. This double feature mirrors the sort of double-consciousness that permeates Hollywood, and by extension the sort of myths Kerouac drew on to produce *On the Road*. The Western stars Eddie Dean, a well-known actor in the 1930s and 1940s, whose films showcased his vocal abilities over plot and cinematography. Kerouac is probably using the term "myth" pejoratively here to contrast Hollywood's version of the West with the true Western-ness of his friend Dean. Earlier in the novel, Sal comes across such clichéd representations while visiting Wild West Week in Cheyenne. The Hollywood Western captures the myth of such freedom, complete with good triumphing over evil, all undertaken in the full light of day.

The second film, *Background to Danger* (dir. Raoul Walsh; 1943), is the Janus-headed unconscious of this myth projected onto the space of the East. World War II Ankara and Istanbul become the space of political intrigue, double-dealing, and shadowy espionage, a world of suspicion where nobody can be trusted. If Hollywood is the dream machine of American consciousness, this osmotic absorption of both myths leaves Sal exhausted. The overly optimistic vision of America as a cowboy land does not fit the "Beatness" of the shabby theater or its patrons. Nor does a singing cowboy represent

Sal's experience of the West. The myth of the East, by contrast, is perhaps too close to the truth of America's real postwar situation. Giving the lie to the reassuring myth of a culture built on mutual trust and camaraderie, *Background to Danger* is a subtle critique of the paranoia and anxiety of containment culture displaced onto Turkey, a film that when released spoke of World War II anxieties but, by the time of Kerouac's experience, made a prescient comment on the shadowy world of Cold War politics. Though ostensibly about the East, this "dark myth" has more explanatory power than America's fictitious Western self-representations. Although Kerouac never visited Turkey, his appropriations of images of the country that *On the Road* unwittingly captures speaks to the fascination Turkey held for Kerouac and other Beats as well as to the East's role as a placeholder for the unconscious anxiety over Western preoccupations.

GENDER AND RACE IN *ON THE ROAD*

While Kerouac unconsciously voices his anxiety in the novel itself, readers have also raised other issues with *On the Road.* Critics in the late 1950s generally attacked it for its narrative style and rejection of middle-class American values, but today's readers are far more concerned with its treatment of gender and depiction of ethnic minorities. Women are often merely objects in the text, placeholders for male desire that are not given voice and quickly discarded in favor of the homosocial bonds between male protagonists. In one scene, Dean is reprimanded by his wife's friend Galatea: "you have absolutely no regard for anybody but yourself and your damned kicks. All you think about is what's hanging between your legs and how much money or fun you can get out of people and then you just throw them aside" (176). Sal goes on to defend Dean, but Galatea's accusation is apt and provides a starting point for discussions of gender inequality, misogyny, and sexuality in both the novel and society at large. Turkish students, along with their U.S. counterparts, are quick to pick up on this theme, and one of the more universal responses to the novel has been female readers' reaction to *On the Road*'s misogynistic passages.

Sal and Dean's often callous treatment of the women they meet provides one type of gender critique in *On the Road*, but the difficulty women have in conducting the sort of open-ended travel that the novel celebrates is another problem. The barriers to mobility prevalent in Turkey prove even more constraining to women. In the Free Girl commercial, Nil's hitching a ride in a truck recalls the tragic story of the Italian "peace bride." In an effort to raise awareness for peace and build solidarity, in 2008 Italian artist and activist Pippa Bacca planned to hitchhike her way from Milan to Tel-Aviv, beginning on International Women's Day. Wearing a wedding dress, she hitchhiked through the Balkans and Thrace but was raped and killed by a truck driver in a city near Istanbul. For women, solo travel in the East would be even more difficult than it is for men. As Yıldız Silier comments in her book *The Illusion of Freedom*, "While 'Free Girl' is roaming across hills and rivers by herself wearing only her shorts and armed only with her cell phone, girls of the same age are becoming victims of honor killings because they talked to boys." While it would be unfair to characterize an entire region based solely on these "honor killings," eastern Turkey does have a reputation as being generally more religiously and socially conservative than the western parts of the country. The idea that a woman could be free to travel by herself, and in shorts and a bra no less, made the ad campaign appear hopelessly naïve to many.[19]

How, then, does the female reader enter into a narrative like *On the Road*? The desire for women to undertake the sort of road trips the novel chronicles strikes many as foolhardy rather than emancipatory. At the time of its publication, the idea of women taking the same sort of trips as Dean and Sal took was difficult to imagine. Joyce Johnson, fellow Beat writer and Kerouac's lover, declared in a 1996 roundtable discussion, "I'm sorry I never got to go down to Mexico with Jack. It wasn't a time when women could really go on the road, in the sense that Jack and Neal went on the road as male travelers. We women could not do that then" (Charters, *Beat Down* 629). Times may have changed, but the masculine bias associated with being on the road remains. Writing in *Salon*, Vanessa Veselka in "Where Are the Women Kerouacs?" discusses her experience hitchhiking, arguing that as a woman she was without "a Melvillean or Kerouacian framework" and therefore remained "unrecognizable" while on the road. For men, such journeys, whether spiritual or physical (or both), become "imbued with heroism," while women's stories are "restricted to a single tragic or fatal choice." Even when women do take to the road, society chooses not to valorize women's self-discovery through the road genre.

Works that seek to invert the male buddy travel format by substituting female characters into the narrative highlight the masculine-centered nature of the genre. The Turkish underground novel *Pogo* is an attempt to rewrite the road narrative for women readers. The back cover of Ural's work draws on the buddy narrative to chronicle life in Turkey's countercultural punk subculture of the 1990s: "Two young girls leading their lives with excitement and self-confidence. They challenge everybody and everything. No credit cards. No first-class journeys. A life with no control, limitless music. The second half of the 1990s: Spider Man, hitchhiking, burglary, love, murder, wine, Prodigy, Sex Pistols, Off Spring: POGO . . ." The novel delivers on this promise, chronicling the travels of Değer and her friend Rüzgar as they become involved in a nonstop series of adventures. In one scene, when Değer and her friend Rüzgar avoid rape by threatening their attackers with a gun, they then proceed to rob the men who tried to rape them. Değer comments, "It's good we taught them a lesson since maybe they would have raped someone else" (182). The pair goes on to rob rich older men by posing as prostitutes. When Değer muses, "We gave seven men seven lessons. Perhaps they thought because they cheated on their wives. Perhaps we've contributed to the feminist movement," Rüzgar quickly dismisses this thought, claiming, "Come on, we do this for ourselves. Fuck the rest. So now are we going to get dominant?" (194). While theirs is clearly not a vigilante cause, Değer and Rüzgar nevertheless feel some solidarity for their fellow women. Yet the novel is not exactly feminist either.

The contradiction between the desire for gender equality and the reversion to masculine models of success is another issue in the narrative. Rüzgar gets a gun from Halil, their drug dealer, by performing oral sex. Later, when Değer comes across Halil, he taunts them with this act, mockingly saying to Rüzgar, "[A]re you afraid of me telling everyone what you did?" Angry that Halil continues to insult a passive Rüzgar, Değer proceeds to beat him over the head with a beer bottle. Halil's bodyguards rush the women out, but one praises Değer, claiming, "[Y]ou did better than us, why don't you become a bodyguard?" (196). Değer is extremely proud of this compliment, going so far as to offer to have sex with the man because of his praise. Success is measured by masculine achievement. The idea is not to reclaim the feminine but to be "strong" enough to adapt to male paradigms.[20] Like the film *Spring Breakers* (2012), *Pogo* embraces the idea of the female rebel and borrows extensively from the buddy film and road trip genre. But despite this replacing of transgressive male acts of bravado with female ones, in the end, Rüzgar manipulates everything to get Değer's Danish boyfriend Kunt to return to her. In fact, whenever anything bad happens, Kunt is there to help. In *Breaking the Rule of Cool*, Ronna C. Johnson discusses Brenda Frazier's novel *Troia: Mexican Memoirs*, another text that complicates the male-dominated road narrative, claiming that the author "deploys a beat antidiscipline in its road tale that achieves female subjectivity even while complying with terms of women's objectification" ("Mapping" 27). The same could be said of *Pogo*. Though it takes acts of transgression even further, Ural's characters are still dependent on masculine standards of behavior.

While *On the Road*'s gender issues get discussed and, to some extent, emulated in Turkey, the novel's racial politics receive less attention. Kerouac celebrates ethnic minorities, and was himself of French Canadian descent, though his discussions of race usually degenerate into panegyric. America's ethnic others exist outside the margins and thus offer Sal a model to imitate: "At lilac evening I walked with every muscle aching among the lights of 27th and Welton in the Denver colored section, wishing I were a Negro, feeling that the best the white world had offered was not enough ecstasy for me, not enough life, joy, kicks, darkness, music, not enough night" (163). While Kerouac's depictions of the ethnic minorities he meets on his travels are couched in positive terms, they are likewise founded on highly problematic stereotypes. Standing outside the American mainstream, such ethnic groups are de facto Beat. But what Kerouac fails to understand is that unlike Sal (and to a lesser extent Dean), they typically do not choose this marginalized lifestyle but rather are forced to live it by a racist society.

One positive aspect of these problematic moments in *On the Road*, especially in the classroom, is that they open up a space for debate and discussion of difficult issues in U.S. cultural life. But in Turkey, Kerouac's treatment of race is never discussed. This is not simply due to a bias—the readers we encountered in our focus groups and study were mainly open-minded when it came to ethnic others. When asked whether they would mind living next to a Kurdish family, 94.7 percent replied that they would not mind (Mortenson, Ergun, and Erdoğan, unpublished data).[21] Could "Kurd" be read for "colored" here, or "Roma" for "poor overworked Jap"? (164). It could, but it wasn't. While a few reviewers such as Demirsü mention feminist issues, none have remarked on Kerouac's treatment of minorities and certainly none compared them to Turkish ethnic groups. The reasons for such an omission are difficult to discern. The treatment of ethnic and religious minorities is a sensitive issue in Turkey, the Armenian issue providing the most obvious example. But the glorification of a supposed authenticity with regard to the life of such marginalized groups would probably also appear odd to the Turkish reader. There is certainly support for the betterment of oppressed groups, and such groups were included in the resistance protests at Gezi Park, but the idea that living such a marginalized ethnic existence would actually be superior might appear strange in the Turkish context.

Nor do the Beats seem to be a catalyst for minority groups in Turkey. Given the problematic treatment of minority groups in the novel, this fact makes a good deal of sense. Yet there may be other reasons why Beats like Kerouac have not appealed to those involved in struggles for ethnic equality. The fact that Kerouac was not picked up by, say, Kurdish groups struggling for equality demonstrates that the Beats are still more important for middle-class rebellion than for minority groups struggling to have their voices heard. This dichotomy seems to be the case in the Turkish underground as a whole. In his study of Turkish hip-hop, Thomas Solomon notes that the term *underground* does *not* refer to the "ethnic and class background of the participants in the Turkish hip-hop community," which is so important to establishing "street credibility" in the United States and European contexts of the genre (8). Turkish underground literature, too, has tended to focus on marginality as it occurs within mainstream Turkish society and rarely delves into the plight of such groups as Kurds, Roma, or other marginalized social groups in Turkey. *On the Road*'s countercultural message clearly seeks to include ethnic minorities as part of a revolt against mainstream cultural values but is mainly directed at disaffected youth who are, for the most part, already included within the very mainstream that is being attacked. Kerouac's usefulness for ethnic minority struggle, both in the West and in Turkey, appears limited.

CONCLUSION

While *On the Road* garners a new generation of readers every year, we need to be aware of the specific cultural context that these readers bring to the work. *On the Road* provides an important model for dissent, but its individualism is by no means universal, nor is the optimism that supports it. Both are a product of the postwar United States. Kerouac's novel speaks to many but finds more ready listeners in a society where individualism and the belief that one's actions can have a positive impact on events are central tenets. Buoyed by the postwar economic boom, Sal and Dean are in a unique position to cast aside relationships that are fundamental to the survival of those in other parts of the world. Thus the novel's rebelliousness is very American in nature, a desire for movement and flux that are seen as liberating in themselves.

Read against the Turkish concerns expressed here, however, Sal's hesitancy to fully embrace Dean's lifestyle becomes easier to discern. Sal's ambivalence is oftentimes lost among the youthful exuberance that pervades a great portion of the text. As John Leland argues in *Why Kerouac Matters*, "Despite the characters' repeated references to God, salvation and redemption, the book's religious dimension has been overshadowed by the image of two wild and crazy guys" (150). For younger readers especially, the focus is squarely on Dean and his anticonformist behavior. This overshadowing is partly due to Kerouac's spontaneous style, which does not seem to privilege one moment over another but provides a sort of running commentary from which readers can choose the reading they desire. Responses from my Turkish students demonstrate just how ambivalent Sal often is about Dean's behavior, a fact that becomes clearer after subsequent readings. Problems like those of gender (and to a lesser extent, race) that can easily be overlooked by a celebration of Dean's character likewise come to the fore when the novel is placed in new contexts. Sal's own visions of the East as a sort of revealing "unconscious" to his Western mythmaking demonstrate the downside to Dean's philosophy of exuberance. While this nuanced reading of Kerouac's classic countercultural novel might denude it of some of its revolutionary force, it also opens it up to a richer reading experience. Rather than an unthinking rebelliousness, Kerouac is offering a challenge to his postwar American society that was itself hesitant about the implications of its message.

This is not to say that *On the Road* does not or should not affect readers. On the contrary, the book has launched innumerable road trips and by all accounts will continue to do so for years to come. But it does mean that we should reconsider the nature of its impact. Kerouac chronicled the materiality of U.S. culture, its cities, roads, bars, and diners, and the logical extension of this type of thinking is a desire to reexperience the places that Kerouac experienced, to measure our experience of this country against his. Thus for a U.S.-based audience, the trip "on the road" is very much a discovery and critique of place itself, the place of America (even if conceived in nostalgic terms). Yet the very American idea of the road trip can also be thought of in more general terms. The road trip is a search—in Kerouac's case, it is nominally a search for Dean's father, but in reality the novel presents a search for America itself and the characters' places in it. The Turkish reception of *On the Road* reminds us that while Kerouac's text deals extensively with the question of defining America, the experience he chronicles can just as easily be read as an inward journey. This allows us to see why the book was received positively by those unable or unwilling to hazard the sort of expeditions that Sal and Dean undertook, and why the book remains in such demand into the present day throughout the world. Readers do not need to go on the road to understand Kerouac's commitment to personal exploration and discovery. In the U.S. context, the book might be used more as a blueprint for physical dislocation and rebellion, but its universality better resides in the idea of a spiritual journey, broadly defined.

Reading *On the Road* refracted through its Turkish reception reveals a book that still has the power to persuade, to foment change in individuals and cultures, but the site and nature of that change undergoes a transformation. Long seen as playing a mediating role between West and East, Turkey is undergoing its own set of cultural changes. By offering a completely different worldview, *On the Road* poses a challenge and provides an opportunity to Turkish culture. For those who want to see changes occur in Turkish society, Kerouac's text provides the means to at least open up a space for dialogue, to bring issues out into the light of day. Instead of aspiring to the wealth and status associated with the West, *On the Road*'s Turkish readers are often looking for a cultural counter to the gross capitalism that appears to be sweeping the planet. Kerouac's book, though itself caught up in consumerist logics, provides a critique of Western capitalism written within that system. With its emphasis on the individual, *On the Road* also offers a means of challenging the top-down hierarchies and rigid social structures prevalent in Turkish society. Although Dean is by no means the perfect role model, he does offer the possibility of renegotiating the personal, familial, and social obligations that are an important part of life in Turkey. Kerouac's text thus has a lot to offer, even if its message is not unilaterally applicable or universally desirable.

Kerouac fantasizes the East, but the East fantasizes the West as well. Although middle-class Turkish students often travel the world, mapping of one's own country through the American-style road trip is far less common. Though the frequency of this practice could certainly change if travel restrictions disappear and disposable money becomes available, the road trip is still more of concept or an activity tied (as in the films discussed) to a destination rather than the journey itself. Kerouac's book is interesting because it maps the spiritual quest onto the material, allowing us to see discovery unfold along the highways and byways of America. Yet this need not be so—Turkish readers can understand Sal's desire to find meaning in life independent of his being American. In focus groups conducted in April 2013 in the Turkish capital of Ankara, a master's student at Hacettepe University observed,

> We live in a conservative country, and people should be more broad about their ideas. . . . Because when you think of a young Turkish person these kind of things like Jack Kerouac or Allen Ginsberg may be the opposites of their beliefs or lifestyles but I think that is necessary for the Turkish youth. For me, I do not practice the book as a lifestyle but I think it changes my mind. But if I could be brave enough I could have practiced it in my life. (Mortenson, Ergun, and Erdoğan, unpublished data)

Beat texts like *On the Road* may not quite fit into Turkish society, but within the disjunctive space they create exists their power to foment change by offering new perspectives and new alternatives.

Countercultural texts like Jack Kerouac's *On the Road* create the possibility that ideas lingering below the surface might one day well upward, cracking the pavements and sidewalks of the dominant culture. Will that challenge succeed? At the present moment, such literature does not seem to pose a fundamental threat to the social order in Turkey. Yet how many people were waiting for a book like *On the Road*, a poem like Ginsberg's *Howl*, or a novel such as Burroughs's *Naked Lunch* to emerge and give expression to an undercurrent of dissatisfaction flowing through American society? Perhaps it is simply a matter of time before *On the Road* or books like it begin to attract the sort of following they enjoy in American culture. Or perhaps the type of oppositional literature that Kerouac's novel represents will be the inspiration for a more Turkish model that will emerge in the future, a new countercultural statement that will give a more Turkish voice to a type of writing that, from time to time, calls society to task for its misdirection and offers new roads into the uncharted future.

4. THE BEATS ON TRIAL
THE CENSORSHIP OF WILLIAM S. BURROUGHS'S *THE SOFT MACHINE*

Censorship is a volatile practice. Consider the case of Sultan Abdülhamid II (1842–1918), whose reign is considered an especially repressive period in Ottoman history due in large part to his desire to stifle and suppress the written word. Anecdotes of Abdülhamid's absurd practices still abound, the most noted being his interdiction concerning noses. The sultan banned any use of the word *burun* (nose) because he felt it was a reference to his own particularly large one. This created problems, because in Turkish "burun" has several meanings. Thus, when the translator of Pierre Loti's novel *Le Pêcheur d'Islande* (*İzlanda Balıkçıları* in Turkish, or *An Iceland Fisherman*; 1886) wanted to translate the geographical term "cape," he had "to give a full definition of the term instead of using the word itself" (Boyer 419–20).[1] The irony is that censorship often calls more attention to the very thing that it is striving to suppress, and noses, rap lyrics, pornographic images, and other banned material often find themselves even better known in the process. This is certainly true of Abdülhamid. The anecdote of the censored nose has made it certain that the embarrassing member that Abdülhamid fought so hard to conceal has become the very thing that comes to mind when his name is mentioned.

This chapter examines another instance of censorship in Turkey and the cultural response it has engendered: the obscenity trial of William S. Burroughs's *The Soft Machine* (1961). The trial process began on April 27, 2011, when Turkey's Committee for the Protection of Minors from

Harmful Publications (Küçükleri Muzır Neşriyattan Koruma Kurulu) decided that the book is an "account of an undisciplined sex addict that holds no moral principle dear" ("Bir kararımız"). Burroughs's book, along with Chuck Palahniuk's equally provocative *Snuff* (2008), quickly became a cause célèbre for publishers, translators, and proponents of underground literature in Turkey. Though the trial is officially about obscenity, what is really under debate is how much license will be given to works that celebrate provocative sexual practices in a country that is traditional, collectivist, and to many, becoming increasingly religiously and politically conservative. An examination of paratextual material such as personal interviews, book jacket blurbs, government reports, news coverage, and Turkish legal proceedings reveals how the book's supporters turned the trial into a cultural event to raise awareness of repressive government practices as well as the often undiscussed issue of homophobia in Turkey.

Tracking the reception of Beat texts such as *The Soft Machine* outside the United States offers insights into how local contexts shape the reception of these countercultural works in new and interesting ways. The Turkish reception of Burroughs's *The Soft Machine* demonstrates that the image of the rebel so beloved in American culture is often downplayed in Turkey. The idea that Burroughs's work poses a challenge to all forms of "control" is a leitmotif in both the scholarship and the popular understanding of his work. In an early study, Timothy S. Murphy argues in *Wising Up the Marks* that "Burroughs's literary career is defined by the central challenge he sets himself: to find an escape route from the linked control systems of capital, subjectivity, and language" (4). This trend continues in Davis Schneiderman and Philip Walsh's more recent *Retaking the Universe: William S. Burroughs in the Age of Globalization*, a collection that frames Burroughs's resistant practices as a challenge to global capitalism's various systems of control. In more popular circles, Burroughs's importance for both the Punk movement and cyberculture has contributed to an image of the writer as a sort of "grandfather" of resistance that still lingers. While Burroughs is acknowledged as an iconoclast in Turkey as well, media coverage tends to downplay such rebellion, preferring instead the image of Burroughs as elder statesman of the Beat generation. But the repackaging of the novel through the mechanism of the censorship trial reignites the countercultural importance of Burroughs's text, forcing the more controversial issue of homosexuality to the fore.

Like its textual cousin, cultural translation reconfigures source materials based on interested, local needs of the present. One of the ironies of *The Soft Machine*'s censorship trial is that a writer marginalized in the

American lesbian, gay, bisexual, and transgender (LGBT) community now finds himself an inadvertent activist for gay rights. Jamie Russell observes that the question of Burroughs's homosexuality has been elided both in the popular press as well as in the critical literature. Because of Burroughs's desire to "ape the dynamics of a masculine, heterosexual dominant that ultimately can never accept him," his work has met with resistance within the gay community (7). Burroughs, by positioning himself outside both homosexual and heterosexual traditions, often remains invisible to both.[2] Yet in Turkey, the championing of *The Soft Machine* as an assault on Turkish heteronormativity has inadvertently reinscribed Burroughs's work within a discussion over homosexuality. Although Burroughs was not a gay rights activist, in Turkey his work becomes part of the cause to raise the visibility of a marginalized lifestyle. Thus cultural context has the power to highlight certain readings that have been occluded in one culture while downplaying others. In a way, then, Turkey "outs" Burroughs.

The Turkish reception also challenges the primacy of language as a means of understanding Burroughs's oeuvre. *The Soft Machine* employs an aesthetic strategy of favoring chance and juxtaposition over crafted meaning and coherence, and the book's "cut-up" method remains stylistically difficult and challenging today. The first chapter, for instance, establishes a fairly straightforward narrative of addicts attempting to score drugs. While characters float in and out of an account filled with changes in perspective, the reader is still able to follow the story. But interspersed within the text are segments that draw on previous phrases shuffled into new configurations:

> He went to Madrid . . . Alarm clock ran for yesterday . . . "*No me hágas casa.*" Dead on arrival . . . you might say at the Jew Hospital . . . blood spilled over the American . . . trailing lights and water . . . The Sailor went so wrong somewhere in that grey flesh . . . He just sat down on zero (14).

Some of these phrases, such as "He just sat down on zero," are new to the text, but most are lifted from earlier passages. Burroughs reworks them into new contexts, creating juxtapositions that lend new meanings to the phrases. The narrator had earlier commented that "Bill Gains" had given him "an alarm clock ran for a year after his death" (13). Thus the phrase "Alarm clock ran for yesterday" recalls the gift of his dead friend, but substituting "for yesterday" suggests that the memory itself rather than the functioning of the clock is being stressed, and invokes the theme of time that the novel will go on to address. By placing this line in a sequence of such dislocated phrases, Burroughs is able to abstract the reader out of the narrative's flow, creating new ways of reading the novel in the process. While Burroughs revised *The Soft Machine* several times to make it more readable, his goal was to use the cut-up technique to challenge accepted notions of the form and function of the genre itself.

Burroughs viewed the cut-ups as revelatory. In a later interview, he went as far as to claim that the method could "show how certain word combinations produce certain effects on the nervous system" and even predict future events (*The Job* 28). Burroughs's insistence that word is a virus, which Oliver Harris convincingly argues in *William Burroughs and the Secret of Fascination* "was not, for Burroughs, metaphoric analysis or poststructuralist platitude but an awareness integral and material to the act of writing," calls into question the role of translation in Burroughs's work (38). Can Burroughs's desire to, as Harris puts it, "*present* rather than represent" the idea of "control and terrors" be conveyed in another tongue? (37). Is Burroughs's challenge to systems of control through the materiality of the word possible in translation? In the Turkish context, these questions are ignored, and the importance of *The Soft Machine* as avant-garde aesthetic practice is downplayed. While both Burroughs and his book are certainly praised by many in Turkey, ultimately the censorship trial presents an opportunity for the book's supporters to publicly raise provocative issues by calling attention to the government's attempt to ban the book, rather than focus on Burroughs's stylistic contributions. Yet such questions are worth exploring.

Through the Turkish censorship trial the social critique that the Beats launched against mainstream American culture at midcentury is once again viable. But in Turkey, the nature of that critique has shifted, inflected by local concerns and presuppositions. *The Soft Machine* has become a means of opening up a space for debate and fostering a discussion of issues, rather than a text to be analyzed in terms of its thematic content or admired for its innovative stylistics. This is not to say that all of *The Soft Machine*'s Turkish audience cannot understand or appreciate the book's thematic or formal aspects. Burroughs has his Turkish admirers, and there is a consensus that he is a legitimate author. The censorship trial, however, has given *The Soft Machine* an afterlife. While in the United States today few would probably argue that the text represents anything more than a countercultural classic that offers a stylistic challenge to prevailing literary norms, in Turkey the discussion of homosexuality during the trial has made Burroughs's novel once again provocative and timely, demonstrating the continual relevancy of Beat texts for countercultural dissent.

MENTIONING THE UNMENTIONABLE

Ultimately, the trial is about homosexuality, a topic difficult to discuss publicly in Turkey. The prosecution claims that *The Soft Machine* violates Article 226 of the Turkish penal code, which prohibits the depiction of "sexual acts performed with the use of force, animals, a human corpse, or in any other unnatural manner" (*Turkish Penal Code* 128–29), specifically citing the depiction of "male-to-male sexual relations" *(erkek erkeğe cinsel ilişkilerin)* in the text as an example of such "unnatural" acts ("Bir kararımız").[3] While homosexuality is not perceived as a polite topic of conversation in contemporary Turkey, such was not always the case. In the Ottoman Empire, for instance, same-sex desire was discussed openly alongside other sexual practices. Dror Ze'evi notes how frank discussions took place not only in literature and poetry (perhaps most notably in Ottoman works dedicated to beardless young men) but also in medical texts, religious tracts, and popular forms such as Turkish shadow theatre. Such manifold discourse came under pressure in the nineteenth century as the Ottoman Empire undertook Western reforms in an effort to modernize. According to Ze'evi, the introduction of the printing press produced fears of increased availability of texts focusing on same-sex practices, and made Western travelogues linking Ottoman sexual practices to political weakness more widely available (46–48).[4] This repression of homosexual discourse continued under Mustafa Kemal's program of modernization. As Serkan Gorkemli explains, "[C]ontinuing modernization in the form of Westernization furthered the silencing of sexual discourses and the rise of heteronormalcy as the one-party Kemalist . . . nationalistic state intensified its efforts to create a loyal and uniform (i.e., exclusively 'Turkish') citizenry, de-emphasizing differences, including linguistic and sexual" (69). Although there were protests by homosexuals in the 1970s and 1980s, government repression meant that such movements were often suppressed. Gorkemli sees a major shift in public sentiment occurring in the postcoup 1990s, when private television channels challenged the hegemony of the state's first station (and mouthpiece), Turkish Radio and Television (TRT; Türkiye Radyo ve Televizyon Kurumu; founded in 1964), with shows depicting cross-dressers, homosexuals, radical feminists, and other "untouchables." This period brought two celebrities to the fore: Zeki Müren, a male singer who dressed in drag, and Bülent Ersoy, a transsexual singer who underwent a sex change operation in London in 1981. But the careers of these two artists demonstrate the power of heteronormativity in Turkey. Müren never publically admitted to being homosexual, since it would have ruined his career, and Ersoy "projected an image of a conservative, Muslim, nationalist, upper-class woman" in her performances (71).[5] Turkish audiences demanded heterosexual norms.

The title *The Soft Machine* is Burroughs's phrase for the human body, and the novel's fragmented narrative explores the multiple ways in which this "machine" can be both enslaved and freed. In Turkish, the phrase unwittingly announces its licentiousness in its very title. "Soft" is translated into Turkish as *yumuşak*, which connotes passive homosexuality. As Tarik Bereket and Barry D. Adam relate in their article "The Emergence of Gay Identities in Contemporary Turkey," the country has "traditionally shared a sex / gender order common to Mediterranean, Middle Eastern, and Latin American regions where male-male sexual relations are expected to embody a gendered division between an inserter partner (*aktif*) considered 'masculine' and a receptive partner (*pasif*) who is expected to show some aspect of the feminine gender" (131). In fact, many men who take the active role do not consider themselves homosexual, and the Turkish language does not have any neutral term for homosexual practices. Burroughs's novel *Queer* (written 1951; published 1985) is translated as *Top*, a word that literally means "ball" but conveys a pejorative sense of passivity. *İbne*, a term borrowed from the Arabic, comes from *iba* or *bin* and is likewise derogatory, translating into "son that is a girl." "Gay" (*gey*), a term introduced from Western discourse, has a more neutral connotation but has not been widely adopted.[6] Burroughs's other books that contain homosexual content have not been brought to trial, which seems to suggest that its title may be what drew the attention of the committee or concerned citizens.

Indeed, *The Soft Machine* does deliver homosexual activity that its translated title inadvertently announces, confirming conservative fears that the text undermines traditional Turkish values. Consider a passage from the novel where the narrator and his friend Johnny join a group of soldiers. After capturing some of their enemies, Burroughs describes how the act of hanging them produced erections in both the victims and their captors, leading to a rehearsal of the act later that night:

> We requisitioned a ranch house and all got drunk and Johnny did this dance with his tie around his neck lolling his head on one side and letting his tongue fall out and wriggled his ass and dropped his pants and his cock flipped out and the soldiers rolled around laughing till they pissed all over themselves—Then they rigged up a harness under his arms and hoisted him up off the floor to a beam and gang-fucked him. (19)

While this erotic description of a hanging is perhaps the most extreme example of a sexual act in the novel, *The Soft Machine* is filled with erotic descriptions.

Much of the novel is given over to detailed accounts of (mainly) homoerotic acts by individual characters, couples, and groups. The committee would not have had to look deeply to find evidence of what it considers "immoral" practices.

While slippage between varying conceptions of "soft" might appear unfortunate, such moments of cultural mistranslation actually work in the book's favor. Turkey has a long list of sensitive topics: religion, nationalism, Mustafa Kemal and his legacy, sexuality and gender, and the Armenian issue. A text like Burroughs's *The Soft Machine* has the potential to impact Turkish society because, as a foreign product, it can raise a topic like homosexuality without directly threatening Turkishness. The reception of the award-winning Turkish film *Zenne Dancer* (dir. Caner Alper and Mehmet Binay; 2012) is a case in point. The film was inspired by the life of Ahmet Yıldız, a homosexual man from eastern Turkey who was allegedly killed by his deeply religious father in 2008. The film depicts this "honor killing" and explores troubling accounts of homosexuals in the Turkish military who are forced to undergo humiliating tests to prove that they are gay. While reviews and responses to the film in Turkey were generally positive, *Zenne* (as the film is known in Turkish) raised the ire of those in religious and conservative circles, demonstrating that the issue of homosexuality, especially when it addresses particularly Turkish concerns, provokes a heated response.[7] Cultural imports can oftentimes circumvent the barriers to openly discussing such topics, since they are "unaware" that these topics are taboo. Underground texts like *The Soft Machine* are therefore promoted as a means of heightening awareness of issues that typically lie outside Turkish debate—an oblique strategy of introducing foreign texts into Turkish culture allows such delicate topics to be discussed. Had such texts been written by Turkish authors and included references to Turkish situations, they would have probably met with even greater resistance.

While there was no way to know that *The Soft Machine* would become involved in a censorship trial, the decision to translate Burroughs's text was political from the start. *The Soft Machine*'s publisher, İrfan Sancı, like most publishers of underground texts, started out in politics. A staunch leftist, Sancı was active in radical politics and even spent time in prison as a result of his activities. But with the 1980 coup, the Turkish left was dealt a huge blow from which it never recovered, forcing many to become more conservative or quit politics altogether. Others, like Sancı, chose to remain politically engaged by moving into publishing. Sancı founded Sel Publishing in 1990 and initially published political works by journalists. By 1993 it had branched out into literature. Sancı is self-consciously taking on the government by publishing books like *The Soft Machine*, declaring, "I set myself a goal of publishing works that are not easily publishable due to censorship or moral constraints" (Sancı, interview). Despite his having been engaged in numerous censorship trials in the past and knowing that the material he publishes will oftentimes attract the attention of the censor, Sancı refuses to bow to precensorship. The back cover of *The Soft Machine*, in fact, includes excerpts from the committee's decision as a means to heighten awareness of censorship and to display the ridiculousness of the committee's position (figure 4.1).[8] As Sancı explains, he wanted "to expose the Committee and to show how useless and even how harmful they are" (Sancı, interview).

Fig. 4.1. The publishers at Sel employ the committee's own words on the back cover of Burroughs's *The Soft Machine* to raise awareness of the censorship trial and to demonstrate the ridiculousness of the committee's homophobic position. The shiny sticker of the Culture and Tourism Ministry (Kültur ve Turızm Bakanlığı) at the bottom appears on all approved books in Turkey. The book remained available for purchase pending the outcome of the trial. *Courtesy of Sel Publishing.*

By publishing works that others are afraid or otherwise unwilling to publish, Sancı continues his opposition through the medium of literature. One of the reasons Sancı chose to publish Beat works like *The Soft Machine* (and other Beat books like Allen Ginsberg's *Deliberate Prose* and Jack Kerouac and Burroughs's collaborative novel *And the Hippos Were Boiled in Their Tanks*) was because he viewed them as a direct challenge to the system. Although he does not really like to use the trial as an advertisement, Sancı views it as a chance to heighten awareness about the issue of homosexuality in Turkey. The Beats are useful in that struggle, since as Sancı notes, the "Beat writers opposed American middle class morality and hypocrisy through their lives and works" (Sancı, interview). Despite this stance, Sancı is nonetheless reticent about the Beat Generation's potential influence in Turkey. Writers like Burroughs, Kerouac, and Ginsberg were not so important to earlier generations of Turkish leftists. Enmeshed as they were in radical politics, they had little use for the cultural revolution that the Beats propounded. Sancı admits that the Beats are an important phenomenon that should be studied, but he believes that their time is past and their lifestyles impossible to replicate. Burroughs is still an important countercultural gay figure, but for Sancı, the future is in work more directly committed to combating homophobia and negative stereotypes, and he is now focusing attention on a new LGBT series that he hopes will heighten awareness of the issue of homosexuality in Turkey.

Snuff's publisher Abdullah Yılmaz, like Sancı, began as a committed political activist before turning to the cultural realm to continue the struggle. It is difficult to imagine, but this mild-mannered, middle-aged gentleman spent ten years in prison for political offenses. According to Yılmaz, almost all leftist publishing houses would tell you roughly the same story (Yılmaz, interview).[9] Ayrıntı Publishing was founded by Yılmaz and two other friends in 1987 to continue the struggle, extending the fight beyond Marx and Lenin and into more postmodern concerns: "In the past, left wing politics meant Marxism, Leninism and even Maoism, but after the 80s, it came to include Anarchism, Feminism, Green and Environmental concerns" (Yılmaz, interview). Not that Yılmaz is particularly delighted with the change. As he himself expresses it in his amusing manner, "If it were up to us, we'd probably continue being political, but they beat us up!" (Yılmaz, interview). For most, the shift from the radically political to the culturally subversive was not made willingly. But as much as publishers long for the "good old days" of leftist political struggle, the future lies in addressing a burgeoning mass of youth.

Sancı and Yılmaz tend to downplay the importance of the Beats' contribution to actual change in Turkey, but the usefulness of their publishing enterprise needs to be measured in ways other than in number of texts sold. When asked about the impact of his publishing house, Yılmaz remarks, "In a country with a population [of] seventy million, if your initial printing is seven hundred copies, even if you have a loyal following it doesn't matter much. We are doing something; we sell one thousand copies a year. That's something, but we are out of the spheres where actual cultural change takes place. The culture doesn't change here, it is not decided here" (Yılmaz, interview). Compared with the products of visual culture or the sales of popular authors, Yılmaz is correct; underground texts represent only a fraction of the material available in Turkish culture. But Yılmaz and others who tend to downplay their contributions do themselves a disservice.

The irony of censorship trials is that they often end up promoting the book better than any advertisement possibly could. Allen Ginsberg's poem *Howl* benefited tremendously from the notoriety it derived from its San Francisco trial. *The Soft Machine* and *Snuff* have proven no exception. Yılmaz remarks that due to the trial, *Snuff* is the most commercially successful of Palahniuk's books for them, selling over twenty thousand copies.[10] Given their usual print run of five hundred to six hundred copies, and the fact that sales for most of their list hover around a thousand, this represents a substantial increase in distribution (Yılmaz, interview). *The Soft Machine*, though it has not done as well as *Snuff*, is on its third printing, with sales beyond expectations at over five thousand (Sancı, interview). But with the advent of the Internet and social media, these numbers represent only a fraction of those who have been made aware of the trial. While *The Soft Machine* will not single-handedly bring more freedom of personal expression and openness in Turkey, the censorship trial and the responses it has generated have opened up a space to debate highly sensitive issues and provides a sort of litmus test to the possible courses and outcomes of dissent in Turkey.

PROTECTING MINORS FROM HARMFUL PUBLICATIONS

As its name implies, the Committee for the Protection of Minors from Harmful Publications is tasked with defending the interests of youth, but it draws on a broader language of safeguarding Turkey and its moral fiber when fulfilling its mission. The committee was originally founded in 1927 under the old penal code that deals with "crimes which include rape by force, perversion towards children and attacks towards chastity" (Doğan). Although the older articles 426, 427, and 428 are no longer extant, the committee is not above quoting from them, arguing that they are targeting any publication "that offends people's sense of shame and honor or are against general morals through the provocation and abuse of sexual desires" (Doğan). While the terms *minors* (*küçükler*) and *harmful publications* (*muzır neşriyat*) both occur in the committee's title, it is clear from their choice of words that the former is merely the pretext for a broad assault on what they consider to be the latter.

To legitimize itself, the committee has recourse to the first clause of the Law on National Education, which outlines the goals of the Turkish educational system. By absorbing this clause into their mandate, the committee seeks to expand their role as defenders of Turkish culture as they define it. Produced in 1983, shortly after the 1980 coup (but still in effect today), the law states that the goal of the educational system is to intertwine education, family, and nation to solidify Turkish national feelings. Its purpose is to

> [r]aise citizens who are devoted to Atatürk's principles of the revolution and Atatürk's nationalism as it is stated in the constitution: adopt, protect and develop national, moral, humane, spiritual and cultural values of the Turkish nation; who love and constantly try to exalt his family, fatherland and nation, and who knows and acts on his responsibilities towards human rights and towards the Turkish Republic which is a democratic, secular, social, lawful state based on the founding principles at the beginning of the constitution. (Doğan)

The committee's decision to censor a book is not simply about adhering to the law but rather about safeguarding what they see as Mustafa Kemal's legacy. By invoking the figure of modern Turkey's founding father, they place a heavy burden on publishers to not only prove the legality of their publications but to overcome criticisms that their work is an assault on the very nation.[11] Educating children is not simply about protecting them from material that might confuse or mislead. The committee is explicitly ideological, envisioning its task as nothing less than defending Turkish conceptions of nation and family.

Homosexuality is seen as lying outside these conceptions of the Turkish state and, as a type of "deviance," posing a threat to the healthy functioning of the nation. This connection between masculinity and nation also formed a backdrop to the initial reception of Beat works in the 1950s. As David K. Johnson elucidates in *The Lavender Scare* and John D'Emilio in *Sexual Politics, Sexual Communities*, homosexuals were perceived as threats to the United States and its principles. Burroughs, as well as Ginsberg, was influenced by this rhetoric of masculinity. Although both were early advocates for gay rights in the United States, these Beats' relationship to progressive homosexual movements was itself vexed. Gay Beats tended to reinforce traditional notions of male behavior, stereotypes that would eventually come under attack by later activists. The gay rights movement was similarly ambivalent. Regina Marler describes Burroughs's contribution to gay liberation in *Queer Beats: How the Beats Turned America On to Sex* as "oblique" and argues, "Curiously, while Ginsberg is a gay icon, he was not necessarily considered a gay rights activist by others in the emerging movement" (xxxv, xxxiii).[12] While their role in gay liberation should not be discounted, the American gay rights movement was oftentimes tangential to the Beats' own goals.

The process of banning a book in Turkey is quite convoluted. It begins with the Media Prosecutor, a division within the Prosecutor's Office in charge of monitoring publications and crimes relating to the press. Two copies of every publication are sent to this office, and if the work is deemed problematic, the Media Prosecutor sends the book to the committee, who issues a report. How the Media Prosecutor determines whether a publication is worthy of further consideration is a subject of intense debate. In any case, if the committee finds the publication obscene, it goes back to the office for prosecution. Conversely, the prosecutor can also send it to other experts, such as professors of literature. But as *The Soft Machine*'s translator Süha Sertabiboğlu mentions, the criteria for what constitutes an "expert" is not stated, and books have oftentimes been sent to business schools or other institutions not exactly qualified to judge literature (Sertabiboğlu, interview). That the Media Prosecutor must, by definition, read thousands of books leads to speculation about how exactly books are chosen for prosecution. Many, such as Sertabiboğlu, believe that the prosecutor relies on "informants," most probably those on the religious right who suggest books for censorship. According to Koç University law professor Murat Önok, other associations may also suggest books for consideration (Önok, interview).[13] Nobody is certain how Burroughs's book was brought to trial, though the randomness of the books chosen does, at times, seem odd. A question, however, remains: Why was *The Soft Machine* chosen and other works of the trilogy that were equally sexual in content allowed to pass unchallenged?

While the committee has been active sporadically since its inception, their increasing willingness to prosecute cases that have little to no legal merit is disconcerting.[14] Most countries, including those in the West, have laws regarding obscenity, but they have not applied them to art, science, or other works regarded as in the public interest since the 1960s. According to Turkey's own laws in Article 226 (provision 7), academic and literary works enjoy protection from such censorship. And while publishers differentiate between "obscene" and "pornographic" works, the committee reduces anything sexual to obscene. As the Turkish Association of Literary Translators (Çevirmenler Meslek Birliği) notes, "In 2010 three books published by Sel Publishers—*Perinin Sarkacı* by the Turkish author Ben Mila, *Genç bir Don Juan'ın Maceraları* ('Les exploits d'un jeune Don Juan') by Guillaume Apollinaire, and *Görgülü ve Bilgili bir Burjuva Kadının Mektupları* ('Correspondance d'une Bourgeoise Avertie') by P.V.—were passed on to the Committee for the Protection of Children from Harmful Publications in spite of an expert opinion which explicitly stated that the three books were literary works and not considered to be obscene" (Çevbir). This willingness to take on such cases has brought the opprobrium of the international community. In February 2010, the European Court of Human Rights condemned Turkey for violating Article 10 of the European Convention on Human Rights with regard to its ban on Guillaume Apollinaire's *Eleven Thousand Rods*, arguing that censorship of this book "hindered public access to a work belonging to the European literary heritage" (International Publishers Association). But these decisions have had little effect on the committee. They are clearly not concerned with conforming to European Union standards; their responsibility is Turkey and the protection of its morals.

But the committee does not need to win its cases to succeed. The pressure it puts on members of the Turkish literary community ensures that each new translation must be thought of in terms of its passability. As many involved in the discussion have noted, this results in a precensorship that is just as damaging as the overt actions of the committee. The Turkish Association of Literary Translators makes this point clear in their press release, arguing that Turkey is faced with a situation "in which self-censorship is incited and in which our profession is readily turned into a criminal offence" (Çevbir). Penalties can be significant—three to nine years in prison and fines up to five thousand days' worth of salary (Doğan). Turkish translators fought hard for the right to be considered owners of their works in an effort to protect their rights and to reap their proper fiscal reward. In an ironic twist, now that they enjoy a stronger legal status they are subject to prosecution along with the publisher. As the association notes, even printers are not immune. Although they are no longer liable for the production of works found "obscene" as they were in the past, they too can still be held legally accountable. In such a climate, everyone must think twice about the legal, financial, and even social consequences to publishing provocative literature. As Yılmaz observes, "The fact that we had five trials that resulted in acquittal before, doesn't mean that we'll be acquitted from the sixth" (Yılmaz, interview).[15] While the committee has had limited success censoring books, they have been influential in creating an environment where publishers, for both economic and personal reasons, have been forced to practice precensorship.

THE HISTORY OF CENSORSHIP IN TURKEY

It is tempting to read the prosecutor's and committee's decisions as the result of a more conservative trend in the Turkish AK Party government. The reality, however, is a bit more complicated. While many see the committee in the service of Erdoğan's move toward the religious right, the fact is that the committee is an inheritance from the days of Mustafa Kemal. Sancı himself does not put the blame directly on Erdoğan. In fact, the previous Kemalist regimes, according to Sancı, deserve their share of the blame as well. As Sancı explains, "People coming from the West arrive with a prejudice. They think there is a religious government in Turkey and the Kemalists are progressive. They think the debate is between the religious [elements] and the progressive Kemalists. On the contrary, I tell them that Kemalism is not progressive but obscurantist. They don't get the answers they are looking for" (Sancı, interview). The philosophy of the republic was that of an elite bureaucracy and not a popular government, and thus to view Turkish politics as simply the struggle between the heroic Republican People's Party (Cumhuriyet Halk Partisi or CHP) and the repressive AK Party would be an oversimplification. While the Kemalists do tend to stand for a more secular Turkey, their willingness to employ draconian practices has given them their own fair share of detractors.

Censorship has been a part of Turkish life since the Ottoman period. As the undisputed ruler of the empire, the sultan enjoyed absolute power over his subjects. Sometimes such autocratic rule could have humorous effects, as was the case with Abdülhamid II. But in many instances, the word of the sultan could mean life or death, or at least the loss of livelihood. Even when reforms finally came to the Ottoman Empire in the nineteenth century, the sultan was loath to cede power. Erik J. Zürcher, in *Turkey: A Modern History*, discusses the emergence of the press: "The first Ottoman newspaper, the Takvim-i Vekai, was started in Sultan Mahmut's days, but was more of an official bulletin than a newspaper in the modern sense. The first newspaper in Ottoman Turkish to be privately owned . . . largely reflected official policies" (71). The idea that the press should be free, however, was not realized until relatively recently in Turkey. As Zürcher notes, the government introduced press and censorship laws as early as 1865 as a means to control the dissemination of ideas and criticism of the sultan

(73). This censorship would continue unabated, and reach into all aspects of publishing. Özgen Felek, in her examination of Ottoman reading practices, discusses the emergence of comics during the Tanzimat (Reform) period. Felek observes that "the first Turkish satirical publication, *Diogenes*, was published in 1870, and many other magazines in the same style emerged. However, because the sultan was unhappy with their humorous approach toward the government, the Palace announced that all comics would be censored" (548). Such censorship practices would continue right up until the end of the Ottoman Empire in 1923.

Mustafa Kemal's new republic fared little better. As Nicole and Hugh Pope explain in *Turkey Unveiled*, "Today, Turkey attributes everything that is deemed modern in the state to Kemal. His radical reforms are well known: he abolished the caliphate and declared Turkey a secular republic (1923), the reform his followers today are most thankful for; . . . he replaced Islamic law by the Swiss civil code and Mussolini's penal code (1926)" (62). Yet Atatürk, too, brooked little dissent. As Zürcher notes, Mustafa Kemal was not above censorship of the press. In 1926, shortly after taking power, "[e]ight of the most important newspapers and periodicals (conservative, liberal and even Marxist) in Istanbul were closed down, as were several provincial papers, leaving only the government organs. . . . All the leading journalists from Istanbul were arrested" (179–80). Mustafa Kemal stifled oppositional voices. Although he twice considered allowing oppositional parties, the Progressive Republican Party founded in November 1924 was quickly shut down, and another party founded by Atatürk's friend Fethi Okyar (the Free Parti or Serbest Fırka), which was supposed to be a mere mouthpiece, was closed less than a year later (Pope and Pope 67). Even after Mustafa Kemal's death his legacy of rule continued. Discussing the rule of Kemal's successor, President İsmet İnönü, Andrew Mango relates that although living standards were low "the government could contain [this discontent] so long as its Republican People's Party (CHP) had a monopoly of power, the press was censored, strikes were banned and associations and demonstrations subject to stringent controls. But the country was used to authoritarian government: most people resented it, but few challenged it" (39). Turkey would not have a multiparty democracy until 1946.

While Erdoğan's AK Party may appear to offer a democratic (and pro-capitalist) face to the West, it too is no stranger to repression. The situation manages to be both unsettling and comic. Sertabiboğlu relates the fairly benign anecdote of the censorship of the "private parts" of Michelangelo's statue *David* on television: "Something I saw on TRT television was hair-raising and I was really panicked. In footage of a museum's interior, the private parts of Michelangelo's famous David sculpture were blurred with smoke" (Sertabiboğlu, interview). Other examples of repression are more disturbing. In a supposed effort to bring to justice members of a clandestine network of high-ranking military officials and select civilian allies whose illegal activities form what is known as the "deep state" (*derin devlet*) in Turkey, critics argue that Erdoğan has used the "Ergenekon" investigations as a means to suppress his domestic opponents. According to the journalist Dexter Filkins writing in the *New Yorker*, "In the past five years, more than seven hundred people have been arrested, including generals, admirals, members of parliament, newspaper editors and other journalists, owners of television networks, directors of charitable organizations, and university officials" (49). This stifling of the press through arrests of journalists and the closing of news organizations has only increased in the wake of the 2016 coup attempt. Ironically, Erdoğan himself faced such censorship during his tenure as Istanbul's mayor. In 1997, Erdoğan was sentenced to ten months in prison and banned from politics for reading a poem in the city of Siirt. Despite the poem having been written by Ziya Gökalp, a secularist, the references to "mosques," "domes," and "minarets" led to a charge of "incitement of religious hatred" (51). But the lesson of censorship in Turkey seems to be not that it should be abolished but rather that one should strive to be the censor instead of the censored.

CENSORSHIP IN THE AMERICAN CONTEXT

Turkey is not alone in its censorship practices. The United States has also had a long history of silencing voices. Michael B. Goodman, in his book *Contemporary Literary Censorship*, relates an anecdote that goes back to Plymouth in 1628, when Governor William Bradford censored Thomas Morton's "lascivious" rhymes and verses with a military expedition that broke up Morton's settlement at Merrymount (171). Donna A. Demac, in *Liberty Denied*, observes that "all thirteen colonies made blasphemy or profanity a criminal offense, yet only Massachusetts had a law, passed in 1712, prohibiting the circulation of sexually explicit material" (39). Boston continued in this tradition to the point where the phrase "Banned in Boston" became a national joke. Despite these instances, censorship in the United States is really a product of the late nineteenth century. According to Felice Flanery Lewis in *Literature, Obscenity, and Law*,

> In spite of federal and state laws prohibiting obscenity, the relative infrequency of cases on record before 1870 indicates that little attention

> was paid to the obscenity issue prior to that date. But in the last quarter of the nineteenth century groups of citizens began calling for censorship action. . . . The abhorrence of any overt expression having to do with sex, extant in elements of the American society since colonial days, seems to have suddenly crystallized into an organized censorship movement. (8–9)

The man credited with galvanizing such a force was Anthony Comstock. In an atmosphere of collective hysteria, Comstock successfully lobbied Congress to pass his namesake act that made it illegal to transport not just obscene materials but also "information about sex education, abortion, contraceptives, and sexually transmitted diseases" through the mail (Peters 7). Comstock was so successful that publishers remained wary into the early twentieth century.

As the United States moved through the first half of the twentieth century, frustration grew against antivice campaigns that kept celebrated authors such as Balzac, Voltaire, and Rousseau as well as emerging modernists like James Joyce and D. H. Lawrence out of Americans' hands.[16] Even many U.S. authors like Henry Miller and Burroughs were available only as contraband, underground books that were smuggled into their own country past the custom inspectors. As Marjorie Heins explains in *Sex, Sin, and Blasphemy*, obscenity cases were judged according to an 1868 English ruling *Regina v. Hicklin*, which set the standard for obscenity as works that might "deprave and corrupt those whose minds are open to such immoral influences" (20). Under this ruling, if the government believed that "children, young women, mentally handicapped individuals, or even potential sociopaths" might be adversely affected by the material, then "the work could be suppressed, regardless of value, and the artist could be prosecuted and jailed" (20). The *Hicklin* ruling set the bar too low, and the public clamored for a fairer standard that would limit truly obscene works while allowing socially meaningful products to circulate. Their call was answered by the U.S. Supreme Court in its landmark 1957 *Roth v. United States* decision.

One of the crucial problems in the censorship debate is how exactly to define obscenity. A vague term open to numerous interpretations, it would take four important Supreme Court decisions to finally specify the legal requirements for a work to be judged obscene. The first, and initially most important, was *Roth v. United States.* Samuel Roth was convicted of sending obscene materials through the mail. The Supreme Court upheld this conviction but, more important, defined obscenity for the courts: "whether to the average person, applying contemporary community standards, the dominant theme of the material taken as a whole appeals to the prurient interest" (Goodman 3). *Roth* created a legal precedent that would be the test for subsequent cases. Basically, the decision demanded that a work not be considered obscene simply because it contained a few obscene words or passages. Works could be found obscene only if they possessed no redeeming social value. But a problem emerged. There were two ways of interpreting the "social value" test: "that the value and the obscenity be weighed against each other, the dominant quality prevailing," and "to mean that a work with any value could not be banned as obscene" (63). Ultimately, Justin Brennan wrote a majority opinion in the *Memoirs of a Woman of Pleasure* (*Fanny Hill*) trial that articulated three tests for obscenity: prurient interest in sex is the dominant theme; it is patently offensive because it affronts community standards; it is utterly without redeeming social value (241). To clarify problems created by the *Roth* case, Judge Brennan stipulated that "each element be applied independently; no single criterion must be weighed against or cancelled by another" (241). As long as a work has value, and is marketed as such, then it is protected. *Roth* remained the standard until the 1973 *Miller v. California*, which shifted the burden of proving the material patently offensive and appealing to the prurient interest away from national standards and allowing these definitions to vary according to locale. While *Miller v. California*, which is the current test today, weakened the Roth decision, nevertheless the censorship of literature in the United States has all but ceased.

The Beats were no strangers to literary censorship. Burroughs's novel *Naked Lunch* (1959 in France; 1962 in the United States) was one of the many censorship cases in the 1950s and 1960s. Selected passages from this novel were involved in a censorship trial for obscenity in Chicago in 1959 when they were released as part of a University of Chicago student journal titled *Big Table*, and again in Boston in 1966 after the novel was published in its entirety.[17] The new relaxed test for obscenity in *Roth* meant *Naked Lunch* was considered not obscene on its next trial. The first two conditions for obscenity had been met, but as it was not without redeeming social value as the testimony of expert witnessed suggested, it was allowed to be published. Goodman relates that "*Naked Lunch* was the last work of literature to be proscribed in this nation's struggle between its belief in free expression and its Puritan heritage" (1). The book's trial was not the decision that made the standard for obscenity clear in U.S. legal history. That distinction goes to John Cleland's 1749 book *Memoirs of a Woman of Pleasure*, often referred to as *Fanny Hill*. But after *Naked Lunch*'s 1966 decision, obscenity cases no longer dealt with literary works.

Unfortunately, censorship is still an issue for Beat works, even in the United States. While overt censorship of literary texts has largely disappeared, censorship supporters have turned their attention to regulating the *channels* through which artistic works are funded, distributed, and viewed. Tipper Gore, the founder of the Parents' Music Resource Center, was able to effectively argue for the creation of warning labels on records with sexually explicit content. Although not censorship per se, Gore's attempts had ramifications for the marketplace, with some firms opting not to sell music with such warning labels. The attack on popular music sometimes takes the form of overt censorship, as when Alabama prosecutors charged the owner of a music store with obscenity in 1988 for selling the album *Move Somethin'* by the rap group 2 Live Crew (Heins 77). Typically, however, censorship is more insidious. As Bill Morgan relates, Ginsberg's poem *Howl*, while acquitted of obscenity charges some fifty years ago, cannot be heard on the radio because of the Federal Communication Commission's (FCC) ban on indecent material. Though censorship groups initially wanted a total ban on such "indecent material" in an effort to "protect the children," such programming is now allowed, but only from "midnight to 6 am" (221). Broadcasters, afraid of the heavy financial penalties the FCC is able to inflict, have chosen to avoid such material. Ginsberg's poem, found not obscene in its 1957 trial, has been effectively silenced on the American airwaves.[18]

THE TRIAL

The Turkish prosecution's argument is based on three points: the book is harmful to minors, it has no literary value, and it is immoral. It must be considered harmful to minors to fall under the committee's purview, though as the defense repeatedly states, as did defenders of *Naked Lunch* in its 1966 Boston trial, the book is intended for an adult audience and is not sold in venues marketing to children. The claim that it has no literary value is due mainly to the fact, again as in the Boston and 1959 *Big Table* trials, that literary works are protected under the law so that to be considered obscene they must be shown to have no literary merit. Ultimately, however, the trial is about morality. The committee saves its most virulent attack for the book itself, castigating *The Soft Machine* as an immoral work. Although they invoke the pretense of defending minors, the rhetoric of both the committee and the prosecution makes it clear that they think the book is unfit for any Turkish citizen.

The prosecution begins by arguing that the publishers of *The Soft Machine* (along with those of *Snuff*) have failed to protect children from this "harmful" publication. Provision 7 of Article 226 of the *Turkish Penal Code* states, "The provisions of this article shall not apply, except section 3, to artistic or literary works where children are prevented from accessing such" (129).[19] The prosecution brackets the question of artistic merit here, focusing instead on the requirement that children be prevented access to such materials: "On the cover of the book *The Soft Machine*, there is no warning regarding this issue. This is one of the reasons the prosecution decided to review this book and send it to the Committee for further review" (Sabitfikir). According to the prosecution, the publishers failed to provide information that would deter children from purchasing the work.

The defense counters that the publishers are not selling to minors. The book is being sold not on the street or at newspaper stands but only in bookstores that are frequented by adults. As Martin de Haan, president of the European Council of Literary Translators' Associations (CEATL) argues, "[I]t is evident that the novels at stake do not address children, that they are not published as 'children's literature' and that they will not be presented as such. CEATL sincerely hopes that Turkish legislation for the protection of children will not be used to restrict the freedom of expression of translators, publishers, readers or any other actors in the literary field" (de Haan). The Turkish Association of Literary Translators puts it even more bluntly: "since it is evident that these publications do not address children, since they are not published as 'children's literature' and since it is out of the question that they will be presented as such, their legal prosecution is the manifestation of a prohibiting mentality that considers every means permitted to interfere in our cultural and social life" (Çevbir). The subsequent arguments of the committee demonstrate the accuracy of these groups' claims. The directive to protect Turkey's youth is simply an excuse—the real goal is to police the general morals of the country.

De Haan's idea that "freedom of expression" should be an assumed standard is a particularly Western touch. The publishers never even attempt such an appeal, and are content to combat the prosecution's accusations point by point rather than through a grand gesture toward such an abstract notion as freedom. The Western response to Turkish censorship inevitably invokes the cry of "freedom" that is notably absent from the Turkish discussion. In a 2011 *Guardian* article titled "European Court Rules against Turkey's Apollinaire Ban," Alison Flood points out that in the case against Apollinaire's *The Eleven Thousand Rods* (*Les Onze Milles Verges*), publisher Rahmi Akdaş complained to the European Court of Human Rights that "the ruling violated Article 10 (freedom of expression) of the European convention on Human Rights" (Flood). The courts found in favor of Akdaş, concluding that while states could intervene to protect morals, Turkey's ban violated article 10 and thus was wrong since the novel had gained literary acclaim and over a century had passed since its publication. The court ruled that the ban "hindered public access to a work belonging to the European literary heritage."

Whether *The Soft Machine* is marketed to minors is admittedly a bit more difficult to determine. The packaging is clearly of a mature nature (the cover is an image from the 1966 underground film *Chappaqua*, which includes cameos by Burroughs and Ginsberg), and Sel Publishing's advertising does not appear to target minors. But the publishers are a bit disingenuous here. Sel has partnered with the publishing house 6:45 to promote the book and its cause (figure 4.2). But 6:45, while not overtly marketing directly to youth, does enjoy a huge popularity with this group, and thus the book's promotion is technically reaching minors. Warnings of the provocative nature of the material can also be alluring. As Yılmaz playfully remarks, "You announce it beforehand that this book is about porn, what better way is there to protect minors? What better way is there to protect minors than to announce it (in the title)?" (Yılmaz, interview). But whether such an announcement is a warning or an enticement is not quite clear. As with Tipper Gore's campaign for warning labels in U.S. popular music, this practice could simply become another means of attracting attention.[20]

The committee, however, is not content to restrict its criticisms to questions of distribution. It also wants to undermine the status of these books as literary works, for two reasons. If the committee can show that *The Soft Machine* lacks literary merit, they can challenge its status as a protected literary text. Thus the language of the prosecution conflates the stylistic and the thematic continuously:

> In this book that holds no moral principle dear, an undisciplined, antisocial, sex-addict type is characterized in a narrative that lacks coherence, is randomly written without unity in the storyline, and utilizes slang expressions with a disconnected style. Especially male-to-male sexual encounters are described in such detail that they are harmful to feelings of morality and chastity. (Sabitfikir)

An assault on narrative style opens the door to a critique of morals. The committee finds that *The Soft Machine* both "lacks coherence" and is the "account of an undisciplined sex addict who holds no moral principle dear." The unstated assumption is that such an immoral figure is incapable of producing great literature. The narrative, according to the committee, is more concerned with depicting detailed descriptions of "male-to-male sexual encounters" than with maintaining "unity in the storyline." The

Fig. 4.2. Publishing house 6:45, partnering with Sel, places an advertisement for Burroughs's trilogy on the back of their *Underground Poetix* magazine. The announcement at the top boldly declares that "Sel Publishing House proudly presents: the 'Immoral' Cut-Up Trilogy by William S. Burroughs," while the statement at the bottom exclaims that the "Beat Generation is standing trial in the Turkish courts!" These announcements are both a means to call attention to censorship issues and an enticement for the curious reader.

accusation is that Burroughs, a writer bereft of moral compass, is simply reveling in "anti-social" events depicted in a "disconnected style." For the committee, it comes as no surprise that such moral degeneracy would be couched in an incoherent form—both are indicative of corruption.

The defense counters that the committee is not qualified to judge such literary matters. In a public statement issued by Sel, they state,

> The prosecution repeats such baseless accusations as "(the work makes) no additional contributions to the intellectual treasury of readers, it has no value as a literary work, and lacks coherence in subject and narrative" of the Committee which is in no way qualified to evaluate a literary text and only makes subjective evaluations. (Sabitfikir)

For the defense, the committee is not composed of literary experts, and even the outside readers they choose are oftentimes equally unqualified. Typically, qualified literary experts are not inclined to support the committee's objections, but the committee has oftentimes pressed on despite expert testimony. As the Turkish Association of Literary Translators notes, "In 2010 three books published by Sel Publishers . . . were passed on to the Committee for the Protection of Children from Harmful Publications in spite of an expert opinion which explicitly stated that the three books were literary works and not considered to be obscene" (Çevbir). The committee's actions seem motivated more by their own conceptions of morality rather than the legal merits of particular cases.

The defense also points out the committee's neglect of social context when targeting works. Focusing solely on words taken out of a larger context has blinded the committee into branding books obscene when, in actuality, their use of such vocabulary is calculated: "the writings are evaluated by the whole world with respect to political and social background, and they are not branded as pornographic just based on the words" (Sabitfikir). According to the defense, words cannot simply be taken out of context and labeled obscene. Beat Generation writers like Burroughs purposely counter rules and norms, and such language is an integral part of their project. Burroughs's cut-up technique, for instance, is meant to challenge accepted notions of language and meaning. To simply write the novel off as "fragmented" and "lack[ing] coherence" is to miss the point entirely. *The Soft Machine* is not supposed to read like a standard novel.

The prosecution acknowledges that the Beats challenged social norms, and that Burroughs is a key part of this taboo-breaking group. They quickly counter, however, that Turkey is not the United States, and that morals are relative. Pornography, for example, has a much more limited scope in Turkey. As the prosecution explains, "If the description is erotic it is not a crime, but if it moves away from eroticism and goes into the details of sexuality such as descriptions of sexual organs or intercourse, it becomes pornography, and that is a crime" (Sabitfikir). The graphic depictions might be acceptable in more liberal societies like the United States or Europe, but in Turkey (so the argument goes) it does not have a place and is unlawful. The prosecution invokes a classic example of moral relativism: the case of drug consumption in the Netherlands. They write, "It is a fact that the understanding of morality is different in different countries. For example, while it is permissible to consume a certain amount of a certain drug in Holland, it is forbidden in our country" (Sabitfikir). Holland may have legalized certain drugs, but that does not mean that they can be consumed somewhere else legally. Ultimately, what is at stake here is a discussion over what should be allowed. The defense is purposely pushing these limits to raise the question of where Turkey's social policy should be going.

The real issue with *The Soft Machine* is its graphic depiction of homosexuality. The fourth provision of Article 226 prohibits the depiction of "sexual acts" in an "unnatural manner" (*Turkish Penal Code* 129). In both their rhetoric and emphasis, the prosecution makes the portrayal of homosexual acts the crux of the issue. In a statement by the prosecution the reason for the trial is made clear from the outset: *The Soft Machine* contains twenty pages of detailed descriptions of homosexual acts. As the prosecution's statement explains, "In the work titled *The Soft Machine*, homosexual relations are included and this inclusion moves away from short descriptions to the details of the relations and their form and this does not occur in a few pages in the book but is observed in twenty separate places" (Sabitfikir). The repeated, detailed descriptions of male-to-male sexual encounters, and the fact that the prosecution bothered to tally these instances, demonstrates a fixation on homosexuality. As Sancı notes, "It consists of old male members, it is a homophobic committee, and they especially cannot tolerate incest and male sexuality" (Sancı, interview). In fact, they have only had one female member, and she did not join until 2007. While both the prosecution and the committee briefly allude to drug use and Burroughs's antisocial image, the homosexual aspect of the novel receives the bulk of attention.[21]

In the U.S. trial of *Naked Lunch*, homosexuality emerged as a topic but soon gave way to discussions of literary style and drug addiction. Although the 1960s were generally a time of sexual exploration, homosexuality was a sensitive topic that came up only sporadically in the book's defense, while the issue of drug use was far more compelling. This is not to say sexuality was elided—obscenity was the reason the book was on trial in the first place. But it was easier to discuss stylistic concerns or drug addiction than male-to-male eroticism. Moreover, since the defense only had to show that the book had redeeming social value, it was free to choose a less sensitive subject such as drug use over homosexuality. Many who defended Burroughs did so under duress; they were not happy with its literary value and thought it close to pornography. As Goodman notes, Burroughs's work "caught the critic between a belief in taste and a traditional revulsion for the censor" (4). Nelson Algren, for example, supported *Chicago Review* but did not like the Beat issue (Goodman 23). Many critics, like Lionel Trilling, discussed it as literary event rather than as literature (161). Ginsberg, of course, defended it, as did others, like Mary McCarthy and Norman Mailer. But critical response was divided and fierce. *Naked Lunch* was either the death knell of humanism or the beginning of a radically new type of novel. That it could be both was perhaps the most troubling thought of all. Not until a few years after the trial, with the Stonewall Riots of 1969, would gay rights be taken up as a battle cry.

The Soft Machine exposes readers to the topic of homosexuality, which is repressed in Turkish cultural discourse. The defense, however, is unable to employ this fact in its arguments for fear of undermining its own credibility. This places the defense in a difficult position. Lack of U.S.-style First Amendment guarantees means they are unable to draw on arguments relating to freedom of speech and expression that Western groups have employed when defending the book. Turkish supporters are likewise restricted from providing direct rebuttals to the issue of "immorality" that the prosecution explicitly raises; to do so would unleash a strong reaction by a majority of the population that considers such sexual practices unethical. The irony is that while the publisher, the translator, and the book's supporters privately admit that the book is important in combating Turkish prejudice, they are unable (or unwilling) to publicly invoke this argument in their defense. Instead, they counter the prosecution's arguments according to the letter of the law, arguing that the book is not being read by minors and has internationally recognized literary merit, and not that such a trial should not be conducted or that such accusations reveal a homophobic tendency running throughout the culture. But beyond the courtroom is another matter.

BURROUGHS AS REBEL

The image of the Beat writer taking a heroic stand against the stifling beliefs of mainstream society has become an accepted cultural legacy in the United States. But it is important to remember that the Beats and their texts are not performing the same cultural function in the same manner everywhere. For many outside the American cultural context, the romanticization of the Beat as rebel holds less appeal. One reason for this difference is that in Turkey, the idea of a "rebel" means something quite different, something far more sinister than celebratory. Implicated in notions of Kurdish resistance best exemplified by groups like the Kurdistan Workers' Party (PKK), the title of "rebel" is associated with violence and looked down on as an aberration. Another reason for Turkey's deemphasizing characteristic American individualism is that Turkish culture is more collective. The importance of familial commitment and traditional neighborhoods, though waning, is still a palpable force in Turkish life. American culture has a long history of glorifying the myth of the individual who takes it on himself to challenge the system. But this go-it-alone stance is less celebrated in Turkey, a point of view that could help facilitate a reevaluation of the Beats and their function as cultural signifiers.

The Turkish media reception of Burroughs acknowledges his controversial status, offering a sort of "cautious praise" that seeks to present him in the most positive light. Burroughs does not receive as much media attention as figures like Kerouac, Ginsberg, or the extremely popular Charles Bukowski, and much of the coverage Burroughs does receive centers on the censorship trial. Reviews of his translated novels predominate and tend to be positive, since typically they are written by those with an interest in his work. Critics routinely address his use of drugs as well as his homosexuality, but it is the issue of violence that garners the most attention. An article in *Birgün*, for example, discusses Burroughs's shooting of his wife Joan Vollmers in a game of William Tell, concluding, "Not a good guy who has good works" ("Kirli"). Nevertheless, the majority of articles on Burroughs's life and work shift the focus away from such scandalous details to focus on his struggles to live life as he saw fit. Because of his extreme positions, Burroughs does not garner the sort of unconditional praise allotted to figures like Kerouac, but he is seen as an important, and interesting, Beat figure worthy of discussion.

One important exception to this staid image of Burroughs is Şenol Erdoğan's article in *Radikal*'s "Weekend Magazine." Erdoğan portrays Burroughs as a Faustian antihero, the dark, evil character whose life is perhaps even more famous than his work. In part as a means to promote *The Soft Machine*, in part as a slap in the face of the committee and the government it represents, Erdoğan flaunts Burroughs's outsider status, playing up his homosexuality, heavy drug use, and stylistically innovative writing. Erdoğan takes up and expands the committee's accusations, mentioning anal sex, orgasm, and violence in the trilogy to shock and entice his audience. This kind of provocative portrayal is typical of Erdoğan's 6:45 publishing house. In his preface to 6:45's *The Beat Generation Anthology* (*Beat Kuşağı Antolojisi*), Erdoğan sarcastically takes the committee to task, writing,

> By collecting together all the necessarily prohibited writers and poets of this harmful generation we hope to help the attempts of the Committee for the Protection of Children from Harmful Publications which draws the borders for the morals of the people and protects our children from harmful publications. We hope we've made their jobs easier. (Giriş)

In fact, the very first page of the anthology boldly announces that the book is a joint project (*ortak yapımı*) between Sel and 6:45. *Underground Poetix*, 6:45's magazine filled with expletives and graphic descriptions, is in much the same vein and has also included advertisements for *The Soft Machine* that utilize the committee's statements (see figure 4.2). But even here, the celebration is not as focused on Burroughs as public figure as it is on Burroughs as mythic type—the outlaw who holds nothing sacred. But Erdoğan's article is the exception that proves the rule, since for most involved in the debate the attention is on the issue of homosexuality and not so much the homosexual writer.

The figure of Burroughs as iconic rebel, gun-loving outlaw, wise-cracking Uncle Bill, or *el hombre invisible* is present in Turkey, but the defense wisely tones down this antihero message. Burroughs's age and conservative appearance help to make him seem more of a curiosity than a threat. Although his reputation as provocateur precedes him, the Turkish media mainly provides a deferential treatment of his work and life. In the photographs that appear in Turkish publications, he is inevitably depicted as an older gentleman neatly dressed in suit and tie. Given this image, the supposedly rebellious figure of Burroughs could easily be lost among the tea-drinking Turks playing backgammon in the local café. In the trial and in their media campaign, the defense is savvy enough to play on such depictions, limiting Burroughs's role to the older, wiser "leader" of the Beat Generation. The cultural situation in Turkey demands a different Burroughs than the one so cherished in the United States.

The Beats are still viable counterculture figures in Turkey, but their function has changed. Beat writers such as Burroughs are more important for some of the countercultural positions they hold and less because they exemplify the American ideal of the lone individual fighting the repressive system. Cultural difference demands a rethinking of what it means to challenge society. Burroughs remains a rebel in Turkey, but not due to his innovative style, idiosyncratic character, suspicion of "control," or even his views on narcotics. Instead, his work has struck the sensitive nerve of homosexuality. Like other cultural products, exported counterculture can be employed in unexpected ways in its new cultural home.

A QUESTION OF STYLE

The Turkish translation of Burroughs's work reveals a very different understanding of his literary contributions. Like most Turkish translators, Süha Sertabiboğlu works more for the pleasure than for the money. It seems strange that this mild-mannered, gentlemanly dentist would be caught up in such a controversy. Sertabiboğlu was also involved in leftist politics, but his career as a translator began during his student years when he was asked to translate Robert M. Pirsig's *Zen and the Art of Motorcycle Maintenance* (1974). Despite translating such countercultural classics, Sertabiboğlu admits that he found *The Soft Machine* more valuable as social statement than as literary classic, stating, "The book doesn't have any aesthetical value, it doesn't give you any pleasure to read it. Whatever there is in literature to attract people, they are doing the exact opposite. Everything is dirty here; whatever people would find repulsive and not welcome is here" (Sertabiboğlu, interview). Sertabiboğlu is no stranger to Burroughs's work. On the contrary, he has reread each book of the trilogy several times to standardize his translations and has also translated Burroughs's book of dreams, *My Education* (1995). Yet Sertabiboğlu dislikes Burroughs's style.

Sertabiboğlu's reaction demonstrates the extent to which underground texts such as *The Soft Machine* push literary and social expectations. The idea that texts are meant to convey fine feelings and to sound pleasurable to the ear is one of the major difficulties Beat and other underground works face in gaining acceptance in Turkey. Ozan Marakoğlu, writing in *Notos*, discusses Turkish readers' perception of the literary and how it impinges on the debate. For Marakoğlu, Turkey's traditional taste is for a literature that is both "overly decent as well as boring," and he concludes sarcastically that "the shameless literature that the reader with this education feels close to is actually a literature that doesn't fit in the syllabus. The thing that doesn't fit the definition of literature at school must be something other than literature—something underground" (49). Routinely decried as "dark," "black," and "dirty," such texts are dismissed as unpleasurable reading, poor constructions, or simply the negative reactions of an unhappy individual. *The Soft Machine*, which revels in detailed descriptions of acts and characters that many readers would consider repugnant, is exemplary in this regard.

The gap between Turkish and English, both culturally and structurally, is part of the difficulty. Sertabiboğlu uses the idea of "squeezing" (the Turkish here is *sığdırmak*, that is, to make something fit into a container) Burroughs's text into Turkish. Turkish makes do with fewer words by expanding the range of meaning of existing words, and by combining words that capture slight variations in connotation. Moreover, spoken Turkish favors polite expression and typically avoids the use of harsh language. To translate a text replete with slang such as *The Soft Machine*, Sertabiboğlu describes how he was forced to resort to nonpolite forms to capture the rough feel of the text. A corollary to this softening of the content is Sertabiboğlu's attempt to soften the sound as well. As a language that subscribes to the law of vowel harmony, Turkish often sounds more melodic than some of its European counterparts. When endings are added, a vowel that corresponds to the preceding vowel in the stem is used. Sertabiboğlu notes, "While translating I tried to put in words that sound similar next to each other to make it sound better on the ear. I also tried to use words that are associated with each other successively so there would be fluidity" (Sertabiboğlu, interview). What all of this demonstrates is that Burroughs's text strikes the Turkish reader as harsh in both tone and content. Although not all Turkish literature conforms to this standard aesthetic, it would be fair to say that underground texts like *The Soft Machine* are received in Turkey as a sort of antiliterature that breaks with aesthetic expectations.[22]

Given such differences in aesthetic values, it is unsurprising that Burroughs's work is less read than that of his underground contemporaries in Turkey. Reviewers such as Fatih Özgün praise his style for its dislocating effects:

> Burroughs deals fanatically with language, with pure, clear language, with spoken, preached, delirious language. He's not interested in the introduction-body-conclusion format. It's possible to start his books from the middle or the end, or even from the beginning, and ask slightly heatedly, "what's he talking about?" It's like a river that flows on its own, concerned about its own flow, not about carrying you somewhere. You are alone as a reader, and must learn to swim. First for dear life, then for pleasure. The Burroughs style is one long, single flow that pulls you in. (Özgün)

But this lack of structure and attention to the flow of language makes for a difficult reading experience. While some may learn to savor such work, others are simply left confused. Such difficulty has led to Burroughs being translated into Turkish very late. The first Burroughs novel translated into Turkish, *Ghost of Chance* (1991; *Şans Hayaleti*), was first published in 1996, and even his classic *Naked Lunch* first appeared in 1998, nearly forty years after its initial publication.[23] The majority of translations are put out by 6:45 press, while Kerouac and Ginsberg have been published by larger and more established presses. In our study, Burroughs is the least read of these three Beats, and only 3.3 percent of respondents claimed to have read *The Soft Machine*, although the trial came up in several focus groups (Mortenson, Ergun, and Erdoğan 103). Fortunately for Burroughs and those who champion his work in Turkey, audiences do not necessarily need to read the book to get its countercultural message of dissent.

THE MEDIUM AND THE MESSAGE

To take their fight outside the courtroom, the defense has embraced social media. As the entire world witnessed in light of the Arab Spring, a highly connected world has the advantage of disseminating information quickly via the Internet, allowing a wide range of geographically dispersed users to be alerted to unfolding events instantaneously. Just as U.S. editions of *Naked Lunch* incorporated trial excerpts into their introductory material, the book's publisher, Sel Publishing, includes excerpts from the Committee for the Protection of Minors' report on the book's back cover and trial transcripts on its website. By these means, the text incorporates its surrounding controversy. As Goodman notes, "In subsequent printings of *Naked Lunch*, the introductory material has included numerous excerpts from the Boston trial, suggesting that the trial can be considered as a part of the book" (5). In this earlier U.S. context, such a strategy worked only after the trial. With the Internet, such dissemination can happen simultaneously, allowing the public to follow governmental attempts to censor the work as they unfold from court date to court date. This study, for instance, relies heavily on documents released by the defense and their supporters on various websites.

Collaborating with others involved in the anticensorship struggle, the defendants have produced a network capable of disseminating their message effectively. Sertabiboğlu, for example, developed his Facebook page in coordination with the page for Ayrıntı Publishing's translation of *Snuff*, and he continues to coordinate efforts of the Turkish Translators Association to disseminate information about the trial. In fact, as Sancı observes, the Internet has enabled him to reach out to journalists across the globe. It has brought journalists together in a virtual space for interviews, and allows them to follow the trial from their own countries as it unfolds. Partnering with *Snuff*'s publisher Ayrıntı, Sel has used the Internet with a great deal of savvy to promote the cause of anticensorship and to raise awareness of both government interference and the countercultural works that challenge the accepted pillars of Turkish society.

In a country such as Turkey where open discussion of homosexuality is difficult, the Internet has taken on greater importance as a facilitator of relatively risk-free communication, allowing such sensitive topics to be discussed with less potential for violence. Sertabiboğlu claims that after the book was on trial, many different people contacted him on Facebook—many of whom identified themselves as homosexual. In fact, both publishers claim that there has been a lot of Internet support from readers for their cause. Discussing the idea of the "digital closet," Gorkemli notes that since its Turkish inception in 1993, the Internet "provided the means by which otherwise isolated individuals with nonmainstream gender identities and/or sexual orientations could connect with each other to form communities" (73). While this technology allowed for greater communication between individual users and fostered the expansion of LGBT groups across Turkey, as Gorkemli explains, this reliance on the Internet's anonymity and invisibility also "became a symbol of homosexual oppression for lesbian and gay activists in Turkey" (79). Nevertheless, the Internet allows for a means of disseminating information and offers the potential for such a movement to emerge.

One of the reasons many of the older publishers and translators involved in the Turkish underground scene downplay their contributions is that they are still working with an older model of revolt that presupposes face-to-face, real-time encounters. But this model does not take into account the Internet's ability to effect cultural change. The Internet also offers a new mode of communication—a model based on the "viral" rather than the "sequential." Given the Internet's ability to distribute an issue exponentially to a worldwide audience, what might seem like an isolated event can quickly gain widespread support. Old Turkish leftists hold on to a Marxist dream of political struggle that leads to a structural change in society. By continually publishing such underground texts, they lay the seeds for a revolution that could come at any time, or could build faster than pre-Internet models of communist cells or party organizations where membership happened slowly, one comrade at a time. The visibility of underground literature and the issues it raises is heightened significantly by the numerous Facebook pages, blogs, and websites devoted to its writers and texts. While our study found that the majority of Turkish underground readers first heard of the genre through friends (82.1 percent), a substantial number (4.6 percent) first encountered these writers and texts on the Internet, and all used the Internet frequently (Mortenson, Ergun, Erdoğan 93). The Internet's importance in disseminating underground literature and the issues it generates will only grow over time.

Many young Americans arriving to the Beats probably do so through social media or other such Internet sites. This phenomenon aligns them more with their young Turkish counterparts than with an older generation whose introduction to the counterculture was most often through word-of-mouth recommendations or chance encounters at the local bookshop or coffeehouse. The nostalgia of older Turkish leftists for more direct political involvement finds its oft-heard echo in baby-boomer reminiscences over more immediate connections to the Beats and the countercultural venues in which they circulated. But listening in person to Burroughs's characteristic drawl as he reads live from a stage and hearing in person the soulful voice of Billie Holiday singing are, unfortunately, things of the past. With the passage of time and the technological change it brings, the Internet will only grow in importance as a tool in disseminating the Beats' antiauthoritarian message. This change is especially true outside the United States, where the only means of accessing the Beats and their cultural products is oftentimes through the screen. For a younger generation, this loss of presence is compensated for by the ease in which Beat images, texts, and the countercultural ideas they raise can be disseminated throughout the world.

CODA: THE VERDICT

The Turkish censorship trial of William S. Burroughs's *The Soft Machine* and Chuck Palahniuk's *Snuff* concluded in a truly inconclusive fashion. Expert opinions for both books were favorable, and the defense expected an acquittal.[24] But fate, or perhaps the Turkish government, intervened. On the day the trial was to be heard, July 5, 2012, a package of laws went into effect that included an article that put all literary obscenity cases on hold for three years. While this would seem to be in Sel and Ayrıntı's favor, the new ruling actually left them in an even more precarious position. According to the verdict, if the accused were put on trial again for a similar crime within three years, the case files for this trial would be reopened (*Edebiyathaber.net*). The threat is that if they continue to publish such provocative materials, they will be retried not only for the new case but for the old one as well. What makes this decision particularly painful for the defendants is that they stood a strong chance of winning their case. Even the judge admits that if the trial had been conducted a week earlier, or the reader reports had not been so late, the verdict would have been acquittal (*Edebiyathaber.net*). Nobody knows for sure whether the timing of this law was intentional or simply bad luck, but the result was the same—Sel and Ayrıntı continued to operate under the threat of censorship.

Fortunately, both publishers chose to continue the fight. Sancı's response was openly defiant: "This law is not amnesty but a threat. . . . When a crime doesn't even exist and we should have been acquitted this judgment only serves to wear us down. Of course we will commit the same 'crime' in three years, that's our job. We will keep publishing these kinds of books" (*Edebiyathaber.net*). Ayrıntı remained equally contentious, handing the judge their latest Palahniuk translation with the statement "since we will keep doing this job, we are informing on ourselves. We are sending the latest Chuck Palahniuk book to the Committee through your court" (*Edebiyathaber.net*). Ayrıntı has stayed out of trouble, but Sel once again found itself facing trial for an earlier translation of Apollinaire's *The Exploits of a Young Don Juan* (*Les exploits d'un jeune Don Juan* in French; 1911).[25] That book was deemed a work of literature in 2010 and acquitted, but Turkey's Supreme Court of Appeals (*Yargıtay*) found it obscene during a 2013 appeal. İrfan Sancı and the translator İsmail Yerguz were then charged with the exploitation of minors (*çocuk istismar*). In late 2013 an Istanbul court again postponed the verdict—if Sel is brought to trial in the next three years on a similar charge, the court will reopen both the Burroughs and the Apollinaire cases ("Genç Bir"). While all this legal trouble appears to place Sel back where they started, some things have indeed changed: they are a bit wiser, a bit poorer, and both *The Soft Machine* and *Snuff*, as well as the issues they raise, are a lot better known.

5. HOWLING IN TURKISH
APPROPRIATING THE MANY FACES OF ALLEN GINSBERG

In the fall of 2014, the publisher 6:45 put together an art exhibit in anticipation of its forthcoming translation of Allen Ginsberg's long poem *Kaddish* (1961). The show paid homage to the company's earlier publication of a limited edition of Ginsberg's *Howl.* Held at Galeri 44A in Istanbul's posh Nişantaşı district, the show highlighted artwork that offered viewers a range of takes on Ginsberg's famous poem. Gaye Su Akyol's work *Tanrın bağımlı ve tedavi* (*Your God Is the Addict and the Cure*), for instance, depicts a man in the act of sniffing a galaxy drawn onto the cover of 6:45's *Howl* translation. The book is under glass, resting on a table next to six lines of what appears to be glittering stardust waiting to be snorted. This piece highlights Ginsberg as a drug experimenter searching for cosmic consciousness. Another work by Eflatun Tatlısu presents a giant eyeball behind which are images of a naked Ginsberg taken during his time in India. This piece stresses the mystical, Buddhist Ginsberg. But the piece that best captured the malleable nature of Ginsberg was by Olgu Ülkenciler. The artist had cut a hole in the middle of the book and inscribed, at the top, "The key is in the window / the key is in the sunlight / at the window," and the viewer was left to maneuver this dangling frame across a range of images taped to the wall. The range of images—the title page of *Das Kapital*, an athlete's fist raised in a black power salute, a picture of Dostoyevsky, a jazz player strumming a bass, to name only a few—demonstrated the possible ways of looking at Ginsberg's classic text. In the end, every visitor to 6:45's *Howl* exhibition could find their own version of Ginsberg.

Ginsberg is a highly adaptable figure, and this chapter explores the various translations of this important Beat poet—both textual and cultural—that have occurred in Turkey beginning as early as the 1970s and continuing today. Of course, translations are always interested, so it comes as little surprise that each reproduction of Ginsberg and his work carries traces of the concerns and preoccupations of the translator. An examination of Ginsberg's Turkish appropriation therefore allows us to see how local conditions influence reception, reminding us that there really is no one final meaning to the signifier "Ginsberg," or to "Beat," for that matter. These various interpretations and translations of Ginsberg into the Turkish language and culture are by no means inaccurate, and should not be judged invidiously. They simply represent different ways of looking at Ginsberg at particular cultural moments that draw on the different possibilities that the poet himself presented.

In his lifetime, Ginsberg cultivated a wide variety of personae—communist sympathizer, political and sexual rights activist, hippie, hipster, seer, Buddhist, and cultural guru, to name only a few. Such an array offers his admirers multiple versions of the poet from which they can craft their own understanding of his life and work. The particular aspect of Ginsberg's multifaceted career that is highlighted by a publisher, an editor, or a translator says much about the cultural moment in which the translation was made. But it also says something important about the translated, and this chapter will also explore what the history of Ginsberg's reception in Turkey might reveal about Ginsberg, the reception of his image over time, and why certain "Ginsbergs" are preferred over others. The cultural reception of Ginsberg, his work, and his image in Turkey demonstrates the ways in which this American cultural icon becomes redeployed in particular moments as translators, poets, and editors choose a version of Ginsberg that best fits their interests and needs.

This chapter begins by examining Turkish translations of Ginsberg's poem *Howl* and the paratextual material that surrounds these translations in order to explore the ways in which Ginsberg's poem becomes redeployed in new cultural contexts. The argument here is that the social world that receives the text plays an integral part in shaping the translation, and thus its meaning. Ferit Edgü and Orhan Duru's 1976 translation, for example, presents a highly politicized Ginsberg that draws on his antiestablishment credentials as a social activist. This point of view comes as little surprise, since pre-1980 coup Turkey was mired in conflicts between a nationalist right and a socialist left. But as Turkey switched from political to cultural forms of dissent, representations of Ginsberg switched as well. Hakan

Arslan's 1991 translation provides a less political Ginsberg, in keeping with a society that left direct political struggle behind. The 1990s were a more transitional moment in Turkish culture, and while Arslan's Ginsberg remains political, he also becomes more personal, as the translator struggles to capture the man as well as the message. Şenol Erdoğan's 2013 version, published by the highly vocal underground press 6:45, updated Ginsberg once again. Ginsberg had become an even more recognizable countercultural figure in Turkey, and 6:45's new version presented a new Ginsberg. Erdoğan's Ginsberg became both a marker of "hip" transgression and a spiritual guru equated with the mystical qualities of Jalāl ad-Dīn Muhammad "Mevlana" ar-Rūmī and Sufism. Each of these translations draws on the needs of its unique cultural moment to highlight a particular aspect of Ginsberg's multifaceted career and persona, and in the process performs a specific type of cultural work.

Ginsberg has also entered Turkish culture through less direct means. The provocative Turkish poet küçük iskender draws on Ginsberg's image as an iconoclastic gay poet to "shock the squares" of Turkish society. An openly gay poet who flaunts a licentious lifestyle of drinking and drug experimentation, küçük iskender has established himself as Turkey's leading underground poet—one willing to directly confront Turkish mores. While not translations per se, küçük iskender's work consciously borrows from both Ginsberg's life as well as the themes and styles in his poetry to challenge the basic tenets of Turkish society. It comes as little surprise that iskender would choose the poet as a mentor. Ginsberg is a highly useful figure, easily amenable to the needs of a Turkish underground that aims to question social norms through the presentation of excluded points of view.

This chapter ends with an examination of Ginsberg's one and only visit to Istanbul in 1990. Although his visit to the country lasted for only a few weeks, Ginsberg had the opportunity to meet with Turkish poets, as well as to visit sites throughout the country. What happened when this countercultural star finally met some of his readers? This interesting moment of cross-cultural exchange ended with both spirited poetic collaboration as well as a bit of miscommunication. The large group of Turkish writers and intellectuals who drank and dined with Ginsberg recall a lively evening of exchange, but whereas they wanted to talk poetry, Ginsberg was more interested in the topics of drug legalization and human rights. Cultural translations are just as difficult to achieve in person as on paper, but they offer all involved the chance to reexamine their expectations and presumptions. Ultimately, both Ginsberg and his hosts were able to find common ground despite their different objectives.

The struggle to bring an author from one culture to another reveals differences that help us to understand how meanings shift across time and place. Thus cultural translations offer an opportunity to better understand the assumptions of the target culture. But such translations can also reveal the assumptions about how a text or an image operates in its original culture as well. Tracing the translation history of Ginsberg and his work provides a sense of recent Turkish cultural history, but it also allows Beat scholars to theorize how the reception of the Beats generates new versions, and thus new readings, of these countercultural texts. Ginsberg's Turkish reception demonstrates that the Beat Generation and their writings will never remain static. As long as new readers bring new frameworks, Beat works like Ginsberg's classic *Howl* will continue to be reinterpreted in ways that both highlight the range of their possible interpretations and allow us to glimpse new possibilities in texts and writers we thought we already knew.

"I USED TO BE A COMMUNIST"

Unlike his other Beat compatriots, Ginsberg was translated into Turkish early. The first major translation of Ginsberg's work was Orhan Duru and Ferit Edgü's 1976 publication *Amerika* (*America*). This volume, which included *Howl* as well as selections from Lawrence Ferlinghetti's poetry, was meant as an intervention into the moribund leftist poetry scene in Turkey. As we have seen throughout this work, pre-1980-coup Turkey was deeply mired in political conflict. In the United States, the Vietnam War had galvanized the counterculture, but Stalinism and McCarthyism had helped to discredit the communist left. In Turkey, however, communism remained a viable political option. A wide spectrum of leftists, from hardcore communists to more progressive socialists, battled right-wing nationalists in oftentimes bloody street battles that claimed lives. Turkey had yet to embrace the sort of identity politics and celebration of individual freedom inaugurated by the 1960s counterculture. Edgü and Duru were both committed leftists, but they were also writers looking for alternatives to hackneyed forms of expression. Beat writers like Ginsberg and Ferlinghetti heralded a new form of protest that was simultaneously political, transformative, and literary.

What made Ginsberg so compelling was that he offered a new way to rebel. Socially engaged writing had degenerated into polemic and propaganda, but Beat writers like Ginsberg offered critiques meant to be taken seriously as literature. Edgü's 1976 introduction to the translation, "Önsöz Gibi" ("Like a Preface"), chronicles his discovery of the Beats and what they might mean for poetry at that time. Growing frustrated with both Turkish and foreign poets, Edgü laments,

> I was asking myself, "What could poetry do today?" . . . If poetry is the act of giving a voice to human reality, this was readily done by those who confused art with political propaganda without batting an eye. I'm proposing two poets of the Beat Generation as a tangible and valid answer to the question: "what poetry can do today?" ("Birinci Basımın")

Edgü's preface highlights the bind socially committed poets were in during the period. The prevailing climate of revolution had generated its own clichéd and stale style of poetry. Writers like Edgü called for a new form of socially engaged writing that went beyond prevailing dogma. The Beats offered a refreshing insistence on lived experience rather than relying on the tired old ways of thinking. Poetry was now seen to "give voice to the human reality" as a means of "Howling" the frustrations of individuals in society.[1] The personal was becoming political.

Ginsberg and Ferlinghetti were the two Beat poets best equipped to facilitate a move from political to cultural critique. Both had the sort of Marxist credentials that Turkish writers could understand, but they sought to go beyond purely propagandistic work. As he chronicles in *Howl* (1956), Ginsberg was involved in communist and socialist activities from an early age. Ferlinghetti was likewise interested in leftist social movements. In fact, both had made trips to Cuba and Nicaragua to witness firsthand the attempts to craft Marxist states.[2] Ben Lee, in "Howl and Other Poems: Is There Old Left in These New Beats?" claims that "Ginsberg's work in the 1950s is shot through with references to political identities supposedly antiquated and actively discredited by intellectuals on both the Left and the Right during the Cold War moment" (368). Although Lee demonstrates that such references have gone unexamined by scholars, they were certainly not lost on Turkish leftists of the late 1960s and the 1970s. Lee undertakes a recovery of Ginsberg's neglected relationship to the leftist tradition that preceded him, ultimately arguing, "We need to reassert Ginsberg's tendency to commemorate the resources of the past, to infuse them with the poetic energies of the present, to reconfigure them in the face of shifting historical circumstance" (368). Ginsberg's attempts in his poetry to fuse the social movements of the past with the changing needs of the countercultural present make him the perfect figure for the precoup Turkish left. For those involved in violent political struggle, Ginsberg probably made little sense. But for Turkish intellectuals looking for a socially engaged literature, Ginsberg and Ferlinghetti offered political poetry that could be both political *and* poetry.

The social thrust of Edgü and Duru's translation is captured on its cover. Although the title is taken from Ginsberg's poem "America," which leads off the collection, Ginsberg is really "bundled" with Ferlinghetti. Although Ginsberg's name appears first, both names appear on the cover, divided by a slash (figure 5.1). In addition, the faces of both poets appear together, in a sort of fusion, with Ginsberg looking to his right in a serious manner and Ferlinghetti staring forward and smiling. The cover not only creates a connection between these two poets but also seems to suggest that they share the title as well as a common purpose—a description of America the reader will go on to discover is highly critical. Ginsberg is bookended by his two most provocative pieces, "America" (1956) and *Howl* (1955–56), with the collection also including the drug-inspired "LSD 25" (actually "Lysergic Acid"; 1959), a poem Ginsberg had written to Kerouac on meeting his lover Peter Orlovsky ("Malest Cornifici Tuo Catullo"; 1955), and his

Fig. 5.1. Edgü and Duru's translation brings together the revolutionary potential of both Ginsberg and Ferlinghetti, as these two poets share a name, a title, and even a face.

rant against government and rationality, "Manifesto" (1974). Ferlinghetti is not as well represented, with only "One Thousand Fearful Words for Fidel Castro" (1961), "In Goya's Greatest Scenes" (1958), and "He" (1958) offered. But as the cover implies, taken together, the volume offers a selection of rebellious poems written in a diversity of styles that challenge the poetic and social status quo.

The emphasis on cultural rather than political critique can be seen in the short biography of Ginsberg the translators offer. After providing the requisite personal data such as date and place of birth, the translators include several details that locate Ginsberg's lifestyle choices in social contexts. Discussing his use of drugs, they quote Ginsberg's claim, "I believe marijuana is a political tool" (Edgü and Duru 11). Although the use of marijuana offers the possibility for mind expansion, the drug also provides a means of offering "political" resistance. Lifestyle choice, rather than membership in a political group, becomes the means of offering a challenge to the status quo. The translators go on to claim, "Because of his rebellious attitude in social issues or personal understanding he often had problems with the judiciary" (11). Not only does this fact provide Ginsberg with a sort of leftist "street credibility" in Turkey as many leftists of the period found themselves in jail or afoul of the law, but it also demonstrates that personal and poetic expression is, in its own way, a social act of defiance. Poets, too, can challenge the system with more than empty slogans and meaningless words—they can let their personal feelings become political tools.

This attempt to carve out a new space for engaged poetry in pre-1980-coup Turkey is present in the translators' decision to include excerpts from Ginsberg's "Notes Written on Finally Recording Howl" (1959) as an epigraph to the volume. First published as liner notes to his sound recording, in the final two paragraphs of this piece, Ginsberg includes "A word on the Academies" and "A word on the Politicians" that provide a definitive statement to those in charge of both the universities and the country (13). Most telling is Ginsberg's admonition that "my poetry is angelic ravings, and has nothing to do with dull materialistic vagaries about who should shoot who" (13). Turning the language of the communist left against itself, Ginsberg denies "materialist" solutions that only exacerbate the sort of left-versus-right divisions that were particularly pronounced in pre-1980 Turkey. Ginsberg opted for a cultural politics that sought to bring a broadly humanistic awareness to social concerns and expand the possibilities of consciousness. Although the translators present these statements without commentary under the heading "Şiir Sanatı" ("Poetics") (and judiciously omit Ginsberg's claim that academics "wouldn't know poetry if it came up and buggered them in broad daylight"), the sort of "third-way" politics that Ginsberg advocated must have found resonance with those artists and intellectuals of the period who wanted to be socially committed but without a slavish dependence on existing political paradigms (13). Ginsberg's own politics, which eschewed alignment with political parties, offered a new model.

Despite the translators' celebration of Ginsberg and, to a lesser extent, Ferlinghetti, as champions of a new type of poetry, the cultural and geographical distance between these young Turkish writers and intellectuals and their Beat colleagues meant that the Beats had to be explained before they could be appreciated. Despite some isolated translations of Beat work that appeared in journals such as *Soyut* (*Abstract*), *Yeni Dergi* (*New Magazine*), and *Yeni Ufuklar* (*New Horizons*) in the late 1960s and early 1970s, the Beats were still largely unknown in Turkey. Duru and Edgü tackle this problem in their translation of one of the later stanzas of *Howl*'s first section, where Ginsberg writes, "the madman bum and angel beat in Time, unknown" (*Collected* 131). Duru and Edgü translate this as "madman, bum, and time's angelically beaten ones, **beat**, unknown" (Edgü and Duru 37). Reading the translation against the source text reveals a slippage in Ginsberg's work that is probably intentional. Is Ginsberg referring to two people here, "the madman bum" as well as "angel beat"? Or is he discussing a "madman bum and angel" who is "beat in Time"? Or are there actually three people, or at least three adjectives referring to the same figure, who is "beat in Time"? The difference is admittedly minor, but it speaks to an ambiguity of language running throughout the poem as Ginsberg switches from the collective "who" of the "best minds of my generation" to the individual cases that compose his litany (*Collected* 126).

Duru and Edgü's translation is still ambiguous, but less so. A comma separates *madman* (*çılgın*) from *bum* (*serseri*), suggesting that these figures are part of a list. Although "*çılgın*" is often used as an adjective to mean "crazy," here it is seems to be a noun, one of a series that will be added to "time's angelically beaten ones," to those who are "unknown," and ultimately to "beat" itself. The translators use the Turkish verb "*dövülmek*" or "to be (physically) beaten" to capture Ginsberg's "angel beat in Time," but they go on to include the English word *beat* in boldface type. This list format provides the Turkish reader with a sense of what *beat* means by explicitly associating the untranslated term with the sort of marginal figures Ginsberg chronicles. Duru and Edgü add an extra "beat" to the line as a means to help define an English term unfamiliar to their readers.[3]

The cultural moment of reception is also an important factor in Duru and Edgü's presentation of communism. While the translators are certainly frustrated with the political situation of 1970s Turkey, the extent to which they omit references to a movement that enjoyed such a strong following at the time is surprising. Shifting social expectations and censorship concerns might account for the lack of reference to "communism" in Edgü and Duru's translation. While they retain the reference to "Supercommunist" in Ginsberg's poem, they omit the entire stanza in part 3 where the speaker and Carl Solomon sing the "Internationale," though both Arslan and Erdoğan include it in their translations (*Collected* 127). In their "America" translation, Edgü and Duru use "I was a gun" (*tüfektim;* 16) rather than "America I used to be a communist when I was a kid I'm not sorry" (*Collected* 146), though both Arslan and Erdoğan use "komünist" (43; Erdoğan, *Uluma* 43). Edgü and Duru also drop "Communist" from Ginsberg's line "America when I was seven momma took me to Communist Cell meetings" (17; *Collected* 147). As we have seen, Duru and Edgü wanted to avoid the sort of sloganeering associated with dogmatic leftist poetry, and thus omitting references to communism might have been their way of disassociating their translation from hackneyed political poetry. But they also might have simply been avoiding the censor. The heyday of Turkish communism was between the 1960 and 1980 coups, but even during this period government repression was rife.[4] "Supercommunist" might have been strange or comical enough to pass the censors, but repeated reference to a movement maligned by the government could have caused problems. The 1980 coup struck a serious blow to the Communist party, and thus Arslan and Erdoğan had no such fears using the term.

Duru and Edgü were not alone in their desire for a new form of revolution through literature. The first extended treatment of the Beats in Turkey, Özdemir İnce's 1977 article "Beat Generation ve 'Amerika' Üzerine" ("On the Beat Generation and 'America'"), also captures this desire for a type of writing free from tired political dogma. Published only a year after Edgü and Duru's translation, İnce's article is important not only because it took the Beat social critique seriously by drawing on both primary sources and secondary ones like John Tytell's *Naked Angels*, but also because it provides insight into the context for the Beats' entry into pre-1980-coup Turkey. İnce likewise recognized the potential of the Beats, arguing, "Theirs was a kind of anti-myth. A myth that turned America inside out. They brought dirt against American cleanliness, laziness against diligence, their own morality with principles but not rules against the official morality which was fundamentally Protestant" (29). Despite İnce's praise for the questions that the Beats posed for U.S. society, ultimately he is reticent about the possibilities for the "anti-myth" the Beats were offering. In a critique that echoes some of their U.S. critics, İnce calls the Beats to task for their excessive individualism:

> In such a social environment that both destroys and is being destroyed, the hope to change the world leads one to scientific socialism; and the lack of this hope to anarchism, nihilism and mysticism. The fact that the cruelty of the capitalist world and the collapse in its culture led the beatniks to the East, especially to Hindu mysticism, is a natural consequence of their choices. Unfortunately, the art of the beatniks underwent this contradiction and at some points became wrapped up in an individualist pessimism.
>
> And that is why I say yes to their rebellion, and no to the conclusion they reached. (31)

Here the Beats are seen through the political frameworks of the time. They are capable of highlighting the problems in U.S. society, but the Beats' focus on individualism leaves them helpless to change the social conditions that drove them to rebel in the first place. The Beats, according to İnce, seek escape from the world and its problems, rather than an embrace of "scientific socialism" that might lead to fundamental structural changes. Literature is important, but for İnce and many other Turkish leftists of the pre-1980-coup era, the writer must also be politically engaged.

Despite this seemingly negative assessment, İnce makes it clear that the more socially engaged Beat writers—Ginsberg and Ferlinghetti in particular—do offer a useful critique. İnce claims, "But no matter what, it would be a great injustice to underestimate their fight. Especially when Allen Ginsberg starts talking" (33). İnce praises Edgü and Duru's translation, then ends his own article with a quote taken from Ferlinghetti's liner notes for *The Impeachment of Eisenhower* (Fantasy Records #7004 LP; 1958) that is included in Edgü and Duru's introduction to the poet: "'*The wig-wearing nihilism of the Beat Generation, if carried to its natural conclusion, will mean the death of the creative artist. The fact that the artist is non-connected is a kind of suicide and is nothing but a muddled version of the same*'" (45). Edgü claims in an interview that he and Duru worked on other Beats as well, specifically mentioning Gregory Corso, LeRoi Jones, and Bob Kaufman (Edgü, "Amerika"). Ginsberg and Ferlinghetti, however, are singled out as two poets worthy of their own volume because both promise a poetry that includes social commitment, pushing their work beyond simple "nihilism" and directly into the social. İnce's article captures a larger zeitgeist among Turkish intellectuals during the period. Ginsberg and Ferlinghetti become exemplars in pre-1980-coup Turkey precisely because they are able to combine an interest in leftist politics with a new form of poetry that celebrates the individual as an engine of political change.

A MORE PERSONAL GINSBERG

The 1980 coup ushered in a new Turkey. The violent clashes between the left and the right that had epitomized the pre-coup years had been suppressed, and the country was opened up to Western influence. Along with the arrival of consumer goods came cultural ones as well, and Ginsberg was again updated for the times. Hakan Arslan, in his 1991 translation of a selection of Ginsberg's poems, sounds a more personal note. Beats like Ginsberg are no longer seen as an unexplored American phenomenon that might provide poetry a "way out." As we shall see, Arslan is himself politically engaged, a communist who spent time in a commune in the Aegean coastal town of Bodrum conducting workshops on Beat writing and Eastern philosophy (Arslan, interview). But the Ginsberg he provides is less a comrade than a companion. In contrast to Duru and Edgü's more political Ginsberg, Arslan makes Ginsberg more familiar and colloquial. Ginsberg is still revealing his thoughts and baring his soul, but readers get the sense that they are listening more to a friend than to a spokesperson.

As with Edgü and Duru's translation, the book's cover provides the first clue to the style of the material within (figure 5.2). The title immediately catches the eye. "*Kuşbeyin*" means "birdbrain" in Turkish, and refers to Ginsberg's poem of the same name included in the volume. Written in a Dubrovnik hotel in 1980 and collected in *Plutonian Ode* (1982), as Arslan rightly comments, it is "one of Ginsberg's most political poems" (Arslan, interview). Thus the title would seem to be in keeping with Duru and Edgü's earlier thrust to use Ginsberg in the service of a new form of resistance. This connection may be true, but only in part. The poem castigates both the United States and Russia, East and West. Birdbrain is "the ultimate product of Capitalism" as well as the "chief bureaucrat of Russia" (*Collected* 738). But the poem is also self-mocking. After proclaiming, "I am Birdbrain!" the speaker later explains, "Birdbrain became a great International Poet and went around the world praising the Glories of Birdbrain" (738–39). "Birdbrain" describes a type of thinking to which everyone is prone, rather than a pointed attack on a particular person or outlook. It demonstrates Ginsberg's ability to use humor to deconstruct the binaries of a postwar world and, in the process, reexamine his own position as poet-revolutionary desirous of both social change and personal fame.

Fig. 5.2. The cover of Arslan's translation is a study in contrasts, as a pensive photograph of Ginsberg is framed by a chaos of Latin script and musical notes, while the title itself screams "Birdbrain!" to the reader.

The rest of the cover picks up on this study in contrasts. "*Kuşbeyin*," as in the English "Birdbrain," comes off as slightly comical, and for those with no knowledge of Ginsberg, its political intent would certainly not be immediately apparent. The rest of the cover material works against its comical title. The front depicts a brooding or perhaps composing Ginsberg, surrounded by musical notations and a cacophony of Latin words pasted in an almost fanzine style. Together, the notes and the Latin text (taken from a liturgy for a Gregorian chant) lend the cover a serious appearance. A picture of a pensive Ginsberg with head downcast and finger to lips indicates a thoughtfully meditative poet hard at work in the act of composing. But the pasted, fanzine style of the Latin words seems to undermine this idea of seriousness. The back cover, by contrast, presents a photograph of an "everyday" Ginsberg sitting on a wood bench in what is probably his Cherry Valley Farm almost smirking at the camera in shorts and a jean jacket (figure 5.3). This photograph captures a sort of familiar, approachable image of Ginsberg. In the end, the volume goes on to promote both Ginsbergs in an effort to reveal not only his revolutionary ideas but also the idiosyncratic man himself.

Arslan's biographical note likewise marks a shift in focus from the political to the personal. There is a nod here to a more socially engaged Ginsberg, and probably to Edgü and Duru's translation, when Arslan notes in the second paragraph, "Of the Beat generation, [Ginsberg] is the most political member after Ferlinghetti" (*Kuşbeyin!*, unpaginated). Arslan is clearly politically engaged. In our interview, he explains, "I'm coming from a politicized generation in the eighties. After September 12 [the date

Fig. 5.3. The back cover of Arslan's translation was taken from this photo of Allen Ginsberg on his Cherry Valley Farm. It presents a more approachable image of the poet, demonstrating the range of Ginsberg personae offered in the collection. *Photo © 2017 Elsa Dorfman. This work is licensed under the Creative Commons Attribution-NonCommercial-ShareAlike license.*

of the 1980 coup] both left and right supporters especially young ones who were interested in intellectual stuff and literature started to seek new ways. They were asking if they were able to find new ways other than established ideological subjects" (Arslan, interview).[5] Although Arslan mentions Ferlinghetti, his translation does not include him. In 2007, Cevat Çapan produced the first full volume entirely devoted to Ferlinghetti's poetry, and even the translator himself notes that his translation received little attention (Çapan, interview). Whereas Ginsberg and Ferlinghetti seem to bleed together in the previous translation, here Ferlinghetti is almost an afterthought. The rest of Arslan's biography demonstrates that he is more concerned with the Beats as a phenomenon and the new lifestyle issues that Ginsberg's work raises. After claiming, "He is a pioneer of the [Beat] generation along with Jack Kerouac and William Burroughs and its most famous member," Arslan relates that Ginsberg "tried narcotics" in order to "research the conditions of changed consciousness" (*Kuşbeyin!*, unpaginated). Marijuana is not stressed as a "political tool" as in Edgü and Duru's translation but has become a matter of consciousness-raising. Arslan concludes with a series of short descriptions involving personal matters: "Exalted sexuality. Believed in love. A Jew" (unpaginated).[6] This is not to say that Arslan does not see the political ramifications of a change in collective consciousness, but rather that the focus of his attention on Ginsberg has left much of the political behind to highlight the personal. As Arslan himself explains, "I tried to explain to a Turkish reader that you can be both political and you can choose a different lifestyle and you can concentrate on very unusual concepts and anxieties and you can be individualistic and political—they are not contradicting" (Arslan, interview).

The new emphasis on the personal is apparent in the two poems Arslan wrote to open the collection, "N'Olmuş Ya?" ("So What Happened?") and "Another Part: A Beatnik's Lament." Like Edgü, Arslan feels the need to chronicle his relationship to Ginsberg. But rather than Edgü's more formal history of his discovery of the Beats as a call for a new poetry, Arslan provides an enthusiast's response, addressing Ginsberg by his first name in a tone that is familial, localized, and filled with slang. Arslan writes in the first poem, "Hey, Allen, I prepared this book while I was almost crying and wailing / Hey, Allen, believe me geezer, you're hunky-dory, you wrote hard, I recall lots of things from the past" (*Kuşbeyin!* 9). The Edgü and Duru translation treat Ginsberg's work as almost exotic—a new form of poetry that needs to be explained and promoted. Arslan's form of personal address, however, brings the reader closer to the man himself.

The same holds true for the second section of "Another Part: A Beatnik's Lament," which is tellingly written in English and heavily influenced by Ginsberg's own style. Arslan begins,

> Allen, what dreams I have of you in the nineties
> for you don't know what a nice thing the Beat scene
> in '84
> in Ankara. (12)

Drawing on the language of Ginsberg's "A Supermarket in California" where the poet addresses Walt Whitman with "What thoughts I have of you tonight" and "America" where he extols the virtues of communism with the line "You have no idea what a good thing the party was in 1835," Arslan relocates the Beat 1950s of Ginsberg's celebrated early work to the mid-1980s of Turkey's capital (*Collected* 136, 147). The tone of playful and respectful mimicry continues throughout. Arslan is concerned mainly with chronicling his own subcultural lifestyle as he lived it in post-coup Ankara, celebrating the sort of Beat lifestyle Ginsberg represents and castigating those with

> fake hearts imitating a drop-out style which they never have,
> unrealized sensibilities, books that weren't read, dreams in which
> nobody believes, hidden desire for money & luxury & being safe
> & exciting experiences to dream or tell or spell or buy
> or lie- (*Kuşbeyin!* 13–14)

Writing from the early 1990s, Arslan can assume a bit more reader familiarity with the Beats and their message and, unlike Edgü, does not need to sell them to his readers. What emerges is the tribute not of a distant admirer but of a fan, devotee, or fellow traveler to a role model.

Arslan's closer familiarity with the Beats and their texts is evidenced in his translations. In Ginsberg's "the madman bum and angel beat in Time" line previously discussed, Arslan gets "closer" to the source with his rendition "madman bum and angel beat in Time" (*Zaman'daki çılgın serseri ve melek beat*; 32). Arslan, like Duru and Edgü, leaves "beat" untranslated here, but while the latter place the term in a series in order to provide context for its meaning, Arslan keeps "angel beat" together as in the source text. Ambiguity is lessened, however, since the phrase "in Time" (*Zaman'daki*) occurs at the beginning of the sentence and thus refers to all the elements in the series, and because "angel" (*melek*) functions as a noun here—to make it a descriptor of the word "beat" would require another formulation in Turkish such as "*melek gibi*" (colloquially "angelic" or "angelic-looking").

For Ginsberg, some combination of these figures is "beat in Time." Arslan, following close to the source text and including the English term "Beat" with all its myriad connotations, is taking a risk. Arslan could have used "*dövülmüş*" (to be [physically] beaten), but his choice to retain the reference to "Beat" speaks to his desire for a closer rendering of the source text, his familiarity with the source material, and his assumption that his readers will know just what he is talking about.

When discussing the three versions during interviews with Turkish writers, editors, and translators, and in a research group composed of five Turkish undergraduates who read all of the versions over the course of a summer, Arslan's was the standout choice for best translation. Comparing translations is a difficult task, of course, and such a decision is not really fair—all three offer their own merits. Arslan's *Howl* and "America," however, are able to deftly bring the openness and challenge of Ginsberg's works into Turkish while staying close to the meaning of the source text. This works in large part due to Arslan's willingness to use a colloquial language suitable to the familiar tone Ginsberg strikes in both poems. Employing words like "*be*" ("hey"), "*valla*" (a word that emphasizes not having lied, like "I swear to God"), and contracting verbs like "*veriyom*" in place of "*veriyorum*" ("I'm giving" instead of "I am giving"), Arslan captures the challenge to traditional notions of poetic language that Ginsberg's work posed and, to a certain extent, still poses.

The varying word choices of the translations are also heavily influenced by changing cultural contexts. The Duru and Edgü translation provides its readers with a Ginsberg that while not bowdlerized, is certainly less offensive and culturally challenging than later translators, resulting in a distance that lends the poem a more formal feeling. When translating Ginsberg's line "who howled on their knees in the subway and were dragged off the roof waving genitals and manuscripts" (*Collected* 128), Duru and Edgü use "manhood" (*erkeklikler*; 31), while Arslan employs "sexual organs" (*cinsel organlar*; 28). Female genitalia receive a similar treatment. Ginsberg's line "who sweetened the snatches of a million girls" (*Collected* 128) becomes "put honey on that place" (*oralarını ballayanlar*; 32) for Duru and Edgü, while Arslan uses the euphemism "honey pot" (*bal çanağı*; 28). As we will see, these differences are not that striking when compared with the profanity of the later Erdoğan translation, but they do demonstrate a steadily increasing leniency in the acceptance of slang and profanity. All three works passed the censor, but it is possible that standards have changed favorably (or unfavorably, depending on viewpoint) over the years, allowing for more provocatively worded translations that allow for both "closer" translations in some cases and retention of the shock value that Ginsberg's poem had for a 1950s U.S. audience.[7]

It is also important to realize that Arslan's version was produced when English had overtaken French as the foreign language of choice in Turkey. English has become the preferred second language for a younger generation of Turks, and while Arslan is a bit older, he was still caught up in this wave of global English that swept French aside. Arslan himself comments in our interview, "I literally plundered the American Library in Ankara." This institution, now unfortunately defunct, provided access to English originals. Duru, too, had more immediate knowledge of both English and the Beats through his sojourn in the United States. According to Arslan, Orhan Duru's wife, Sezer, once recalled, "Orhan Duru stayed in America for a year at the beginning of the sixties. He had been in many states along with New York and Los Angeles and was affected by them. Since he was a writer and a[n] open-minded person he discovered the Beat Generation over there and was influenced by their writings" (Arslan, interview). But Edgü was versed in the French tradition, as was most of his generation. As Çapan, Ferlinghetti's translator, recalls, "Turkish translators or Turkish intellectuals were more interested in French poetry before that. I think this interest in English and American poetry came rather late" (Çapan, interview). American studies were unheard of in 1960s Turkey, and only a handful of universities offered English literature. Foreign literature meant French works. Edgü himself describes the process of translating, stating, "During the winter of 1966–67, I used to stay at Orhan Duru's house in Ankara where I spent my weekends. At late hours, if we didn't have any guests, we would spread the new published French translations and original version of Beat Generation authors' books and tried to translate them into Turkish" (Edgü, "Amerika"). Journalist Demir Özlü recalls that during his interview of Ginsberg in Stockholm in January 1982, "I always asked in French and he always answered in English" (Özlü, interview). Arslan's knowledge of English allows him a closer intimacy with Ginsberg and his texts, lending his translation a more personal feel that many I interviewed considered better.

Despite, or perhaps because of, English's current dominance, Arslan favors an older Turkish style when translating. Personal preference plays an important role in any translation. Arslan is committed to the use of *Arı* or *Öz türkçe*—older, more "pure" Turkish words—and this penchant comes through in his translations. As he relates in our interview, "When I'm speaking Turkish I prefer pure Turkish way or '*Arı türkçe*.' I use it in my poems and in other literary stuff like essays, or theoretical works. I always use pure Turkish. It's one of my poetical visions, my poetical way, focusing on pure Turkish concepts" (Arslan, interview). In *Howl*, for example, Arslan translates the line "who were expelled from the academies for crazy & publishing obscene odes" (*Collected* 126) using "*koçaklamalar*" for "odes" (*Kuşbeyin!* 25). While not exactly incorrect, this choice refers to a specific type of ode prevalent in Old Turkish folk poetry performed by Turkish bards. For the Turkish reader, it would signal *Howl*'s connection with an older Turkish poetic variant that existed before the Turkish people encountered Islam in their steady migration across Central Asia. Duru and Edgü simply use "*şiirler*," or "poems," which, while perhaps basic, has the advantage (if one considers it so) of not introducing extra meanings into the translation (28). Erdoğan employs "*methiyeler*," or "panegyric," a form of petition to a patron called a *qasida* prevalent in Ottoman divan poetry but also employed by Sufis like Jalāl ad-Dīn Muhammad "Mevlana" ar-Rūmī for more mystical purposes (Erdoğan, *Uluma* 12). But Arslan does not see any contradiction in translating American countercultural texts in a "pure" Turkish style. On the contrary, they are complementary: "Beat language is a new language in terms of American literature. So is pure Turkish" (Arslan, interview). Arslan sees a connection between the stylistic innovations of the Beats and his own desire to write in a more Turkish style.

Translation necessarily involves personal choices, but those choices speak of desires firmly rooted in the political, social, and cultural moment of the translator's era. Cultural context does have a determining effect on the range of possibilities open to a translator. Arslan is heir to the sort of pre-1980-coup politics of Edgü and Duru, but he was also intimately involved in the sort of cultural exchange with the West that characterized post-1980-coup Turkey. His Ginsberg is thus an amalgamation of both political rebel and cultural guru. Here Ginsberg offers more than just a new means of writing politicized poetry—he likewise advocates a revolution of consciousness, capable of empowering each individual to explore their own desires and interests. In a sense, both translations capture the same elements of Ginsberg, but it's a matter of focus. For Arslan, the potentials Ginsberg offers for individual growth are the real attraction of the poet.

THE MYSTICAL HIPSTER

While previous translations of Ginsberg sought to introduce the poet to their audiences, by the time of Altıkırkbeş's 2013 translation, Ginsberg and his work, while certainly not known to everyone in Turkey, had been around for some forty years. The press plays on this fact, issuing the book in the City Lights Pocket Poets Series style, complete with a translation of the William Carlos Williams foreword and without any of the introductory front material that these previous translators relied on to acquaint readers with Ginsberg and his work (figure 5.4). The only other additions are a curious drawing that depicts Ginsberg with his beard made into a map of the United States (taken from a David Levine illustration in the *New York Review of Books* in 1970) and back advertisements for the first two titles in this 6:45 poetry series, Batuhan Dedde's *Morfinsiz Çekilen Düş Sancıları* (*Morphine Withdrawal Dream Pains*) and umay umay's *cevapsız ağrı* (*Answerless Pain*). The publishers thus fold Ginsberg seamlessly into the 6:45 program of "underground" writers presenting clandestine and highly personal revelations to their readers. In a special limited edition of the book, Ginsberg appears on the cover in the stencil style of a Banksy, further solidifying his outsider status and updating him for a new generation. The result is an interesting mix of the classic rebel and the contemporary renegade, sending

Fig. 5.4. Publisher 6:45 (Altıkırkbeş) presents its translation of Ginsberg in the iconic Pocket Poets series style made famous by City Lights Publishers. This classic cover invokes Ginsberg's cult status as both a leading member of the Beat Generation as well as an ageless hipster of the counterculture.

a message that Ginsberg is not only a countercultural forebear whom the reader should know but at the same time an extant, vital member of an ongoing cultural rebellion.

Erdoğan plays up Ginsberg's outsider status in the translation, drawing attention to the transgressive aspects of the poem. The translator tends to reduce the ambiguity in Ginsberg's *Howl,* making use of more direct and literal expressions that anchor Ginsberg in a world of outcasts, drug users, and illicit sexuality. Take, for example, the line "who wept at the romance of the streets with their pushcarts full of onions and bad music" (*Collected* 129). While the Duru / Edgü and Arslan translations are practically identical, Erdoğan changes "onions" into "rolling paper" (*sarma kâgıdı*) while "pushcarts" become "the cars of drug dealers" (*mal satıcılarının arabalarında*) to get "with rolling paper and bad music they cry for the romance of the streets in drug dealers' cars" (Erdoğan, *Uluma*, 20). The Erdoğan translation tends to create literal scenes out of lines that convey an abstract mood or experiential situation or feeling. The result is an emphasis on the lifestyle of the marginal, outcast, or illegal. The use of drugs is highlighted throughout the translation to heighten the transgressiveness of the text. Where Ginsberg writes "ashcan rantings" (126) Erdoğan adds "marijuana ash curse" (*esrar külünün laneti*; 13), and instead of "narcotic tobacco haze" (127) of the source text the translation reads "*ot tezgâhını*" or "joint-rolling preparations" (16). The same desire for a more transgressive text can be seen with regard to sexuality. When translating the previously discussed line "genitals and manuscripts" (128), Erdoğan opts for the even more provocative "dicks" (*sikler*; 17) instead of "genitals."[8] Erdoğan also takes Ginsberg's "returning years later truly bald except for a wig of blood, and tears and fingers" (130) and makes "finger" into a verb that, with the addition of a bracketed "(n)," makes it simultaneously "to finger" and "to be fingered" (*parmakla(n)mak*; 24). This is certainly a clever play on words, but it also carries with it a sexual connotation in Turkish that Duru and Edgü's and Arslan's simple plural noun "*parmaklar*" (fingers) do not convey (36; 31). These choices, which are not at all necessary for the translation, demonstrate Erdoğan's desire to highlight *Howl*'s transgressive aspects.

This equation of Ginsberg with a hip outsider status is displayed in other places as well. Given Erdoğan's publishing house's celebration of all things "underground," it is unsurprising that Erdoğan translates the "subways" (126) of Ginsberg's poem using the term "*yeraltı*" (13), though "metro" is the standard usage in Turkey and suffices for both Duru / Edgü and Arslan (29; 26). That Erdoğan has arrived later allows him to also use "hipsters" (11) in English where Duru and Edgü revert to "believers" (*inançlılar*; 28) and Arslan to "queers" (*götlekler*; 25). While a more knowing public makes such slang terms easier for Erdoğan, it also introduces instability as well—it is doubtful that even Erdoğan could have predicted the arrival of skinny pants and facial hair that have added to the term's meaning. Nevertheless, like any translator, Erdoğan uses Ginsberg for his own purposes. With 6:45 presenting itself as a major player in the Turkish underground, Erdoğan's translation capitalizes on Ginsberg's star power by highlighting its countercultural credentials.

But Erdoğan also provides a more spiritual Ginsberg that is lacking in the other translations. To return to the "madman bum and angel beat in Time" line, Erdoğan renders it as "mad bum in Time, and sanctified angel, unknown" (*Zaman'daki kaçık serseri, ve kutsanmış melek, bilinmeyen*; 26). Erdoğan's use of the comma after "Time" makes it clear that these are two separate individuals, though whether they are both "in Time" is ambiguous in the Turkish. What is important, however, is that Erdoğan chose to translate "beat" into "*kutsanmış*," an adjective derived from the passive form of the verb "*kutsamak*" that means "to sanctify, to bless, to consecrate." Erdoğan could have left "beat" untranslated, or used "*dövüşmüş*" to convey the sense of "beaten" by life or "downtrodden," but instead chose the more spiritual meaning championed by Jack Kerouac when he equated "beat" with "beatific." Can Kantarcı, the translator of Kerouac's *On the Road*, used "*bitik*" as his choice for "beat." Literally "finished," this term is even more negative than "*kaybeden*" (loser). To be "*bitik*" is to be literally at the end, finished, done for, and in Turkish would have absolutely no redeeming possibilities or hope for a future. Erdoğan's decision to translate Beat as "sanctified" speaks to his desire to promote a more spiritualized Ginsberg. This message of a spiritual Ginsberg is reinforced by the limited edition's back cover, where a spiral is formed from repetitions of the word *Holy* (figure 5.5). These words, left in English, derive from Ginsberg's "Footnote to Howl" where he declares everything "Holy": "Everything is holy! everybody's holy! everywhere is holy! everyday is in eternity! Everyman's an angel!" (*Collected* 134). Duru and Edgü do not even include this poem in their collection, and though it appears in Arslan's volume, Erdoğan's decision to reprint the word *Holy* on the back cover demonstrates his commitment to a more mystical Ginsberg that is lacking in the other translations.

This mystical reading of Ginsberg is given added force in a filmed reading of Erdoğan's translation of *Howl* produced by 6:45 in 2008. Directed by Mehmet Ada Öztekin and starring Erdoğan and 6:45 owner Kaan Çaydamlı, the film presents Erdoğan's public reading of the translation in 6:45's bar in the university town of Eskişehir. The film begins with shots

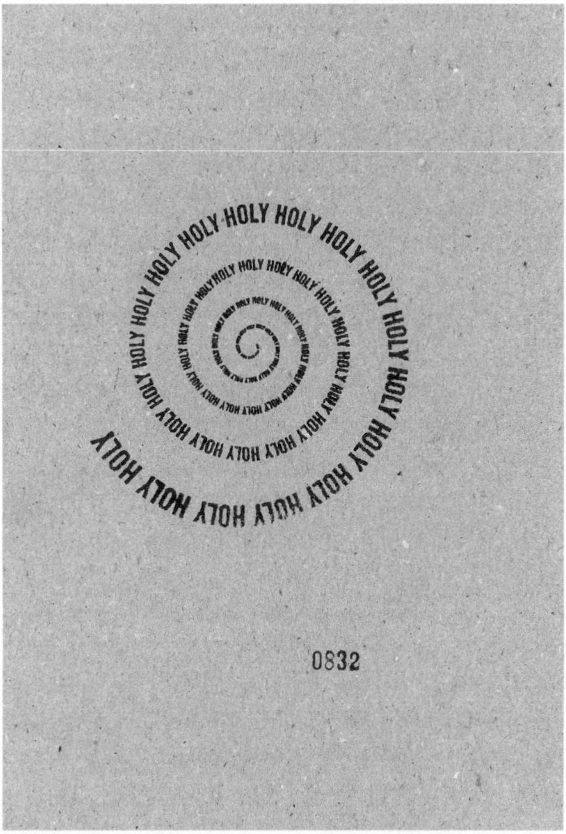

Fig. 5.5. The spiritual nature of Ginsberg's work highlighted in the 6:45 translation of *Howl* is reinforced by the seemingly endless spiraling of the word *Holy* found on the limited edition's back cover

taken from the Bosporus, the strait that divides the European from the Asian side of Istanbul, as a reed flute plays in the background. A voice then begins to recite the first eighteen lines of Jalāl ad-Dīn Mevlana ar-Rūmī's classic *Mesnevi* (composed 1258–73), a "masterwork of poetic narration and Sufi wisdom" according to Turkish literary critic Talat Halman (35). This well-known "Song of the Reed" is a metaphor for Sufi longing for union with God, "reed" being understood as both the plant cut from its surroundings and the *ney* or flute that it creates. The film then cuts to an interview with Çaydamlı and, later, another one with Erdoğan conducted "on the road" to the reading. This series of scenes provide an introduction to the reading, setting the mood of the film and offering a framework for understanding Ginsberg and other Beats discussed in the film like Jack Kerouac, Neal Cassady, and William S. Burroughs.

The recitation of Mevlana and the playing of the reed flute during the opening scenes place *Howl*, both film and poem, in a religious context. Mevlana is perhaps the best-known Sufi poet, and his lines would certainly be immediately recognizable to a Turkish audience. The *ney*, or reed flute, is known generally in the Middle East but was the instrument of choice in Sufi lodges. While Ginsberg was almost certainly aware of the Sufi tradition, he looked farther east to Buddhism for his spiritual guidance. Nevertheless, Sufi mysticism, with its insistence on a more personal relationship between the disciple and their God, is certainly in keeping with the sort of Gnosticism that Ginsberg, Kerouac, and many other Beat and countercultural figures embraced, and there is indeed a strong gnostic element in Islamic mysticism. In his interview during the film, Çaydamlı goes on to make this connection explicit, explaining to the viewer that "the primary intention that drove [the Beats] here was their appeal to Eastern philosophy, to immanence and this I think can be traced in many works" (*Uluma*). As we have seen, this is not entirely accurate—although Istanbul was a stop on the overland trail to India, only Ginsberg and his lover Peter Orlovsky (separately) made it to the country. Nevertheless, Çaydamlı's point is well taken. There is a connection between Eastern philosophy, broadly defined to include Sufism, and the sort of mystical self-exploration that Beat writers like Ginsberg championed.

The Sufi use of the reed flute also aligns these mystics with the sort of breath rhythms that helped define both Beat writing and the jazz music that inspired it. As Çaydamlı nicely comments, "The point that jazz will eventually reach is the sound of the ney. Thus what these people seek out is the sound of the ney" (*Uluma*).[9] Inspiration, with its double meaning of breath and spirituality, links the ney to the jazz tradition so celebrated by the Beats for its spontaneity and heightened states of ecstasy. Sufi dervishes, with their transcendent style of whirling dance and use of music, are clear forebears of the Beat desire for spiritual transcendence, even if the Beats seldom (if ever) referenced them directly in their work.

Equating Ginsberg's *Howl* with the Sufi mystical tradition helps the Turkish reader understand the sort of spirituality that Ginsberg and many of his fellow Beats promulgated. Like the venerated master Mevlana ar-Rūmī, Ginsberg is offering a new conception of religiosity that does away with dogmatic conservatism. If everything is "holy," then we are already living in Heaven—we just need to open our eyes and see God's immanence around (and within) us. To achieve such visionary experience, Sufism embraced alternative practices that fell outside clerical prescription, and became open to the sort of "derangement of the senses" that the Beats practiced. While "drunkenness" in Mevlana's poetry is a metaphor for euphoric union with

God, the use of wine and hashish was a part of some Sufi traditions.[10] The link between Sufism and *Howl* allows Turkish readers to make the Beats their own by placing them within a religious tradition that emanated from Anatolia and is very much still venerated in Turkey.

This recourse to Sufism also carries with it a political dimension. The promotion of a more open, gnostic practice by 6:45 could be seen as a challenge to what many believe to be a growing insistence on more rigid interpretations of religion encroaching on daily Turkish life. Invoking Sufi mysticism thus allows Erdoğan to supplant a growing Islamicization occurring in President Recep Tayyip Erdoğan's Turkey with a type of spirituality more personal and inclusive. This antiauthoritarian attitude meant that Sufism had to endure persecution. Although some lodges were state-supported, Mevlevi Sufism was banned by Mustafa Kemal and the Alevi tradition likewise suffered repression. Mustafa Kemal's program of modernization attempted to weaken the grip religion had on the Ottoman Empire, and Erdoğan's AK Party regime has done little to support a tradition that does away with the support of the clergy or the state in its adepts' struggles for a personal union with God. The Mevlevis exist today mainly as a tourist attraction for foreigners wishing to see these "whirling dervishes." By invoking an older model of religious "extremism" that was formed in Turkey some eight hundred years ago, Erdoğan is attempting to call the AK Party and their conservative religious politics to task by recuperating a former Islamic practice that still strikes a chord with many Turkish citizens even today. Beats such as Ginsberg, just like their Sufi forebears, offer a new way of being spiritual that avoids the narrow-minded prejudices of institutionalized religion.

INSPIRING THE NEXT GENERATION—KÜÇÜK ISKENDER

Ginsberg's influence occurs not just through the various translations of his work but also in the power of his charismatic persona to affect those living both inside and outside U.S. borders. In the early postwar years, Ginsberg was an important voice in the international counterculture, and was instantly recognizable in underground circles throughout the world. While this early fame has abated, Ginsberg remains an important figure for a wide variety of people engaged in countercultural struggles. In Turkey, Ginsberg's influence can clearly be seen in the life and work of perhaps the most famous underground poet alive today: küçük iskender. This provocative poet is openly gay, flaunts his use of alcohol and drugs, is proud of his use of profanity and slang, and is also outspoken about the influence of

Ginsberg and other Beat writers on his work. Küçük iskender demonstrates the fascination Ginsberg continues to hold for younger poets looking for a model of freedom in their lives and in their work.

Küçük iskender has always been something of a rebel. Born Devran İskender Över in 1964, he left Istanbul University's Cerrahpaşa Medical School in his senior year to study sociology, only to quit the university for good in his third year. Both times he explained his actions with the statement, "I've learned what I needed for my poems" (Doğa). Över published his first article in 1985 in *Adam Dergisi* under the pen name küçük iskender, and since then has gone on to become Turkey's best-known, and most controversial, underground poet (Avcı). This rebellious streak is present even in his name. As the poet himself has explained, "küçük iskender" has three meanings. The first references the son of Alexander the Great, or "little Alexander," and demonstrates the scope of the poet's aspirations. "küçük," as "little," was also used to designate the pupils in traditional Turkish art, and thus shows küçük iskender's willingness to learn from his elders. The final meaning is Turkish slang referring to the penis, the "little Alexander," or little conqueror ("Küçük Iskender" 14). It is this last reference that is particularly shocking in Turkish society, and given the poet's willingness to write in the confessional mode about his homosexuality, makes küçük iskender a highly controversial figure in Turkey.

Unsurprisingly, the Turkish media has taken sides in the debate over küçük iskender's work and his appropriateness for Turkey. The controversy surrounding his reading at the 2008 Frankfurt Book Fair provides an example of the sort of response his actions and his work receive. Hüseyin Kulaoğlu, writing in the right-wing newspaper *Vakit*, expresses outrage that someone like küçük iskender would be invited by the Ministry of Culture to read at Turkish Poetry Night. His article "İşte Küçük iskender bu!" ("This Is küçük iskender!") seeks to expose the poet for the socially unacceptable nature of his work:

> We have found the books of gay-Kemalist Küçük İskender who had been prominent during that meeting. In poetry circles, he is known as "the master of suicides that do not result in death" . . . It has been established that in his books, he makes statements that encourage obscenity, homosexuality, and drug use; that his books titled *Flu'es* and *Methods for Going to Hell* (*Cehenneme gitme yöntemleri*) are full of obscenity and curses with "sinkaf." The book titled *Methods for Going to Hell* is notable in that it encourages drug use and contains pornographic elements.

Kulaoğlu is voicing a common condemnation of küçük iskender's work. The poet is attacked for both his life and his art, for being a homosexual drug user who then writes about his personal experience. Kulaoğlu is unwilling to even mention the sort of words iskender employs, instead using the two Arabic letters "sin" and "kaf" to designate "sexual intercourse," an abbreviation used in official documents and court proceedings to emphasize that a curse includes sexual content.[11] Although the titles mentioned in the article are indicative of the type of provocative language küçük iskender uses, they are chosen for their transgressive nature—"Master of Suicides" and "Methods for Going to Hell" are certainly not going to play well with those on the religious right. Nor is küçük iskender's Kemalism, which is equated with his homosexuality ("*gay-Kemalist*") in order to doubly discredit the poet in the eyes of *Vakit*'s readership. Kulaoğlu's critique reveals a litany of complaints that are generally heard when the poet's works are attacked.

Küçük iskender, however, is not a universally maligned poet. He also has a large fan base and a myriad of supporters who view his work as a necessary intervention into the social anxieties that plague Turkey. The left-wing *Radikal*, for instance, came to küçük iskender's defense. In the anonymous book review of *Ölü Evinde Seks Partisi* (*Sex Party in the House of the Dead*), the author responds,

> İskender is the first poet who takes the humiliated and marginalized underground culture of the city and the emotional conflicts experienced in that cultural milieu and makes them essential for his poetry. The various aspects of his homosexual lifestyle are featured in his work. For the first time, an urban discourse that included jargon and obscenity became part of poetry. ("Çoğalmayıp Yetkinleşen Şiir")

Radikal defends küçük iskender on two grounds. Against the charge of obscenity, the author argues that iskender's work (much like that of his Beat mentors) is actually reflecting underground life in the cities, and thus should be celebrated for its willingness to engage the issues and problems of a social sphere excluded from public discourse. Perhaps more tentatively, *Radikal* insinuates that as part of his life and personal choice, the issue of homosexuality is necessary to iskender's work. Given the Turkish anxiety with homosexuality that we have seen evidenced throughout this study, the author appears reticent about celebrating this aspect of iskender's work. Nevertheless, küçük iskender and his work are seen as raising important literary and social issues in Turkish society, and are thus championed as a breath of fresh air in an otherwise stultifying climate of repression.

Given the issues that küçük iskender raises, Ginsberg is an obvious choice as a mentor figure for the poet. While Ginsberg and the Beats are certainly not the only influence on küçük iskender, they are certainly the most prominent, as the poet himself willingly announces. In a *Lacivert* interview in 2010, küçük iskender replies to the question of Tümay Çobanoğlu, "Which writer from the Beat Generation did you first read and were impressed by?" with the response,

> Allen Ginsberg. He is an incredible poet. . . . I had a little New York trip. During that trip I had a chance to see both Allen's and Kerouac's houses, hanging around the same streets that they walked on. . . . Beat might be the only movement from abroad I envy. Not that I wanted to be part of it, because I belong to this land. But I'd like to have a movement here in Turkey too which is similar to the Beat Generation.[12] ("Küçük Iskender" 14)

In another article by the poet himself titled "The Strained Comraderie of the Bad with the Good" in the journal *Sabitfikir*, küçük iskender goes on to explain the reasons for his fascination with Ginsberg. According to the poet, Ginsberg "did not neglect to become one of the most aggressive speakers of Beat Generation inside the Buddhism / Communism / Jewish triangle. By adding the strata of sexual freedom, freedom of identity, and the freedom of drugs, he created the most radical language of the independence of the individual" ("'Televizyon okuyan'"). Küçük iskender's love of Ginsberg stems from his mentor's openness toward homosexuality and his willingness to explore and announce in his poetry all facets of his life, including his use of drugs. The poet is also impressed by Ginsberg's creation of an "independent language" to convey his experience. Küçük iskender is still very much a Turkish poet, but his debt to Ginsberg and the Beats is openly acknowledged.

Ginsberg's influence is undeniably present in küçük iskender's poetry. For Turkish underground writing, the Beats' social transgressions are usually more important than their stylistic contributions. But küçük iskender is an exception. The clearest example of this occurs in his 1994 poem "Türkiye" ("Turkey"). The poem references Ginsberg's "America" in both line and theme. İskender begins the poem, "When I have time from boys and alcohol, I think about you, Turkey" (*Periler Ölürken* 189). Like Ginsberg, iskender personifies his native land in order to critique it. "Türkiye" goes on to admonish the country, calling it to task for its various problems in a sarcastic and ironic manner. Ginsberg does the very same in "America," asking his homeland, "America when will you be angelic? / When will you take off your clothes? / When will you look at yourself through the grave?"

(*Collected* 146). İskender translates this into the Turkish context with the query "Turkey, I'm sorry to ask but when will we snap out of it; when will we let go of Cyprus, Turkey, and when will we be worthy of the thousands of our revolutionary martyrs" (*Periler Ölürken* 192). The Cyprus question mirrors U.S. imperial designs, and like Ginsberg, küçük iskender calls attention to the "revolutionary" martyrs that typically go unrecorded in a nation's celebration of accepted heroes. "America" works so well because it uses humor to avoid becoming a simple didactic complaint. Instead, the poem forces its readers to see the ridiculousness of the "official" version of America. By drawing on a similar style, iskender's "Türkiye" updates that critique for a Turkish society.[13]

Küçük iskender draws not only on Ginsberg's unique style in "Türkiye" but on his content as well, updating typical Ginsbergian concerns like homophobia and the use of drugs for his contemporary Turkish audience. These issues, along with iskender's use of profanity and slang, are a leitmotif in his work, and come together in one of the longer lines of his poem that outlines his vision of a new Turkey:

> I want sex-shops, a communist party, a Muslim democrat party, a rock party, all sorts of gay bars to be opened; the abolishing of the mandatory military service Turkey, I wanna see Nobels, Oscars, LSD, freedom and cock monuments in this land, I'm returning my share from per capita income so that you can spend it on the changes that I want; evacuate jails, zoos, camps, asylums immediately; I wanna be a traveler who travels around your cities with peace, grace, human rights and great joy. (*Periler Ölürken* 194)

It is important to realize the force that these lines have in Turkey. While planning a questionnaire for our study, we had originally hoped to provide this quote to respondents. When we presented it to those responsible for hiring the interviewers, they immediately refused to include it. When asked why, they explained that there was a real concern for the safety of the staff that would be conducting the interviews. We redacted the quote by cutting references to drugs and "cock monuments" (*sik anıtları*), and withdrew other passages that touched on the sensitive concerns of homosexuality, nationalist issues such as military service, and quotes such as iskender's that employed profanity. This quote is indeed highly inflammatory. Iskender's reference to "gay bars" (*gay barlar*) and "cock monuments" are perhaps the most eye-catching (194). Homosexuality in Turkey, as we have seen, is tolerated if it remains hidden, but İskender's strategy in the poem (and in his other works as well) is to call attention to and even celebrate a gay subculture that is just now finding its voice in Turkey. The poet hopes to travel the country in "peace, grace, human rights, and great joy," but that would require Turkey to openly acknowledge and accept the sort of lifestyle that iskender is promulgating.

Homosexuality meets resistance in Turkey. In our study, this passage was judged less positively in most categories than the rest of the passages. For instance, when asked to respond to the statement that the passage "contained literary value," the response "entirely disagree" hovered at or below 10 percent for all the other passages, while for iskender it was 28.4 percent (Mortenson, Ergun, and Erdoğan 94). The same was true for the statement that the passage was "obscene." İskender's passage garnered double the rate of the other texts. Overall, nonreaders were still basically positive about iskender's passage, yet the fact that they were less positive about it than they were about the other passages is telling. It is difficult to know the exact reason for these results. Iskender's passage also includes reference to several political parties and makes disparaging remarks about the army, which could account for such a response. The title of the poem is, after all, "Türkiye" ("Turkey"), and might have raised the ire of Turkish respondents who normally would have not found anything disagreeable with the text. Yet the second-least-favorable passage was from Allen Ginsberg's poem *Uluma* (*Howl*), which also contained homosexual references (15.4 percent agreeing that it is "obscene," versus the other passages at 6.2 percent [Hakan Günday], 8.8 percent [Jack Kerouac], 9.5 percent [Kanat Güner], 10.8 percent [both William S. Burroughs and Süreyya Evren], and 9.5 percent [Chuck Palahniuk]; 95). Thus it seems fair to conclude that while nonreaders were overall very positive concerning the underground literary texts they were offered, homosexuality still remains the one issue raised by the genre that finds a more difficult reception.

Küçük iskender is also asking Turkey for the freedom of its citizens to explore the use of drugs like LSD. While drug policy in the United States has been liberalizing, in Turkey the situation is quite the opposite. Despite hashish and opium having been sold legally in the Ottoman Empire, films like *Midnight Express* (1978) that paint the country as awash in controlled substances, and references by Burroughs to widespread heroin use in Istanbul, the fact is that even alcohol is coming under stricter bans from Recep Tayyip Erdoğan's AK Party. İskender openly admits to the use of alcohol and drugs, and even advocates for their consumption. Though he is quick to claim that he is not an addict, it is clear he believes in the benefit of such substances, telling Özcan Erdoğan in a 2008 interview in the journal *Bireylikler*, "For the academic research of poetry, drugs should be in every poet's laboratory" (Ö. Erdoğan). This aligns iskender with Ginsberg, who advocated the use of drugs for consciousness expansion, and even took to the streets with a sandwich board to question the U.S. government's criminalization of marijuana. Drug legalization was a cornerstone of Ginsberg's antiestablishment message, and even into later years the poet remained concerned with drug policy and wrote several prose pieces discussing both his personal use of drugs as well as U.S. drug policy and its international effects.[14] With the legalization of marijuana in many states it appears as though Ginsberg's fight has paid off, but küçük iskender is facing the sort of virulent antidrug and even antialcohol rhetoric in Turkey today that characterized the early postwar period in the United States.

İskender also champions a permissiveness of language that runs counter to the sort of "polite" discourse expected in Turkish poetry. This desire to infuse his work with the language culled from the margins places his writing squarely in the Beat mode. Speaking with Özcan Erdoğan, iskender explains, "Though I used dead words, I also included the words of this century into the literature. I added the experiences of vernacular, pornography, metropolitanism, technology, jargon, subjacent, medicine, contemporary folk who are at the Tigris and Euphrates, different sexual identities. . . . I am the first user of many of these words in Turkish poetry" (Ö. Erdoğan). İskender clearly sees himself as a maverick, saying the unsayable things in Turkish culture. Ginsberg, too, faced the same sort of challenges when discussing taboo subjects in a language drawn from the various subcultures chronicled in a poem like *Howl.* Both poets believe that to truly record their experiences in the underground culture, they need to employ the language spoken there. While this strategy brings küçük iskender closer to the sort of poetry Ginsberg espoused, it also distances him from many Turkish readers who feel such topics and language have no place in poetry, or even in public discussion. But in the end, like his mentor, küçük iskender is able to force these topics into the open, thus creating an opportunity for normally muted issues in Turkish public discourse to be broached.

GINSBERG IN ISTANBUL

Despite the Turkish interest in Ginsberg and his work from the late 1960s onward, it was not until June 1990 that the poet finally made it to Turkey for a visit. For the counterculture, India was a site of spiritual pilgrimage, and there were two ways to get there—by sea through the Suez Canal, and overland through Turkey, Afghanistan, and Pakistan. Ginsberg took the former. Although he had traveled extensively throughout the Middle East before his celebrated trip to India, Ginsberg had never made it to Turkey. According to Burak Fidan in his article "Ginsberg'in Istanbul Günleri" ("The Istanbul Nights of Ginsberg"), before he came to Turkey, Ginsberg claimed there were three countries left that he really wanted to see: "Iceland, South Korea, and Turkey" (49). Meeting his Turkish translators in the summer of 1990 was a chance to rectify that situation. Traveling with composer Philip Glass, Ginsberg visited Istanbul and made a short trip down to the coast to see Efes, Didim, and Bodrum, before journeying to the capital at Ankara. As with his other trips, Ginsberg was interested in more than seeing the sights; he also wanted to connect with the culture and the people of the countries he visited. Although everyone involved had fond memories of the occasion, it is clear that this attempt at mutual understanding also posed difficulties. Ginsberg's expectations for the meeting were different from those of his guests, and while the visit was far from a disappointment for either party, it does demonstrate the difficulties in cross-cultural communication. The irony of Ginsberg's visit was that while his image and work were becoming widely disseminated, the real-life Ginsberg was not exactly the Ginsberg Turkish readers had built up in their minds.

The Turkish writers and intellectuals who met with Ginsberg saw the meeting as a chance to finally connect with an important poet who had made an impact on their lives. As we have seen, Ginsberg was a significant influence on an earlier generation of leftist writers who saw him as part of the countercultural pantheon. The stakes were high. As küçük iskender, who was not there, laments, "Here is one of my biggest regrets in life: Allen came to Istanbul, I didn't know Can Baba [Can Yücel] at that time either. They drank rakı together at Kumkapı, I'd really like to sit with them and drink rakı together. If I had a picture, I'd even frame it and hang it on my wall. Being at that table would have been a great honor for me" ("Küçük Iskender" 21). Meeting Ginsberg was considered a great honor for many there that night, and provided a chance to discuss Ginsberg's work with the poet himself. Turkish writers were also interested in Ginsberg's opinions on Turkish poetry. Duru, Özdemir, Can Yücel, and Melih Cevdat Anday thus eagerly awaited a chance to talk poetry with one of the world's best-known poets.

Ginsberg seemed eager to address Turkish poetry as well. According to Sezer Duru in her article "Allen Ginsberg'le Anılar" ("Memories with Allen Ginsberg"), he had brought copies of Melih Cevdet Anday's work (translated by Talat Halman) and wanted to meet the Turkish poet and get a signature. Ginsberg was also aware of the work of Orhan Veli Kanık. Burak Fidan relates that Ginsberg "pulled out an English translation of Orhan Veli from his pocket and asserted that Veli's poetry was a relative of the type created by

Jack Kerouac," claiming that Veli's style is much in keeping with Kerouac's work (Fidan 49). Ginsberg's interest in Veli and Anday makes sense, as both were part of what came to be called the "Garip" (Strange) movement that occurred in Turkish poetry in the 1940s and 1950s. Although the Beats seem to have been unaware of a movement contemporaneous with their own, Ginsberg appeared excited by the discovery of it and wanted to connect with its writers.[15]

Ginsberg had made it a habit of familiarizing himself with the poets and writers of the regions he visited, but he was also interested in talking politics as well as poetics. Ginsberg was particularly keen on the issues of drug legalization and human rights violations. One of the more comical cultural mistranslations of the visit was that despite Ginsberg's promotion of marijuana over the evils of alcohol consumption, the Turkish writers took him to a *meyhane*, a traditional restaurant or bar, in the Kumkapı district of Istanbul. *Rakı*, the famous anise spirit of Turkey, flowed freely during the courses of little plates of *meze*, or appetizers, and despite his belief in abstinence, Ginsberg gave in to the moment and became inebriated with his Turkish guests. The party was large, roughly twenty-five people, and included Anday; Can Yücel and his wife, Güler; Ülker and Özdemir İnce; Glass; and others. In the published version of Duru's interview with Ginsberg in June 1990, Ginsberg speaks repeatedly about the benefits of marijuana and the problems of other drugs, both legal and illegal, at length. He even tries to broach the subject of whether Orhan Veli smoked pot, but Duru chose not to answer that particular question (Duru, "Gezegen antika" 56).

Ginsberg was also interested in the question of human rights. According to the writer and translator Güven Turan, while Glass was fascinated by the gypsy music performed on the street, Ginsberg was more interested in authors' freedom of expression and writers in prison ("Allen Ginsberg" 46). This topic was of particular relevance to Turkey, whose visibility on the international scene had prompted increased scrutiny of the country's human rights record. According to Turan, Ginsberg was aware of what had been going on in Turkey since the 1970s (Turan, interview). Ginsberg was not the first American writer to explore Turkey's human rights abuses. In 1985 Harold Pinter and Arthur Miller visited jailed writers and politicians there. They stayed a week and also met with Orhan Pamuk; inspired by the trip, Pinter wrote his famous play *Mountain Language* (1988). According to Sezer Duru in her article "Memories with Ginsberg," Ginsberg asked specifically about the case of Ismail Beşikçi, a Turkish scholar who spent seventeen years in prison for his Marxist work on Kurdish society. Ginsberg's hosts were of course familiar with such issues and certainly sided with the opinions of their guest, but were probably far more inured to the violation of human rights and were, in any case, much more interested in hearing Ginsberg's thoughts on poetry.

Nevertheless, the evening was enjoyed by everyone, and even included the production of poetry that sought to capture the tensions inherent in the evening's cross-cultural exchange. Collaborating with the Turkish poet Can Yücel, Ginsberg spontaneously created a poem:

> Mirrors are not people
> People are mirrors
> both at once, at the same time
> Whether in the Lower East Side Manhattan
> or on Kumkapı on the Bosphorus city—
> everybody is a liar everybody tells the truth
> even drunk mouths at the Yeni Rakı table ("Bir Kumkapı Gecesi," 23)

Ginsberg's short poem seeks to bridge the cultural gap. Though appearances seem to suggest difference, deep down everyone is really the same, no matter where they are. "People are mirrors," because those looking into them see parts of themselves reflected there, either as the "liars" they sometimes are or the "truth" tellers that they strive to become. Thus difference ends up being similar, regardless of whether it is in "Manhattan" or "the Bosphorous City." Ginsberg's spontaneous poem thus "mirrors" the argument made here—cultural translation works because everyone can find part of themselves in someone else.

Yücel, a member of the "İkinci Yeni" or "Second New" group of Turkish poets interested in poetic innovation, picks up on Ginsberg's theme in his own spontaneous response, titled "Uygunsuzerler" ("Misfits," purposely, perhaps, misspelled in the Turkish). Although the title suggests a breakdown in communication, Yücel's poem is equally concerned with questions of comprehensibility:

> You should not resemble people
> They already resemble each other
> You should not water the flowers
> If it looks too much like a flower
> There is a saying in Turkish:
> There can be no errors in simile!
> It's burnt!
> You shouldn't liken each other

You should beat them!
Only one statement is valid!
PREGNANT is LIKE
AND LIKE is PREGNANT
You won't even use that! ("Bir Kumkapı Gecesi," 23)

The question of communication across cultures was clearly on everyone's mind that evening, and both poems seek to "mirror" the tensions and possibilities of cultural exchange.

One could read this encounter as a misunderstanding. From a Western perspective, the Turkish hosts did not "get" Ginsberg. But it would be just as accurate to say that Ginsberg did not "get" what his hosts wanted from the encounter either. Thus Ginsberg's visit to Turkey encapsulates the stakes of cultural translation—each side presents its own biases, interests, and concerns. Ginsberg was interested in Turkish poetry, at least in a certain kind of Turkish poetry that he had gleaned from his readings, but he wanted to talk about politics. Turkish writers wanted a certain Ginsberg that they had formulated in their minds, and to hear his thoughts on their authors. Despite Ginsberg's careful promotion of his image, gaps and slippages are bound to occur, especially when traveling outside U.S. borders. In the end, however, both found something new. Ginsberg arrived more interested in the poet Melih Cevdet Anday but ended up collaborating on a poem with Can Yücel. Turkish writers wanted more discussion of poetry but were provided with an outsider's view of their country's politics. The benefit of cultural translation is that it shifts expectations and assumptions, and in the process reveals something new. It would be simple, and incorrect, to talk about a right and a wrong way of cultural appropriation. As with its textual cousin, cultural translation is not about finding the "best" or the most "true" rendering of a source text. All translations have their own merits and their own purposes.

CONCLUSION

After a Bob Dylan show in 1965, Ginsberg took the poet Michael McClure, the Hell's Angel's leader Sonny Barger, and other members of the motorcycle gang backstage to meet the singer. To everyone's surprise, Dylan began to berate the Hell's Angels for not expressing themselves better and not having thought through their message clearly. This was a pivotal moment for Ginsberg's understanding of the role image plays in shaping public opinion. As Ginsberg explained years later in his 1977 prose piece "Coming to Terms with the Hell's Angels," the members of the motorcycle club

> realized that they had nothing to say, or else if they did, they hadn't found the right theater. And we'd had the same realization: our march had to get its theater together, just as the police and the government did. I think that was the beginning of our realization that national politics was theater on a vast scale, with scripts, timing, sound systems. Whose theater would attract the most customers, whose was a theater of ideas that could be gotten across? (*Deliberate Prose* 17–18)

The message itself was not enough; it had to be presented in such a way that the audience would not just understand but respond enthusiastically. Ginsberg learned his lesson and deployed it in subsequent marches, protests, and demonstrations that he was involved in throughout the rest of his life.

Ginsberg was acutely aware of the power of image, using such knowledge to his advantage when promoting himself, his friends, and his various causes. While Ginsberg's poetic work has rightfully earned its place in the pantheon of world literature, this mutability of personae also helps to account for his lasting power. The world is awash in images of Ginsberg available for consumption and reappropriation—young aspiring Beat poet exploring a postwar New York, naked activist seeking rapport and mutual understanding, suit-and-tie-wearing Brooklyn College professor, "ohm"-chanting Buddhist, bearded hippy with his "Pot Is a Reality Kick" sandwich board, and wise old mystic guru, to name a few instantiations. Depending on age, issue, and disposition, we can choose the Ginsberg that makes the most sense to us. As Arslan remarked in my interview of him, "Everybody finds something different in Ginsberg that resonates with himself and translates that part" (Arslan, interview). There is a Ginsberg for everybody.

Despite this wide range of Ginsberg personae to choose from, the man, his image, and his texts must still be translated. The issue of translation has seldom been discussed in Beat scholarship, but it might be time to consider what happens when provocative works such as *Howl* are carried over into another language and culture. While nobody would argue for a translation that strives to appease the censor or public taste, the act of placing a text into a new language also offers opportunities. We have come to see bowdlerization as naïve and negative, but sometimes a judicious backing away from highly inflammatory words might, while losing fidelity to the original, gain accessibility in the process. Take the issue of Beat misogynism. Edgü and Duru's translation in some ways denudes the sting of the original. But it also makes the text more widely acceptable, especially for female readers who might bristle at the word *snatch*.[16] This might seem a minor point, but it does raise questions as to what to do with Beat gender and racial "problems" as new translations emerge—should a translator keep misogyny or correct it? While one could argue that Duru and Edgü are being politically correct, the reality is that they were probably more concerned with the censor or the public (or both) than with challenging Turkish gender inequalities. But their translation inadvertently raises a larger issue. If translations are always interested anyway, should they go ahead and bring the Beat social critique more in line with prevailing gender, race, and other social practices, or should the faults of Beat works remain for all to see? An analysis of the Beats in translation offers food for thought.

An emphasis on transnational reception challenges the sacrosanct notion of the poet as personal figure that often colors the reception of the Beats in the West, particularly in the United States. With their insistence on chronicling the details of their lives and experiences, the Beats are often ripe for emulation. Being "Beat" has often come to entail living a lifestyle similar to those of the Beats. Witness all of the books that seek to retrace Kerouac's *On the Road* journey. But the irony of this fascination with the lives, experiences, places, and drugs of the Beats obscures their fundamental point—they were on a quest for personal understanding and consciousness expansion. Though they too emulated certain romanticized figures (Rimbaud comes immediately to mind), ultimately theirs was an idiosyncratic search for wisdom and understanding relevant for their own lives as they intersected with the Cold War world. While the cult of personality that surrounds the Beats makes sense given their insistence on personal experience and its expression, ultimately the entire point of their lives and writings was not to provide heroic images that others could repeat but to admonish and entice others to seek their own path outside the confining narratives offered by American culture. The reception of the Beats outside the West, while containing some elements of this hero worship, for the most part seeks to utilize and transform the Beats based on cultural specificities of the moment, rather than emulation.

Tracing the transnational reception of Allen Ginsberg demonstrates the importance of local conditions, cultural expectations, and the needs of the particular cultural moment as factors in the making of a text's "meaning." Ginsberg's U.S. reception is likewise multifaceted, but the proximity to Ginsberg and his legacy in the United States sometimes obscures the myriad ways in which his work can be utilized. Ginsberg's Turkish reception demonstrates the poet's own success at crafting a variety of useful images. By offering such a broad range of possibilities, Ginsberg has made himself useful for several generations of Turkish writers, intellectuals, and activists. What that malleability demonstrates, however, is that one never knows how one's image will be used. That was probably not a problem for Ginsberg—one assumes that he would have been delighted with the causes his name supported in Turkey. For writers like Jack Kerouac, who battled for control of his image and lost, the ramifications were more severe. By ceaselessly exploring new avenues of being, Ginsberg ensured that his image and his work would continue to be highly amenable to the needs of the present, wherever that present happened to be.

CONCLUSION
THE LESSONS OF COUNTERCULTURAL DRIFT

There will always be new moments for older texts. During the "Standing Man" protests that followed the Gezi Park demonstrations, a photograph of a young woman (Özge Dursun) defiantly reading George Orwell's *1984* in front of heavily armed riot police was widely circulated in both Turkish and international media and helped draw attention to the protestors' cause. The image became a means of critique, drawing clear battle lines between the Turkish state's use of unnecessary force and a well-read youth movement that wanted to pursue its own interests without government interference. Orwell's book, a condemnation of totalitarianism that became a staple in high school English classes, has proven highly amenable to the post–Cold War world. After Donald Trump's election to the U.S. presidency in 2016, sales of the novel spiked on Amazon.com. Decades after *1984* was seen as an apt characterization of the Soviet threat, many felt that the book's attack on totalitarianism and doublespeak had become applicable to internal U.S. politics. Much like Orwell, the Beats too have enjoyed an afterlife. Because of the intensely personal nature of the writing and its ability to challenge constraints to personal freedom and self-expression, Beat works seem destined to find an audience. But the ways in which that audience uses Beat works, how the works are deployed in a culture, and the lessons drawn from these texts are always changing.

What can we learn by exploring the reception of a countercultural movement over half a century after its inception in a culture so unlike the one that produced it? What is the payoff for looking at the Beats in Turkey?

An examination of the Beats' reception as "underground" figures in Turkey provides insight into how oppositional literature functions in the world today. In the West, the idea that lifestyle choice can be a revolutionary means of social critique has already been accepted—we might question a particular choice but not the right to choose difference. But in Turkey, this idea is still under debate. This is not to set up an invidious distinction between Turkey as a place where the Beats still matter and the West as a place where they have become just another cultural commodity or literary movement. Rather, what this difference reminds us is that different cultural contexts make for different receptions, different readings, and to the extent that the reader is involved in the creation of meaning, different texts.

One of the primary reasons for the Beats' continued relevance is that they provide a valuable space for readers to negotiate their responses to constraining social norms. This is especially true for those whose lifestyles strain against accepted standards of behavior. Thus young people exploring their sexuality can often benefit from a writer like Allen Ginsberg, or women struggling to reconcile personal desires with social demands can gain insight from Beat women writers like Diane di Prima. The Beats can often help negotiate the difficult line between the mainstream and the marginal. But it is important to remember that different cultural contexts provoke different readings. Beat texts fulfill the myth of American rebellion, and thus they remain both classic and countercultural, as publishers and marketing executives have figured out long ago. But the Turkish context presents a situation where the Beats pose a direct challenge to many of the basic tenets of society. Such a situation reminds us of the Beats' power to challenge social expectations and to foment change.

In the end, generational shift is perhaps the most powerful engine of this social change. The Beats represented a vanguard that sought to inspire a cultural revolution in the United States. Their contributions should not be minimized, but their message of dissent was delivered in the right place at the right time. Postwar America, with a generation discontented with the lifestyles of its parents and facing the impact of a televised war in Vietnam, was ripe for a countercultural revolution. American youth was ready to reject its parents and to question the ease and comfort that its mothers and fathers so cherished. The Beats were instrumental in disseminating the message, but it had to fall on ready ears—luckily, it did.

The Turkish case is different. Underground literature, as even its promoters are quick to concede, will not bring about an immediate sea change in Turkish culture. The question for underground literature in Turkey is whether the next generation is ready for its message, and how far the conservative government will go to stop it. The recent 2016 coup attempt calls into question the parameters within which the Beats can function. Does the sort of countercultural rebellion the Beats offer make sense in an increasingly autocratic state such as today's Turkey? Beat works are still available, but whether they will remain a viable means of social resistance remains to be seen, especially given Turkey's willingness to stifle and suppress free speech and the press. In such a climate, rebellion in Turkey may once again turn violent or be crushed altogether. The current situation in Turkey thus presents a test case for whether the Beats need an open, democratic society to function as generators of social change. The Beats were used by students and dissenters to challenge autocratic rule in the postwar Soviet bloc. Can they be useful in challenging today's repressive and despotic regimes?

Placing the Beats in a global context also provides a novel means of thinking about the importance of language in the reception of Beat texts. The Beats are championed as literary innovators who drew on both high and low culture to craft a new style of writing inspired by the breath rhythms of jazz and the spoken word. But texts change when translated, and it behooves us to pay closer attention to what happens when Beat works are brought into another language. Unfortunately, translations have thus far received scant attention in Beat scholarship. But it might be time to discuss what is at stake when a Beat style that is now accepted as formally innovative becomes reformed in another language. William S. Burroughs, for instance, believed that by challenging the reader's linguistic expectations, his cut-up method literarily revealed a deeper truth concealed in his texts. But as we have seen, stylistic innovation is not always so easily carried over into translation. This is not to say that the Beats are untranslatable, or that Burroughs's claims should always be taken at face value. Translation studies, however, has demonstrated that every translator makes choices that impact a text and its possible interpretations. The Beats in Turkish are not exactly the Beats in English, and that gap highlights the sort of assumptions we tend to make about the Beats and their use of language.

Consider, for example, the often haphazard translation histories of Beat texts in Turkey. In Western Europe, where translation tends to follow initial publication fairly closely, it can be assumed that translations of an author's works arrive in the same chronological order that the original books first appear. But in countries where that is not the case, a reader's first encounter with a Beat author might be through a more obscure work that a translator just decided to translate, or through some other medium, such as a sound recording, a film, or even an Internet meme. As we saw in the second chapter, one of the first Turkish fanzines included Jack Kerouac's review of the film *Nosferatu*. Those coming to this text without much knowledge of Kerouac might conclude the novelist was actually a film critic. Such readings could be amended through subsequent exposure to the Beats and are less likely to occur as knowledge of their work grows, but the initial context of reception is important for guiding reader expectation, a point worth considering when examining how the Beats are received globally.

Beat texts have benefited tremendously from the upsurge in English as a global language, which not only gives many nonnative English readers direct access to these works but also increases the number of possible translators of them. While the increase in translations of Beat works, in both Turkish and other languages, is due in large part to the sort of universal themes of resistance that Beat works provide, the rise of global English has also played a part in their dissemination. The rise of English as a lingua franca raises important questions for thinking about the Beats' global visibility. Is their message of rebellion tainted through their association with the exportation of American cultural products throughout the globe? Would their work be as popular (or as subversive) in a world speaking Chinese, Arabic, or Swahili? These are, of course, unanswerable questions, but they do allow us to begin thinking about the importance of cultural and historical conditions in the global reception of the Beat countercultural message.

Examining the Beats outside conventional geographic and cultural boundaries is crucial, not only because, in our globalized world, the Beats are no longer simply an American phenomenon but also because such study helps clarify how we have arrived at our present understanding of the Beats and how we have chosen to frame their social and literary relevance. There is a divide, felt palpably in Beat circles, between an older generation who has "been there" and a younger one who only knows of the counterculture through appropriation. Yet the Beats, with but few exceptions, are no longer with us, and we are on the cusp of an era that will see such personal connections to Beat luminaries come to an end. This inevitable change, however, need not mean the end of the Beats' significance. Nostalgia for the postwar moment of the Beats' initial reception will always to some extent remain, but the Beats and their work will live on in forms and venues dictated by the needs and desires of a new generation facing new challenges. Beat thinking and concepts are more important and timely than ever, but the nature of their challenge to social and cultural models needs to be rethought, and the purely celebratory tone toward their accomplishments needs to be tempered. Part of this rethinking is already under way, as critics continue to explore gender, race, and class issues and how they might help us to rethink Beat contributions. Thinking about Beat texts through their Turkish reception reminds us of their function as cultural objects available for use in new contexts, and provides a way of understanding what is transformative about Beat writing.

The U.S. reception of the Beats is intimately connected to the glorification of their image as rebellious outsiders who purposely transgressed social and literary standards. While this portrayal is accurate and laudatory, it is time we took a broader view of their legacy. Our investment in the Beats and the counterculture as the celebration of the lone genius struggling to achieve self-expression has sometimes blinded us to the role that reception plays as an instrument of social change. Perhaps we should also be exploring what the Beats have to say about our current situation rather than simply glorifying their exploits. For those who want to recapture the earlier spirit of Beat rebellion and save the Beats from becoming simply Cold War curiosities, looking at how the Beats function in countries outside the United States could provide new ways of meaningfully redeploying them in contemporary social struggles.

Ultimately, *Translating the Counterculture* speaks to more than just the Beats' reception in Turkey. It allows us to think about how resistance travels. In a globalized world where many of the problems and difficulties humans face are beginning to look a lot alike, it seems intuitive that forms of resistance will appear similar as well. Given that the Beats have proven useful in the past, it also makes a great deal of sense that their countercultural message of dissent would be redeployed, especially when cultural conditions seem similar. But cultural products produced in one setting will always mean something else in another place or time. While conditions must be right for a strategy of importing rebellious works from another culture to be viable, those works will always bear the imprint of a host culture that will choose and amend them to conform to the needs of the present. The lasting power of the Beat critique resides in its malleability. Despite carrying the outward marks of the postwar era, deep down Beat works are perfectly adaptable to diverse needs, thus ensuring that the Beats, their texts, and their message will remain useful to anyone with a desire to "counter" the dominant culture.

APPENDIX 1:
AGE AND GENDER OF READERS' FIRST HEARING ABOUT THE UNDERGROUND GENRE

How old were you when you first heard about underground literature?

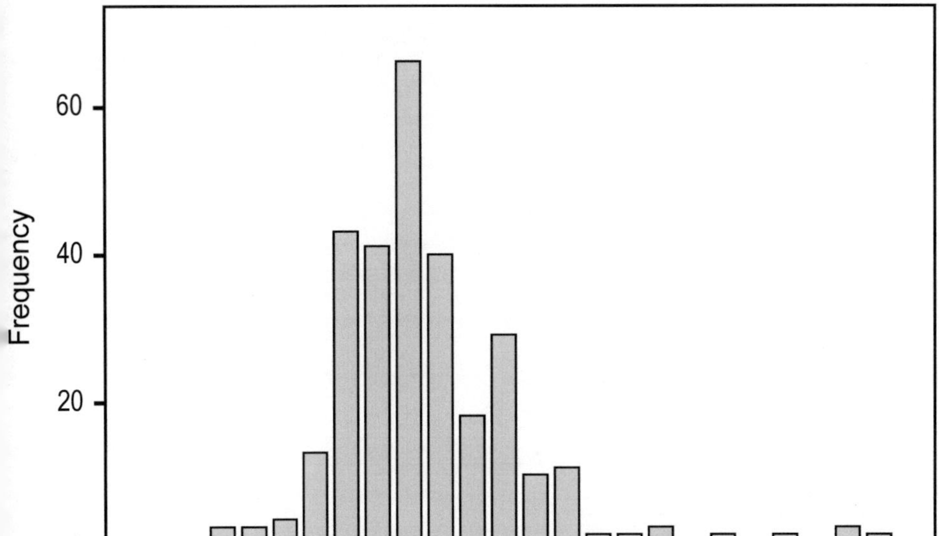

*No answer.

How old were you when you first heard about underground literature?

Gender	*Mean age (y)*	*No.*	*Standard deviation*
Female	17.10	141	3.027
Male	19.35	161	10.031
Total or Overall	18.30	302	7.682

APPENDIX 2: WHERE READERS FIRST BECAME AWARE OF THE GENRE

	Frequency	*Percentage*	*Cumulative percentage*
High school	175	57.9	57.9
University	67	22.2	80.1
Bookstores	21	7.0	87.1
Second-hand booksellers	4	1.3	88.4
Internet	14	4.6	93.0
Café / Bar	10	3.3	96.4
Family / Friends	10	3.3	99.7
No answer	1	0.3	100.0
Total	302	100.0	

Note: All percentages are statistically valid.

Where did you first hear about underground literature?

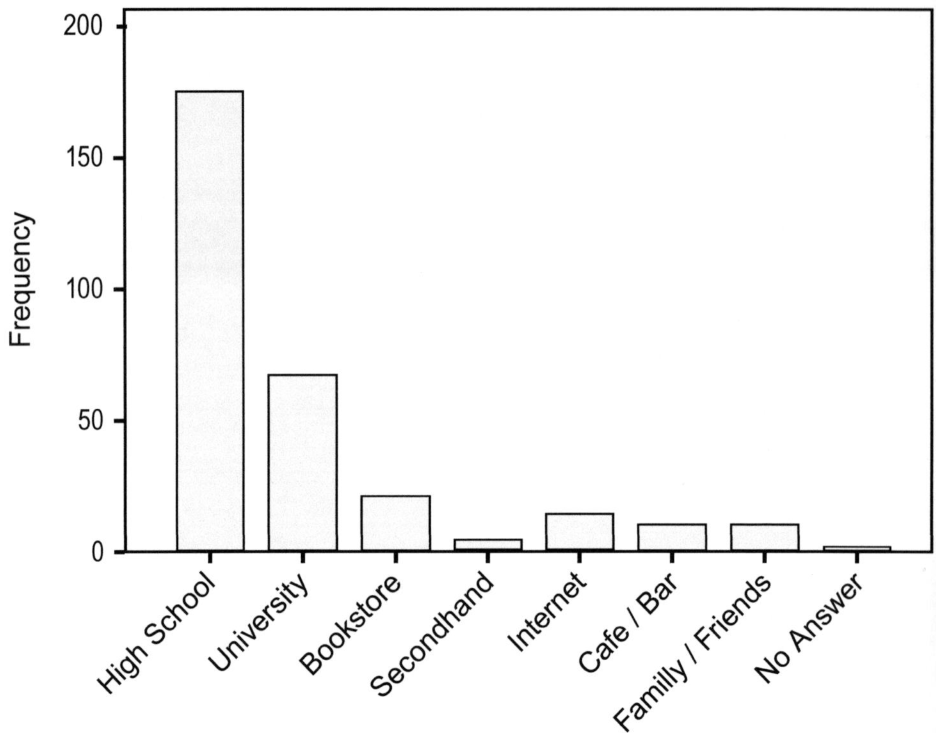

APPENDIX 3: FAMILIARITY OF READERS WITH VARIOUS UNDERGROUND TEXTS AND AUTHORS

Texts and Authors	*Read / Watched (%)*	*Heard of (%)*	*Never heard of (%)*
U.S. countercultural texts			
"America" (poem)	3.3	39.1	57.6
And the Hippos Were Boiled in Their Tanks	2.0	45.0	53.0
Big Sur	2.0	41.7	56.3
Dharma Bums	5.6	49.0	45.4
Fight Club (book)	40.1	45.7	14.2
Fight Club (film)	54.6	36.8	8.6
Hollywood	12.9	46.7	40.4
Howl (poem)	5.3	41.4	53.3
Howl (film)	4.0	43.0	53.0
Naked Lunch	5.6	40.7	53.6
On the Road (book)	16.2	43.4	40.4
On the Road (film)	13.6	43.7	42.7
Pulp	5.0	50.0	45.0
Snuff	19.2	51.0	29.8
Soft Machine	3.3	43.4	53.3

Appendix 3, continued

Texts and Authors	*Read / Watched (%)*	*Heard of (%)*	*Never heard of (%)*
The Subterraneans	11.9	51.3	36.8
Women	22.8	44.7	32.5
U.S. countercultural authors			
Charles Bukowski	40.4	37.7	21.9
William S. Burroughs	6.6	40.1	53.3
Lawrence Ferlinghetti	2.6	37.7	59.6
Allen Ginsberg	8.3	34.4	57.3
Jack Kerouac	9.6	44.0	46.4
Chuck Palahniuk	19.2	33.4	47.4
Hubert Selby Jr.	1.0	41.7	57.3
Turkish underground texts			
Ağır Roman (book)	44.0	44.0	11.9
Ağır Roman (film)	45.0	42.7	12.3
Eroin Güncesi	17.9	56.0	26.2
Kinyas ve Kayra	23.2	51.3	25.5
Piç	37.7	47.0	15.2
Pis Moruğun Notları	11.6	52.6	35.8
Pogo	4.3	49.7	46.0
Travesti Pinokyo	10.6	44.0	45.4
Tutunamayanlar	54.3	30.8	14.9
Underground Poetix	6.6	38.4	55.0
Turkish underground authors			
Hikmet Temel Akarsu	4.0	47.0	49.0
Şenol Erdoğan	5.6	49.3	45.0
Süreyya Evren	3.0	50.3	46.7
Hakan Günday	29.5	49.7	20.9
küçük iskender	43.7	48.0	8.3
Metin Kaçan	11.9	60.6	27.5
Altay Öktem	8.9	56.0	35.1
Sibel Torunoğlu	4.3	53.0	42.7
Ayça Seren Ural	2.0	48.7	49.3

NOTES

INTRODUCTION: WHY THE BEATS? WHY TURKEY? WHY NOW?

1. Tony Trigilio, in his excellent article "The Beat Goes On—But How?" examines what he considers the "stunning divide between Beat scholars and Beat fans" that unfortunately characterizes the discipline (12). It is hoped a scholarly approach that takes fan appropriation seriously might offer a chance for rapprochement.

2. There is a third option, that of the "cosmopolitan." The term is derived from the Greek *kosmos*, or "world," and *politēs*, or "citizen"—thus, a citizen of the world. *Cosmopolitan*, however, is less a description of the world than an ethical project meant to counter the social problems created by nationalist tendencies. The hope is that placing global responsibility above concerns of immediate locality will result in a stronger commitment to humanity as a whole. For a more extended discussion of the nuances and problems of cosmopolitanism, see *Cosmopolitics: Thinking and Feeling beyond the Nation*, edited by Pheng Cheah and Bruce Robbins.

3. While the 1990s marked a general shift to the transnational, Rolf Lundén notes in his contribution to the volume *Beyond the Crisis in US American Studies: Scandinavian Perspectives* that while "[t]ransnational American Studies thus seems to have a longer history than what is commonly held, going back to at least the 1950s," nevertheless there are "strong indications that American Studies in the United States in the 1960s and 1970s contemplated moving in the direction of an internationalized perspective, which did not come about" (43). As we will see in regard to Beat scholarship, many of these early practitioners

were scholars working outside the United States. As Lundén explains, "If not the majority, at least a substantial number of non-American, particularly European, Americanists seem to have invested early in comparative, trans-Atlantic studies, more so than their colleagues in the United States" (43). It makes sense that those working outside the United States would be the first to embrace such techniques, and part of the transnational turn includes an attempt to better acknowledge work conducted beyond the country's borders.

4. The work of Amy Kaplan and Donald Pease is especially important in this regard. See, for example, their jointly edited volume *Cultures of United States Imperialism.*

5. There is also a substantial body of work by European scholars and enthusiasts that does not directly bear on transnational concerns but nevertheless demonstrates the global reach of the Beats and their work. The work of Eric Mottram, especially his study *William Burroughs: The Algebra of Need* (1971), was an important catalyst for Beat studies in the United Kingdom. In addition to works such as Yves Le Pellec's *Beat Generation* (1975) that collect translations of essays, interviews, and other source materials, there is a wealth of material that offers more personal reactions to the Beats, including Victor-Lévy Beaulieu's *Jack Kerouac: A Chicken Essay* (1975), an impressionistic treatment of Kerouac as a French-Canadian author, and Chris Challis's *Quest for Kerouac* (1984), an Englishman's attempt to come to terms with Kerouac's work and legend through accounts of visits to places and people associated with the writer.

6. While these studies examine the transnational dynamics of the Beats in a more critical vein, there are a variety of studies that document the Beats' various sojourns abroad. Deborah Baker's *A Blue Hand* (2009), for instance, offers an account of the interactions and travels of Beats like Ginsberg while in India. Barry Miles offers a history of the Beats in Paris in his book *The Beat Hotel* (2001), and Jorge García-Robles's *At the End of the Road* (2014) chronicles Jack Kerouac's time in Mexico. Bill Morgan's *The Beats Abroad: A Global Guide to the Beat Generation* (2016) offers references for international travelers wanting to visit Beat haunts. This desire to chronicle the lives of Beat figures stems both from a fascination with their international experiences as well as a general interest in the personal details of a group of writers whose exploits have become the basis of myth and legend.

7. These texts are far too numerous to mention individually, and include even more specific subgenres such as walking tours of old Beat haunts and compilations devoted to specific Beat concerns like Buddhism. Nor is this trend restricted to U.S. publications. Fernanda Pivano's *Beat & Pieces: A Complete Story of the Beat Generation* (2005) includes photographs by Allen Ginsberg and short essays and book covers of first editions in both Italian and English. The vast number of publications relating to the Beats both in the United States and abroad demonstrates their continued cultural relevance.

8. The center-periphery model, so dominant in postcolonial studies, does not seem to hold for Turkey either. Critics instead turn to issues of modernization, and it is telling that in his defining study of postcolonialism, Edward Said ignores Turkey. This omission makes sense, given that the Ottoman Empire was itself a colonizer, thus complicating Said's critique of Western attempts to appropriate the Oriental other. See Meltem Ahıska's contribution "Occidentalism: The Historical Fantasy of the Modern" in the *South Atlantic Quarterly* special issue on Turkey.

9. Islam has an extensive history in Turkey and includes an extremely heterogeneous array of attitudes and practices. For a more detailed account of the role of religion in Turkey, see Şerif Mardin's *Religion, Society, and Modernity in Turkey*.

10. See Murat Ergin, "The Racialization of Kurdish Identity in Turkey," in the journal *Ethnic and Racial Studies*.

11. Gürbilek is careful to note that this call for a more open sexuality was still conducted in the service of the state and mediated by "the language of newspapers and news magazines, television and advertising" (69). Nevertheless, the 1980 coup ushered in a more liberal cultural climate where a variety of voices could be heard.

12. It is difficult to ascertain the exact contribution of the Beats to such a diffuse uprising, but their texts were available at the makeshift Gezi library, and the demonstrations were clearly in the spirit of Beat protestors such as Allen Ginsberg.

13. See Erik Mortenson, Duygu Ergun, and Selen Erdoğan's "Underground Literature and Its Influence on Youth in Turkey" in *New Perspectives on Turkey*.

14. The acceptance of the reader as worthy of consideration did not come easily. Although interest in the reader can be traced back to Immanuel Kant and Friedrich Schiller as well as to the English Romantics and even into the classical period, it was not until the late 1960s and early 1970s that the role of readership began to be seriously theorized. In a reaction to the textual formalism espoused by the New Criticism, University of Constance theorists such as Wolfgang Iser in his *The Implied Reader* (1974) and *The Act of Reading* (1978) began to discuss the reader in a serious manner. Try as they might to shift focus toward the act of reading, these early theorists were loath to abandon the primacy of the text, and the authority of the work itself still held sway. It was not until the work of Stanley Fish that the activity of reading became of value. Fish redefined literature as an experience and not simply as a decoding of an object. The text was no longer independent of a reader's conception. Critics like Roland Barthes took this even farther. In *S/Z* (1970) and *The Pleasure of the Text* (1975), Barthes emphasized a reader who challenged the text rather than passively accepted its dictates. The move toward the reader was likewise under way at the Media Group at Birmingham University's Centre for Contemporary Cultural Studies. Throughout the late 1970s and early 1980s, critics

like Stuart Hall, David Morley, and Angela McRobbie examined interactions between popular texts and audience reception. This group likewise posited a reader who was capable of producing meaning. Unlike the Frankfurt School theorists who saw the "culture industry" as a monolithic, hegemonic force that easily influenced its audiences, these Marxist-inclined critics found redemption in a viewer who was able to challenge ideological messages instead of accepting them—the reader became the "bricoleur" rather than the "dupe." A new era of cultural studies was born, with critics such as Hall and John Fiske focusing on consumers who used cultural products to arrive at their own meanings. This study, while not specifically underpinned by reader response theoretical formulations, shares in the belief that a full understanding of literature and its function can be achieved only through an examination of readers.

15. See Sandra Bermann's introduction to the edited volume *Nation, Language, and the Ethics of Translation* and Emily Apter's *The Translation Zone: A New Comparative Literature* for attempts to theorize the importance of ethical considerations to the field of translation studies.

16. The truth of this claim can be seen in the fact that admirers today can still think of themselves as "Beat," while it would be extremely odd for devotees of the Victorian novel or the work of Shakespeare to consider themselves "Victorian" or "Shakespearean."

1. LABELING A PHENOMENON: THE BEATS AS "UNDERGROUND" FIGURES

1. For a more extended discussion of the term *Beat* and its implications, see Steven Belletto's introduction to the *Cambridge Companion to the Beats.*

2. For an account of modern underground spaces and the myths associated with them, see David L. Pike's *Metropolis on the Styx: The Underworlds of Modern Urban Culture, 1800–2001.*

3. Suárez quotes Andrew Ross, *No Respect* (New York: Routledge, 1989), 84. Given its title, Dostoyevsky's novella understandably occupies a central place in debates surrounding underground literature both in the United States and in Turkey. Underground literature's other forebears are varied, but certain names do appear with frequency: the Marquis de Sade, Louis-Ferdinand Céline's *Journey to the End of the Night*, Jean Genet's works, much of the Gothic genre, and for the Turkish critic Hasan Bülent Kahraman, Emily Brönte and Georges Bataille.

4. Suárez quotes Stan Van Der Beek, "The Cinema Delimina," *Film Quarterly*, Summer 1961, unpaginated.

5. *On the Road* was first translated as *Yolda* by Güzın Özkan and Ferruh Armutçuoğlu (Kıyı Yayınları, 1993), while *Naked Lunch* was translated as *Çıplak Şölen* by Üçel Birlik (Altıkırkbeş Yayınları, 1998). Bukowski, though perhaps

not strictly a Beat writer, has fared better: his *Hot Water Music* was translated as early as 1983, and he is by far the most translated figure (*Sicak Su Müziği*, trans. Avi Pardo, Parantez, 1983).

6. See Mortenson, Ergun, and Erdoğan, "Underground Literature and Its Influence on Youth in Turkey" in the journal *New Perspectives on Turkey*.

7. To accomplish this task, we first developed a sense of reader demographics through in-depth interviews and media analysis, and then formed focus groups that allowed for the construction of more detailed questionnaires that examined reader beliefs about important issues in Turkey today. These focus group responses were honed into two longer questionnaires that were distributed to a group of underground literature readers (n = 302) and similar nonreaders (n = 306). In addition to the same demographic questions asked of readers, nonreaders were given a series of eight quotes taken from both Western underground texts in translation (n = 4) and Turkish underground works (n = 4). The result was a useful comparison of how underground literature's readers viewed the genre and how nonreaders exposed to such texts felt about the issues that they raise.

8. The cross-tabulations showed no significant differences based on gender, except when it came to social perceptions of women. Unsurprising perhaps, when presented with the statement "women should get permission to work from their spouse," 67.4 percent of women completely disagreed while only 44.7 percent of male participants did. Only 7.1 percent of women completely agreed with this belief, and 16.1 percent of males did. In terms of readership of particular underground texts, differences in gender were unimportant, except in the case of the journal *Underground Poetix*, which had nearly triple the rate of male readership compared with female, and Bukowski's novel *Post Office*, with almost five times as many male readers (91).

9. While 62.1 percent of nonreaders believe that the United States has a negative impact on Turkey, the percentage among readers was higher, at 70.2 percent. In reflecting on European culture, 41.7 percent of nonreaders believe it poses a threat to Turkey, while the rate is slightly higher for readers at 50.6 percent. This finding is best explained by their left-leaning political positions. As befits the Turkish left in general, readers of underground literature tend to be critical of the West while embracing its countercultural literature (95).

10. By the time the *Notos* dossier on underground literature was published, the debate over what constitutes underground literature and whether it even exists had taken a more definite shape. While the *Varlık* article does include mention of the Beats, when the *Notos* issue came out six years later, they were regularly invoked by critics as obvious examples of underground writers.

11. Another is that no author, with the exception of iskender, considers himself or herself underground. As Ozan Marakoğlu observes, "What is weird

is that many writers whose names are mentioned as 'one of the important representatives of underground literature in Turkey' by other writers participating in the inquisition were claiming that their writings had nothing to do with what's called underground literature a few pages later" (47).

12. This critique holds especially true for the 1990s, when the Beats reached what was perhaps their marketing zenith with Kerouac and Ginsberg appearing in Gap khaki ads and Burroughs promoting Nike shoes. Today it seems as though the Beats have taken a more subdued place as classic examples of rebellion, along with other 1950s icons like Marlon Brando and James Dean. With many of their texts rereleased in anniversary editions and marketed as twentieth-century classics, perhaps our acceptance of the Beats as rebels has become a rarely questioned fait accompli.

13. This tension plays out in the Turkish context as well, with older fans often decrying the debasement of the genre through saturation and marketing. But who gets to decide what others read? There are self-imposed gatekeepers everywhere who feel it is their duty to protect the integrity of the genre and attempt to do so by striving to separate the true from the ersatz. There is a strange desire in the debate for discussing which texts are and which texts are not underground (and the reasons why) that has shifted attention away from the ramifications of this increased exposure the underground has received and the possible benefits it might offer to the culture at large.

14. Reader response to underground literature reaches its zenith in Turkey's famous website *ekşi sözluk*. This "sour dictionary," which was created in 1999, allows anonymous users to respond to topics uncensored and uninhibited. While it would be impossible to chronicle the various entries that appear under the topic "*Yeraltı Edebiyatı*" and attempt to define, explain, and comment on underground literature, most of them are admiring in tone. Nor is the subject of underground literature a minor consideration on the site. All the major authors associated with the genre, both foreign and domestic, have their own threads. The Turkish poet küçük iskender, for example, generated 589 responses, with discussion of his homosexual lifestyle and poetry prompting heated debate. Terms like "Beat Generation" (*Beat Kuşağı*), journals such as *Underground Poetix*, and even publishing houses Ayrıntı Yayınları and 6:45 have topic threads that can contain hundreds of entries. Given that *ekşi sözluk* is considered a site where the youth of Turkey can voice their concerns uninhibitedly, it appears as though underground literature is a topic worthy of consideration for this group.

15. The work of Çiğdem Kağıtçıbaşı is especially relevant here. See "Social Norms and Authoritarianism: A Turkish-American Comparison" in the *Journal of Personality and Social Psychology*, as well as her *Gençlerin Tutumları: Kültürler Arası Bir Karşılastırma* (1973).

16. One other Turkish text is a touchstone for the genre: Oğuz Atay's masterpiece *Tutunamayanlar* (1971). Translated as "The Disconnected" but literally

meaning "those who could not catch hold," this massive tome is considered the first modernist novel in Turkish. Written in a stream-of-consciousness style heavy with colloquialisms, Atay's work is often cited as an underground text despite having been published years before the genre was established.

17. Although many involved in the debate raise the issue of style, none provide a concrete sense of what characterizes underground literature textually. Given its countercultural stance, the genre unsurprisingly poses a challenge to literary conventions. As Ayrıntı's editor Abdul Yılmaz declares, "In terms of style, it makes a stand against the established norms of literature." (Yılmaz interview). The use of slang is also a touchstone in the debate. But beyond this critics have surprisingly little to say. In terms of Turkish underground texts, a distinction is often made between purely autobiographical, diaristic accounts and those that attempt a more innovative presentation.

18. For a more detailed account of the underground literature phenomenon in Turkey and its importance for the reception of Beat writers and texts, see Erik Mortenson's article "The 'Underground' Reception of the Beats in Turkey" in the journal *Comparative American Studies.*

2. BUILDING COMMUNITY OUTSIDE THE MAINSTREAM: *UNDERGROUND POETIX* AND THE TURKISH ALTERNATIVE PRESS

1. Humor was also rampant. In contrast to the staid journalistic style of the mainstream press, the underground prided itself on its wit. The publication *Renaissance*, for example, included a cut-out coupon titled "Safe Conduct Pass" addressed to "Policeman, soldiers, parents, bosses, housewives, presidents, queers, teachers, . . ." that offered "safe conduct pass to Hippie-Land. Hand this to the first friendly looking, long-haired boy or girl (it doesn't matter if you can't tell them apart[;] we'll teach you) you meet. Good luck. This is the first day of the rest of your life" (*Renaissance*, no page). Such humor entertained as well as undercut the seriousness of more established publications.

2. The Beats, for the most part, made the switch from the alternative presses of the late 1950s and early 1960s into the often more provocative publishing environment of the late 1960s and early 1970s. Ginsberg becomes a mainstay in later 1960s journals as well as in the underground newspaper format, and McClure appears regularly as well. Snyder makes appearances in both, especially in Buddhist or ecologically inspired publications, and his article "Why Tribe?" has continued to be an underground press classic. Burroughs has perhaps been the most successful, having his work appear in countless underground periodicals and using Jeff Nutall's *My Own Mag* (1964–66) and the widely disseminated London underground paper the *International Times* (later changed to *IT*; 1966–82) to debut much of his early cut-up work. The notable exception here is Kerouac. Despite the odd article or poem, he was

conspicuously absent from the postwar underground scene, due in large part to his early death but also because his more conservative political views did not align with the general outlook of the counterculture.

3. This interdependency between alternative journals and presses can be seen in their advertising strategies. Publications mentioned and promoted one another extensively, and it was not uncommon to find announcements for new books and journals within the covers of like-minded publications. The fourth issue of *Big Table* (Spring 1960), for example, contained an ad for Kerouac's *Poetry for the Beat Generation* album with Steve Allen; another for Donald M. Allen's *The New American Poetry 1945–1960*; one for New Directions' *Happy Birthday of Death* by Corso, Denise Levertov's *With Eyes at the Back of Our Heads*, and Ferlinghetti's novel *Her*; another ad for the Pocket Poets Series from City Lights; an announcement for *The Beat Scene* anthology edited and introduced by Elias Wilentz; and ads by Totem / Corinth for Snyder's *Myths & Texts*, Whalen's *Like I Say*, and Kerouac's *Scripture of the Golden Eternity*. Such mutual support created a tight-knit group of editors, writers, and publishers who knew each other's work and promoted it.

4. This critique extends to the contributor page, where Sanders's descriptions are an assault on both literary expectations and, often, good taste. Describing the poet John Wieners, for instance, Sanders writes, "Coke head and boy-hawk. Auerhahn due to secrete his second book also, if the motherfucker ever completes it" (vol. 2, no. 5, December 1962). While these playful biographies are in keeping with both the journal's stance and the counterculture's sexual playfulness, it is difficult not to feel a slight discomfort when Sanders describes Carol Bergé as "One of the 4 Young Lady Furburgers of the Totem / Corinth collection. The entire Editorial Board wd love to freak a dick in her" (vol. 3, no. 5, May 1963). In the counterculture, the border between taste and transgression was easy to cross.

5. Beat Generation authors and their works were often used to challenge the literary status quo of a host country as well. In his editorial "against the monstrous regiment" published in the 1959 issue of *Edinburgh University Review*, editor Alex Neish writes, "[O]nce again Scotland lies in creative stagnation, redeemed only by the works of one or two artists. The links with the wider context of world literature have been lost, while for the past twenty or thirty years we have been urged to excommunicate all that is not one hundred per cent Scottish." (7). As with Turkey, the Beats are imported to shake up the establishment and provide new possibilities in what the editor sees as a moribund culture. Neish continues by attacking Scottish poets for their unwillingness to engage the people, arguing that in such a case the Beats, with their insistence on the vernacular and the street, are a group worth appreciating.

6. See also Öktem's *Şeytan Aletleri* (*The Tools of Satan*) and *Şehrin Kötü Çoçukları* (*Bad Kids of the City*) for further examples.

7. Ascribing authorship and editing credits as well as proper publication information is, obviously, difficult for a journal self-consciously opposed to such niceties. Nevertheless, this issue of *Kadıköy Underground Poetix* is listed as "#99" with a publication date of "2040." The author's best guess is that it was the second issue, printed in 2008.

8. For a more detailed discussion of the Turkish underground journal *Şizofrengi*, which conducted the same sort of critique on the Turkish mental health establishment, see Erik Mortenson and Rafet Karaoğlu's "Diagnosing the National Neurosis, the Underground Journal *Şizofrengi*, and Its Critique of 1990s Turkish Society" in the journal *Turkish Studies*.

9. The editors clearly view the Beats as a means to challenge the repressive norms of the Turkish government. As Erdoğan explained in our interview, "Turkey, in every context, politically, literally, and morally, is at the point of explosion, and that creates an interest towards the Beat Generation" (Erdoğan, interview). The Beats function as a potential catalyst that could help crystallize a general feeling of discontent into a serious challenge to restrictive norms. For Erdoğan, the Beats are important not only because they offer a means of thinking revolution but also because the sort of problems they struggled against are eerily reminiscent of the current situation in Turkey. As Erdoğan declares, "America's 55 period and Turkey's situation right now have terrifying similarities" (Erdoğan, interview). Given Erdoğan's belief that Turkey is in much the same position as the United States during the culturally repressive Eisenhower 1950s, the Beat social critique has become as timely as ever.

10. Erdoğan claims that *Underground Poetix*'s representation in the East of Turkey is severely limited, however: "In three months we only sold one book in Diyarbakır" (Erdoğan, interview).

11. Şenol Erdoğan, the editor of the journal, joins this textual community by contributing his own poetry that reinforces this antireligious message. Employing a litany of images both transgressive and surreal, it is sometimes difficult to know whether Erdoğan's work should be taken seriously or as evidence of a type of spontaneous scatology. Nevertheless, the shocking nature of phrases like "afternoon prayer masturbation" (*ikindi namazı otuzbirleri*) and "sperm and blood sand ablution" (*meniyle ve kanla teyemmüm*; vol. 9, no date; p. 13) command attention. Erdoğan, too, places himself outside God's purview by issuing a self-imposed fatwa, claiming in one poem that he is "Wanted by Allah" (ibid., p. 15; written in English).

12. The verb here is *sikmek*, meaning "to fuck," derived from the vulgar noun *sik*, which means "dick" or "cock." Given its source in the male genitalia, the verb would never describe the sexual act from a women's point of view. A more literal translation would be something like "to dick," with the more polite reciprocal verb *sevişmek* meaning "to love one another" or "to make love with one another."

13. The Turkish reads:

biliyorum ki türkçe konuşamıyorum
kürtçe söylenemiyor adım
dudaklarımdan süzülemiyorsa kelimelerim
affet beni
sana söylediklerimden ötürü
yalanlarım
bilemediğimden
ülkelerim, giysilerim
öğrenemediğimden amerika
ya da
gidemediğimden avrupa
giyemediğimden gülemiyorum seni.

14. Our study revealed that 60.9 percent of the readers read underground texts only in translation, while 31.5 percent sometimes read them in the original and only 6.3 percent always read the originals. Although most read in translation, the number of texts read in the original seemed somewhat high to us. But many of underground literature's readers are university students who probably have some knowledge (and in some cases a strong knowledge) of the English language, and thus would choose to read in the original rather than in translation. This is an important finding, since it demonstrates that the spread of global English means an increased attention to untranslated Beat texts (Mortenson, Ergun, and Erdoğan 92).

3. "WHAT'S YOUR ROAD, MAN?": JACK KEROUAC'S *ON THE ROAD* IN TURKEY

1. The existence of the Free Girl advertisement campaign first came to my attention through a Turkish colleague in Koç University's history department. But the advertisement was mentioned several times in various focus groups, exclusively by women respondents. While data is not readily available, it seems safe to say that a large portion of the population watched at least one of the commercials over its run. The commercials can still be viewed by using the search terms "özgür kız" on YouTube.

2. When the translator sent Ginsberg a copy of the book in Turkish with its cover depicting a sitting Buddha wearing sunglasses and holding an American flag, Ginsberg's thank-you note was upbeat but included a warning: "The Turkish cover Buddha—Moloch with a flag will mislead any young kid reading for understanding" (postcard reprinted in the 1997 edition by Söz Yayın publishers). Ginsberg's point is well taken. Translations, especially the initial ones of an author, set the tone for a readership's understanding of an author.

3. Even when such larger questions of *On the Road*'s contemporary importance do emerge, discussion is often limited and the results contradictory. Thus Ferhat Uludere's review "Kutsal serserinin yol maceraları" ("Holy Bums' Road Adventures") argues that the novel belongs in postwar America, while Sevda Duman, in "Yaşamayı seven isyankarlar" ("Legislation Loving Rebels"), believes that its message is universal. But these articles are anomalies—the majority are content to simply provide readers background information.

4. Can Kantarcı is not the first person to translate the novel into Turkish. Though earlier translations exist, Kantarcı's version is the most recent (published in 2008 by Ayrıntı Yayınları in Istanbul) and the first to be based on the original *On the Road* scroll.

5. Recent scholarship argues that the 1980 coup ushered in a period of individualization in Turkey, though the dynamics of this change are still under debate. Nurdan Gürbilek, in *The New Cultural Climate of Turkey*, argues for an irony to this push for individualism: "All these factors combined to usher Turkey into a belated period of subjectivity, of individuality, of inwardness, all the more vehement for its belatedness. Here lay the power of the 'promise of freedom': private life opened wide its gates, as if it were freedom itself. . . . But here was a dilemma also: as private life expanded into the space left empty by politics, it found itself encircled by the most public of discourses" (69). The discourse of individualism, while it claimed to provide freedom by allowing the free expression of individual desire, actually worked to recontain it through other means. Gül Özyeğin examines the effect of individualism on women, making the claim that this trend broke down "women's family-bound class identification: women engage in a very individualized process of self-construction in their focus on bodily health and beauty. The focus for women's consumption is no longer limited to family and class. A growing emphasis on cosmetics and beauty products, reinforced by the proliferation of magazines, advice literature and advertising, has increasingly changed the terms of the cultural constitution of female identity. . . . It signals the emergence of a new feminine self, more 'individualized,' set apart from other family members" (56). Thus many critics challenge the supposed freedom that the turn to individualism claimed to inaugurate. This holds especially true for more conservative critics, who see individualism as an attack on accepted notions of family, religion, and community that had served as the backbone for Turkish identity. Focus on the individual undermines religious solidarity as well. Of course access to the benefits of a more individualistic society is not available to all, and is still mainly a middle-class prerogative.

6. For a psychological discussion of the importance of collectivism in Turkey, see Çiğdem Kağıtçıbaşı, "Autonomy and Relatedness in Cultural Context: Implications for Self and Family" in the *Journal of Cross-Cultural Psychology*. Kağıtçıbaşı offers a good review of the social and psychological literature on

this topic, arguing that Western notions of individuality have come to dominate the field and rehearse the argument of autonomy's importance for human development. She argues, however, that autonomy need not be equated with individualism, and thus collective societies can consist of interdependent subjects who still retain agency.

7. When I taught this book in Germany the result was similar, though not as pronounced as in Turkey. This variation was due mainly to the similarities between the United States and Germany, both Western countries in the broadest sense. German students understood the book's insistence on travel and discovery. In fact, many had made similar trips themselves, though usually by train and never with the sort of open-endedness that characterizes Sal and Dean's travels. But Dean's willingness to jettison relationships in his quest for unencumbered personal freedom met with resistance in Germany as well. Taking a road trip was one thing, but living a life according to Dean's principles was quite another.

8. See the fifth chapter of Erik Mortenson's *Capturing the Beat Moment: Cultural Politics and the Poetics of Presence* (2011) for a discussion of how the Beats attempt to establish collectives that are based on temporary experiences rather than on longer-lived traditions and social structures.

9. Ethnic and linguistic origins are fiercely debated, but the general nomadic wandering across the plains of Central Asia over several centuries is a consistent feature in descriptions of early Turkish history. Almost every treatment of Turkey, including discussions of the modern-day republic, begins with such a sketch. See Nicole and Hugh Pope's *Turkey Unveiled: A History of Modern Turkey*, Andrew Mango's *The Turks Today*, and Lord Kinross's *The Ottoman Centuries: The Rise and Fall of the Turkish Empire* for examples.

10. Interestingly, these earlier translators opt to retain the term *Beat* and generally provide a translation with the controversial passages intact, proving that while censorship was a concern in the early 1990s, it did not stop their fidelity to Kerouac's text.

11. In his article "Yeni Garip ve Beat Kuşağı," Şenol Erdoğan also cites the Turkish poet Orhan Veli Kanık's use of the road motif, as well as his reference to trains and railroads, claiming that the poet uses them "almost as much as Kerouac does."

12. A notable exception here is Orhan Pamuk's *The New Life* (1997). The novel chronicles the adventures of Osman, a young university student who becomes obsessed with a book and gives up everything to search out its meaning. The protagonist leaves home on a quest that shares similarities with Kerouac's work, though the result is as much metaphysical detective story as road novel. Given that Pamuk's work is often inspired by Western models, *The New Life* is the exception that proves the rule—the American-style road novel is absent in Turkey.

13. For an extended treatment of the importance of spontaneity in Beat writing (as well as its limitations), see Mortenson's *Capturing the Beat Moment.*

14. Not everyone shared this wealth, of course. Minorities and women were often excluded from these opportunities. Memories of the Depression, as well as fears of nuclear war, were still in the minds of many. Nevertheless, postwar America can be described as a period of abundance when living standards for a majority of Americans were on the rise. See Stephanie Coontz's *The Way We Never Were: American Families and the Nostalgia Trap.*

15. Of course the same could be said of North America. Terrorist acts are on the increase, and given the recent violence associated with drug trafficking and organized crime in Mexico, it would be foolhardy to repeat Sal and Dean's forays into that country given the current climate.

16. References to the "Turks" also appear in Gregory Corso's poetry as a means to evoke a pan-Mediterranean backdrop to his work. See "How Happy I Used to Be" and "Clown" in *Mindfield: New and Selected Poems.*

17. For an extended discussion of this figure, see the third chapter of Erik Mortenson's *Ambiguous Borderlands: Shadow Imagery in Cold War American Culture.*

18. For a discussion of the influence of Edward FitzGerald's nineteenth-century translations of twelfth-century Persian poet Omar Khayyám on Kerouac's oscillation between the beauties and vicissitudes of life, see Michael Skau's "Jack Kerouac's Rubáiyat: The Influence of Omar Khayyám" in the *Journal of Popular Culture.*

19. Yet some find the commercial a powerful statement in support of women's rights and opportunities. Nil Karaibrahimgil, the actor who plays the female protagonist, is perhaps the most vocal supporter. Karaibrahimgil went on to establish a singing career and have a family, and in another commercial for Orkid women's pads in 2003, she sings a jingle that claims that she can have both a career and a child, a phrase that became a popular motto for working mothers. The debate hinges on the role that cultural representations can play in fomenting social change. Karaibrahimgil does not argue that the advertisement is plausible, only that is provides a feeling of empowerment. Women viewers can identify with the desire for freedom regardless of whether it is available to them. The question remains as to whether this desire can then be actualized. In the imaginary space of the commercial, it is. Whether that will translate into increased freedom and mobility in Turkey, for all its citizens, remains to be seen.

20. Despite this uplifting (if conflicted) story of two women living their lives as they see fit, the novel is received not as strict memoir but as a sort of enhanced autobiography—readers are incredulous about two women performing such acts in Turkey. In an interview with Sibel Arna in *Hürriyet*, Ural makes clear that the book contains both autobiographical and fictional accounts of her travels (Arna).

21. Readers were only slightly more open-minded than nonreaders, 91.8 percent of whom also would not mind living next to a Kurdish family. Living next to homosexual people, however, was another matter. Only 67 percent of nonreaders would not mind such an arrangement, compared with 81.8 percent of readers who felt comfortable living next to members of this sexual minority.

4. THE BEATS ON TRIAL: THE CENSORSHIP OF WILLIAM S. BURROUGHS'S *THE SOFT MACHINE*

1. Boyar provides a detailed account of Abdülhamid's use of censorship but concludes that the sultan's financial support of the press was nevertheless instrumental in allowing it to survive.

2. Russell is reticent about Burroughs's possible inclusion in the queer canon, arguing in the afterword that "his inclusion would be politically problematic and could only ever be regarded as a historical recuperation of a novelist whose work expresses desires that the contemporary gay movement has long since sought to distance itself from" (191).

3. In the case of *Snuff*, a novel that depicts the struggles of a porn star to break a serial fornication record, discussion likewise revolves around the issue of sexuality. *Snuff* arrives in Turkish as *Ölüm Pornosu*, which can be back-translated into English as "Death Porn." It is interesting to speculate what exactly caught the reviewer's attention first, "death," "porn," or porn linked to death? One assumes porn, since although the novel ends with the death of many of its protagonists, the real emphasis is on the six hundred sexual acts that the leading character plans to perform and the impact it has on her daughter, a boy who thinks he's her son, and an ex-lover. The selection of *Snuff* as a target for obscenity has more to do with its open portrayal of sexual activity than with homosexuality, which is absent from the novel. Given Turkey's insistence on the importance of family, the book's depiction of a porn star as a mother and the quest of various characters to establish patrimony are other possible reasons the book raised the ire of the censor. Ultimately, it could simply be that a title with *porn* and *death* was bound to attract attention.

4. See also Khaled El-Rouayheb's book *Before Homosexuality in the Arab-Islamic World, 1500–1800*, where he discusses three strands (role-based, platonic love of human beauty, and religious-juridical) of same-sex desires and practices.

5. For a more extended discussion of Müren, see Martin Stokes, "The Tearful Public Sphere: Turkey's 'Sun of Art,' Zeki Müren," in *Music and Gender: Perspectives from the Mediterranean*. For a detailed treatment of Ersoy, see Rüstem Ertug Altınay, "Reconstructing the Transgendered Self as a Muslim, Nationalist, Upper-Class Woman: The Case of Bülent Ersoy" in the journal *Women's Studies Quarterly*.

6. For a more detailed discussion of the multiple homosexualities to be found in Turkey, see Hüseyin Tapınç, "'Masculinity, Femininity, and Turkish Male Homosexuality," in Ken Plummer's *Modern Homosexualities.*

7. Consider, too, the same-sex marriage of Ekin Keser and Emrullah Tüzün that took place on an Istanbul ferry in September 2014. Although such marriages are not allowed by Turkish law, both men received death threats and were evicted from their home when this purely ceremonial union was featured in the news (Alkaç).

8. For a discussion of how the *Naked Lunch* trial contributed to the marketing of the book in the United States, see Meagan Wilson's article "Your Reputation Precedes You: A Reception Study of *Naked Lunch*" in the *Journal of Modern Literature.*

9. Yılmaz's choice of words is telling. He uses "bulaşmış insan" to describe those who were involved with leftist struggles. But "bulaşmış" could also be translated as "infected." There is an ambivalence here in Yılmaz's comment that sheds light on the generally negative ways in which the left has been portrayed. Leftist politics is a contagion, something that one catches by becoming too close to undesirable elements in society. Of course Yılmaz, a leftist himself, is probably using this ironically or gesturing to the sort of rhetoric that was foisted on him in his activist days. According to local legend, Ayrıntı was supposedly established with funds from a jewelry heist, though your author thought it best not to question Yılmaz on the veracity of this rumor. The left still carries a stigma in Turkey, a mark of outsider status that some still wear proudly, others a bit sheepishly, and far more have left behind in an attempt to embrace capitalism.

10. Unlike Sel, Ayrıntı has chosen a more subdued response to the trial. They do not include the Committee's statements in their advertising, and while Yılmaz was forthcoming about the trial in a personal interview, their website, unlike Sel's, contains no updates on the trial's progress. Funda Uncu, *Snuff*'s female translator, is equally reticent, perhaps due to the fact that she is named in the indictment and was threatened to be taken by force to the Bodrum police station to give her statement if she did not go willingly. But despite being harassed at the station by officers who asked her if she was the model for the book's main character, she has filed charges against the officer, and in an email interview she remains undaunted: "I've translated nearly all of Palahniuk's novels into Turkish and I plan to continue to translate his or other underground writers' novels" (Uncu interview).

11. To understand the stakes involved in such a debate, the reader should realize that Turkey still carries on its books the infamous Article 301, which makes the denigration of "being a Turk, the Republic or Turkish Grand National Assembly . . . the Government of the Republic of Turkey, the judicial bodies of the State [or] the military or security organizations" a crime (*Turkish Penal Code* 165–66). Although an allowance is made for "the purpose of criticism"

(166), this article has been used most notably in the trial of Nobel Prize–winning author Orhan Pamuk, who dared to mention the killing of Kurds and Armenians in Turkey. As Ahmet Beşe notes in "Thoughts on Censorship in Turkey and the West," the difficulty is that "the concepts of 'Turkishness' and 'denigration' and what is protected under freedom of speech is continually being interpreted and reinterpreted by the Turkish judicial system" (149).

12. For a discussion of the connection between masculinity and the Beat generation, see David Savran's *Taking It Like a Man: White Masculinity, Masochism, and Contemporary American Culture* (1998).

13. Önok also discusses the committee's composition: the president is appointed by the prime minister, one member by the minister of justice, one by the minister of the interior, two from the Youth and Sports Ministry, one from the Ministry of Health, one from the Ministry of Culture and Tourism, one from the Committee of Higher Education, one from Religious Affairs, and a final member from among a ballot drawn by the Ankara, Izmir, and Istanbul Council of Reporters. The first three appointments, and especially the president, are government ones, and one can assume that they would generally follow the interests of those in power. The others, however, are supposedly nonpartisan but would obviously have their own political leanings.

14. There is a distinct possibility that the prosecutor, and perhaps even the committee, are simply going through the required motions without hope for success. Sertabiboğlu claims, for instance, that the prosecutor is not really conservative: "I talked with the prosecutor personally, he wasn't a conservative man. The prosecutor told me that 'We put this book on trial as a formality so that we are not questioned later on why we didn't do it.'" (Sertabiboğlu, interview). Perhaps most of those involved in this process are simply doing their jobs. Given the inertia of Turkish bureaucracy, this is not such a wild claim as it might first appear. *The Soft Machine* and *Snuff* might simply be two books that were clear standouts for censorship, the perfect texts with which to generate the appearance of proper government functioning.

15. This seems to have been the case in the U.S. context as well. According to Michael B. Goodman in his study *Contemporary Literary Censorship: The Case History of Burroughs' "Naked Lunch,"* while the first printer, Grove Press, contacted for the U.S. edition of *Naked Lunch* refused, claiming that he would "not allow my name to be associated with this type of literature for reproduction in my plant," the second printer "included a clause which indemnified the company in the event of legal action" (157). In the end, this protection was unnecessary, as the book was tried "in rem," or "the thing itself." According to Goodman, this meant that "a book had to be found obscene before a dealer could be arrested on criminal charges for selling it" (174). The book stood trial, rather than the bookseller, printer, or author. It was a solution that benefited everyone. Rather than creating a culture of fear where others would

be afraid to print or sell such work, the in rem procedure allowed "an official the opportunity to be simultaneously perceived as tough on smut, and liberal on the criminal prosecution of the bookdealer" (176). Turkey, unfortunately, lacks such a procedure.

16. For a detailed account of U.S. censorship before the 1930s, see Paul S. Boyer's *Purity in Print: The Vice-Society Movement and Book Censorship in America* (1968). Boyer, writing from within the 1960s debate, notices an interesting shift from the defense of an earlier licentiousness to a more difficult and complicated embrace of postwar sexuality. Boyer notes that "in the 1920s, most of the 'shocking' books which aroused the censors treated sexual relations, whether heterosexual or homosexual, in a context of love, tenderness, and respect for human dignity" (xiv). In such a climate, it was easy to deride censorship and champion the free expression of explicit material. The postwar era, for Boyer, marks a sea change. As he explains, "It is now writers like William Burroughs, Hubert Selby, Jr., 'Pauline Réage,' and—ultimately—the Marquis de Sade for whom one must take a stand. Under these circumstances, the old cheerful faith in the obvious desirability of complete permissiveness has faded" (xiv). Ultimately, Boyer makes that stand but is reticent and undecided about how permissive U.S. censorship should be given this new cultural situation.

17. In addition to these two trials, *Naked Lunch* was involved in a third case in Los Angeles in the fall of 1964. Isaac Galanti, the distributor of the book, and Earle Frank, a bookseller, were charged with violating the state's obscenity statute (Goodman 232). But as Goodman notes, the case was quite different. *Naked Lunch* itself was not on trial, but in order for these defendants to be found guilty, the book had to be proven to be obscene. Judge Alan G. Cambell ruled that *Naked Lunch*, considered as a whole, did not meet the standard for prurient interest and the charges for distributing and selling it were dropped (although the two continued to stand trial for another book) (234).

18. Procensorship forces are not content with just the airwaves, however. Debate has intensified over public funding of the arts, with many critics trying to have funding pulled from "controversial" artists or exhibits. Artists like Andrés Serrano and Robert Mapplethorpe, for example, have seen their works attacked as lacking in value and thus undeserving of funding from the National Endowment for the Arts. Museums and other venues have likewise felt the pressure to avoid exhibiting works that might attract the ire of such groups. Again, this threat creates an atmosphere of precensorship that is just as problematic as outright attempts to ban works.

19. Section 3 is a provision against "[a] person who uses children in the production of obscene written or audio-visual material" or who "conveys such material into the country, who copies or offers for sale such material or who sells, transports, stores, exports, retains possession of such material or offers such material for the use of others" (129). This provision legitimately protects

minors from being involved in the production of works that would otherwise not be considered obscene because of their status as artistic.

20. While it is easy to side with the defense against the oftentimes ludicrous claims of the committee, a legitimate question arises: Why not put warning labels on these books? The publishers of both Sel and Ayrıntı have admitted that they are willing to do so if necessary. Of course this does not address the deeper questions of censorship and whether such labeling is right, and it certainly amounts to a form of precensorship. But for the publishers, this is clearly the last line of defense—they believe these works have the right to be sold without disclaimers.

21. Consider an exemplary sentence from a typical committee report: "From primitive times to the present, everywhere and in every society, as an indispensable rule, people have covered their sexual parts and protected the secrecy of their sexual affairs" ("Bir kararımız"). Statements such as this not only demonstrate the rather outdated notions of decency entertained by the committee but become fodder for their opponents, who are extremely fond of pointing out the ridiculousness of the committee's positions. Despite such anachronistic ideas regarding sexuality, the possible one- to four-year jail term and the five-thousand-day fine stipulated in the fourth provision mean that the committee's charges have to be taken seriously.

22. The street language the Beats employed probably sounded harsh to their initial postwar audience as well. Part of the rebelliousness of figures like Burroughs is their willingness to say the things nobody else is willing to say in a language nobody else is willing to speak. Stylistically, Burroughs's cut-up method is considered innovative in the United States even today, though his use of harsh language has lost some of its bite over the years. In Turkey, however, such language still has the power to shock, as the reception of Burroughs's work makes clear.

23. The decision to publish a rather obscure text in the Burroughs oeuvre before the more obvious choice of *Naked Lunch* highlights the oftentimes haphazard nature of the Turkish publishing industry. A single author is often represented by multiple presses who do not always coordinate their publishing schedules, and the decision to publish a particular work might be due simply to the fact that a translator happened to choose that work to translate, for any number of reasons. This institutional situation means that a given author's presence in the culture can be constructed quite randomly, rather than as a planned strategy of introducing the more important or representative texts before publishing lesser works.

24. The book was reviewed by three professors, Esra Melikoğlu and Canan Şavkay from İstanbul University and Hasan Sınar from İstanbul Kemerburgaz University. In a joint statement, they concluded that Burroughs's text is a work of literature and the author is making a social statement rather than simply

arousing readers' sexual desire. The reviewers draw extensively on Burroughs's international reputation, citing comments by writers like Norman Mailer and Jack Kerouac to demonstrate that *The Soft Machine*'s groundbreaking narrative style and use of sexuality as a theme serves the purpose of social critique. ("Bir kararımız").

25. It is impossible to know whether the committee has brought more books to trial in Turkey. The only reason that the Burroughs and Palahniuk trial made headlines was that Sel and Ayrıntı chose to promote it. Unfortunately, without media exposure, it is difficult to track the committee's decisions.

5. HOWLING IN TURKISH: APPROPRIATING THE MANY FACES OF ALLEN GINSBERG

1. Güven Turan, a Turkish poet likewise involved in the leftist scene in the 1960s and 1970s, claims that Ginsberg was an integral part of Turkish counterculture: "As in *Howl*, he said 'put those missiles up your ass,' and this was almost a motto for young Turkish leftists. Because there were missiles in Turkey too and leftists were against them. So Ginsberg was our revolutionary model too. Like Che. We were hanging the poster of Ginsberg or the cover of *Howl* on the wall next to Che. Young university students!" (Turan, interview).

2. For an extensive treatment of Ginsberg and Ferlinghetti's interest in the Marxist revolution in Nicaragua, see Michele Hardesty's "'If the Writers of the World Get Together': Allen Ginsberg, Lawrence Ferlinghetti, and Literary Solidarity in Sandinista Nicaragua," in Nancy M. Grace and Jennie Skerl's *The Transnational Beat Generation.*

3. Critics in other cultures struggled with the term as well. In his afterword to the important collection *Junge Amerikanische Lyrik* (*New American Poetry*, 1961), which introduced the Beats to a West German audience, Walter Höllerer attempts to explain the term *Beat* itself:

> First of all, "beat" means "dead-tired" (*todmüde*) "non-resistant" (*widerstandslos*), exhausted by the public notices of propaganda arguments and contradictory approved slogans. The same generation in Germany offers a parallel. But at the same time connected with this term is less the German "beaten" (*geschlagen*) and more "concentrated" (*auf sich konzentriert*) or "inwardly directed" (*nach inwärts gerichtet*), in such a manner "impulsive" (*impulsiv*). American critics, namely politicians, even use the word "mystical" (which is used over there as rashly as we use "nihilistic") . . . but with that comes a double-meaning in the word, which is more in keeping with the texts of these authors: hard passivity (*harte Passivität*) and a new, taut activity (*neu gerichtete gespannte Aktivität*). (256)

Most translators leave the term *Beat* untranslated, but that strategy still requires them to explain it to their readers. For Höllerer, the Beats may be "beaten" by society, but contrary to their critics, they do not give up hope but rather respond actively to their oppression.

4. For an extended discussion of the history of the Left in Turkey, see Murat Belge's article "Nationalism, Democracy, and the Left in Turkey" in the *Journal of Intercultural Studies.*

5. Arslan was not the only one looking for a new mode of dissent. The book was actually published by Islamicists looking to challenge the current government. Arslan relates that he warned them about the book's provocative content, but "[i]t was not a problem for them because Ginsberg was a milestone in the history of opposition. They said we are an oppositional group also; maybe we have no intimate contacts with Ginsberg's thought and poetry, but he is an important one and had to be expressed in Turkish. They were even okay with the uncensored version and we got no penalty for that translation" (Arslan, interview). Oppositional politics, at least in Turkey, makes for strange bedfellows.

6. Arslan's invocation of Ginsberg's Jewishness should by no means be taken pejoratively. In fact, Turkey has had a long history of accepting Jews into its society. Mehmet the Conqueror requested the Jews of Constantinople to remain after he had taken the city, and furthermore invited Jews from the Christian persecution in Spain in 1492 to settle in the Ottoman Empire (Pope 27). Most of Turkey's Jewish population traces its roots back to this period, and even speak a version of Spanish called "Ladino." This tolerance continued through Mustafa Kemal's reign, and even though the government admittedly instituted heavy taxes on Jews during World War II (with those unable to pay being sent to labor camps), according to Hugh and Nicole Pope, "The republic maintained Ottoman traditions, protecting some Jews from Nazi Germany by giving them Turkish passports and welcoming 150 Jews among the more than 200 German professors two took refuge in Turkey during the Second World War" (242). To this day there is still a small population of Jews remaining, though their numbers are slowly dwindling.

7. For a discussion of how Ginsberg's queerness has been silenced in Polish translations of his work, see Jack Hutchens's article "Translating the Queer Voice: Problems with Polish Translations of Ginsberg's 'America' and 'Message'" in *The Journal of Popular Culture.*

8. Erdoğan does, however, get closer to Ginsberg's "who sweetened the snatches of a million girls" (128) with the use of an interesting diminutive, "little pussy" (*amcık*; 18).

9. Çaydamlı likewise invokes religious imagery when discussing a trip he took to former Beat haunts. Calling his trip a "*hac*" or "pilgrimage," Çaydamli asks himself what took him there, and responds, "it was again the reed flute and breath" (*Uluma*).

10. The use of hashish in particular was an integral part of Hassan-I Sabbah's Assassins, a Persian group that had an influence on the thinking of William S. Burroughs.

11. This sort of word construction can also be seen in the Turkish slang for masturbation, "otuz bir" or the number "31," which refers to the numeric value of "elif" and "lam," which spell "el," or "hand" in Turkish.

12. Küçük iskender also had fond memories of his host. The poet explains, "There was a professor, who also lived in Turkey for a period of time, Ed Foster, he was giving Beat Generation classes at the university. He hosted me in his house. It was a great journey" (14).

13. The power of Ginsberg's personal revelations are the major draw of his poetry, but it also helps that his style is easily reproducible. Many foreign poets have chosen to use his work as almost a template in their poetry, retaining the formal structure of poems like *Howl* or "America" but replacing details that customize the work to the particular place. Christopher Gair and Konstantina Georganta, for instance, have demonstrated the close parallels between the Greek poet Lefteris Poulios's "An American Bar in Athens" (1973) and Ginsberg's "A Supermarket in California" (see "Greece and the Beat Generation: The Case of Lefteris Poulios" in Grace and Skerl's *The Transnational Beat Generation*). Ginsberg also had a huge impact on the Bengali poets of what came to be called the Hungry Generation, especially in the poem "Stark Electric Jesus" by Malay Roy Choudhury. Both these examples demonstrate the countercultural force that Ginsberg's work has in its reproducibility.

14. See the second section of *Deliberate Prose: Selected Essays, 1952–1995*, as well as *Allen Verbatim: Lectures on Poetry, Politics, Consciousness* for Ginsberg's thoughts on the subject of drugs.

15. An extensive review of U.S. underground journals from the late 1950s and the 1960s revealed only one reference to a Turkish poet: Nazım Hikmet. Turkish poetry, from all periods, appears not to have circulated widely in the postwar American context.

16. Beat writers did learn from critiques of their work. Gregory Corso, for instance, relates in an interview with Gavin Selerie, "Now this is before Women's Lib. Dig the ball game: when you use the word 'Man' it entails everybody, but today you gotta be careful. After Women's Lib, I have to put two more vowels with it—'Humankind.' I can't say 'Mankind,' I can't say 'Man,' I gotta say 'Humankind'" (Schober 154). While it might seem unfair to soften such rhetoric after the fact, it is true that Beat writers did acknowledge problems in their work.

BIBLIOGRAPHY

Agel, Jerome, editor. *The Radical Therapist*. Ballantine Books, 1971.

Ahıska, Meltem. "Occidentalism: The Historical Fantasy of the Modern." *The South Atlantic Quarterly*, special issue, vol. 102, no. 2/3, Spring / Summer 2003, pp. 351–79.

Ahmad, Feroz. *Turkey: The Quest for Identity*. Oneworld, 2005.

Akarsu, H. T. "Dosya: Türkiye'de Yeraltı Edebiyatı Var mı?" ["Dossier: Is There an Underground Literature in Turkey?"] *Varlık*, February 2005, pp. 14–24.

Alkaç, Fırat. "Gay Couple Faces Threats after Symbolic Wedding." *Hurriyet Daily News*, Oct. 13, 2014, www.hurriyetdailynews.com/.

Altınay, Rüstem Ertug. "Reconstructing the Transgendered Self as a Muslim, Nationalist, Upper-Class Woman: The Case of Bülent Ersoy." *Women's Studies Quarterly*, vol. 36, no. 3/4, pp. 210–29.

Altun, Murat. "The Photocopied 1990s: Youth, Culture, and Fanzines." Master's thesis, Boğaziçi University, 2005.

Andaç, Feridun. "Dosya: Türkiye'de Yeraltı Edebiyatı Var mı?" ["Dossier: Is There an Underground Literature in Turkey?"] *Varlık*, February 2005, pp. 14–24.

Apter, Emily. *The Translation Zone: A New Comparative Literature*. Princeton UP, 2006.

Arna, Sibel. "Yeraltından Notlar" ["Notes from Underground"]. *Hürriyet Daily News*, Feb. 8, 2003, www.hurriyet.com.tr/yeraltindan-notlar-126965.

Arslan, Esat. "Özgür Kız ve Postmodernlik" ["Free Girl and Postmodernism"]. *Radikal*, Jan. 25, 2004, www.radikal.com.tr/radikal2/ozgur_kiz_ve_postmodernlik-870945.

Arslan, C. Hakan. Interview by author. Translated by Cansu Soyupak. Digital recording, Istanbul, Apr. 26, 2014.

———, translator. *Kuşbeyin! Seçme Şiirler 1949–1985*. [*Birdbrain! Selected Poems, 1949–1985*]. By Allen Ginsberg. Istanbul: Şehir Yayıncılık, 1991.

Ash, Mel. *Beat Spirit: The Way of the Beat Writers as a Living Experience*. Tarcher Press, 1997.

Avcı, Ümran. "Şairlik Çok Yönlü Fahişeliktir" ["Being a Poet Is a Versatile Form of Prostitution"]. *Haberturk*, Nov. 29, 2010, www.haberturk.com/kultur-sanat/haber/575933-sairlik-cok-yonlu-fahiseliktir.

Baker, Deborah. *A Blue Hand: The Tragicomic, Mind-Altering Odyssey of Allen Ginsberg, a Holy Fool, a Lost Muse, a Dharma Bum, and His Prickly Bride in India*. Penguin, 2009.

Barthes, Roland. *The Pleasure of the Text*. Translated by Richard Miller, Hill and Wang, 1975.

———. *S/Z: An Essay*. 1970. Translated by Richard Miller, Hill and Wang, 1975.

Beaulieu, Victor-Lévy. *Jack Kerouac: A Chicken Essay*. Coach House, 1975.

Belge, Murat. "Nationalism, Democracy, and the Left in Turkey." *Journal of Intercultural Studies*, vol. 30, no. 1, February 2009, pp. 7–20.

Belgrad, Daniel. *The Culture of Spontaneity: Improvisation and the Arts in Postwar America*. U of Chicago P, 1998.

Belletto, Steven. Introduction. *The Cambridge Companion to the Beats*. Cambridge UP, 2017, pp. 1–22.

Bereket, Tarik, and Barry D. Adam. "The Emergence of Gay Identities in Contemporary Turkey." *Sexualities*, vol. 9, no. 2, 2006, pp. 131–51.

Berk, Özlem. *Translation and Westernization in Turkey: From the 1840s to the 1980s*. Ege Yayınları, 2004.

Bermann, Sandra. Introduction. *Nation, Language, and the Ethics of Translation*, edited by Bermann and Michael Wood. Princeton UP, 2005, pp. 1–10.

Beşe, Ahmet. "Thoughts on Censorship in Turkey and the West." *The Transnational Turn in American Studies: Turkey and the United States*, edited by Tanfer Tunç and Bahar Gursel. Peter Lang, 2012, pp. 141–52.

Bhabha, Homi K. *The Location of Culture*. Routledge, 1994.

"Bir Kararımız Bile Yok Ama Iki Raporumuz Var" ["We Don't Have a Decision, but We've Got Two Reports"]. *Sel*, July 5, 2012, www.selyayincilik.blogspot.com/2012/07/bir-kararmz-bile-yok-ama-iki-raporumuz.html.

"Bir Kumkapı Gecesi" ["A Kumkapi Night"]. *Millliyet*, Apr. 14, 1997, p. 23.

Boyar, Ebru. "The Press and the Palace: the Two-Way Relationship between Abdulhamid II and the Press, 1876–1908." *Bulletin of the School of Oriental and African Studies*, vol. 69, no. 3, 2006, pp. 417–32.

Boyer, Paul S. *Purity in Print: The Vice-Society Movement and Book Censorship in America*. Charles Scribner's Sons, 1968.

Burroughs, William S. *The Job: Interviews with William S. Burroughs.* Grove Press, 1974.

———. Preface. *BAMN: Outlaw Manifestoes and Ephemera, 1965–70*, edited by P. Stansill and D. Z. Mairowitz. Penguin, 1971.

———. *The Soft Machine.* 1961. Grove Press, 1966.

Burroughs, William S., and Jack Kerouac. *And the Hippos Were Boiled in Their Tanks.* Penguin Classics, 2008.

Can, Jan Ender. "Son" ["End"]. *Kadıköy Underground Poetix*, vol. 18, 2020 (actually 2008).

Çapan, Cevat. Interview by author. Digital recording, Istanbul, Apr. 18, 2014. In English.

Çaydamlı, Kaan. Interview with author. Translated by Sinan Ünver. Digital recording, Istanbul, May 14, 2010.

Celâl, Metin. "Dosya: Türkiye'de Yeraltı Edebiyatı Var mı? ["Dossier: Is There an Underground Literature in Turkey?"] *Varlık*, February 2005, pp. 14–24.

Çevbir. "'Yumuşak Makine' için İngilizce Basın Açıklaması" " ["A Press Statement in English for 'The Soft Machine'"]. Last modified 2011. http://www.cevbir.org/index.php. Accessed Feb. 9, 2013. No longer accessible.

Challis, Chris. *Quest for Kerouac.* Faber and Faber, 1984.

Charters, Ann. *Beat Down to Your Soul: What Was the Beat Generation?* Penguin, 2001.

———. *Kerouac.* St. Martin's Press, 1973.

Cheah, Pheng, and Bruce Robbins, editors. *Cosmopolitics: Thinking and Feeling beyond the Nation.* U of Minnesota P, 1998.

Clay, Steven, and Rodney Phillips. "A Little History of the Mimeograph Revolution." In Clay and Phillips, *A Secret Location on the Lower East Side: Adventures in Writing, 1960–1980.* New York Public Library and Granary Books, 1998, pp. 12–54.

Clifford, James. *Routes: Travel and Translation in the Late Twentieth Century.* Harvard UP, 1997.

"Çoğalmayıp Yetkinleşen Şiir" ["Poetry That Matures but Doesn't Multiply"]. *Radikal*, Oct. 31, 2008, www.radikal.com.tr/kitap/cogalmayip_yetkinlesen_bir_siir-905940.

Çoğulu, Halime Öcal. "Türkiye'de Yeraltı Edebiyatının İzleri: Kanat Güner, Ayça Seren Ural, Sibel Torunoğlu, Mehmet Kartal" ["Traces of Underground Literature in Turkey: Kanat Güner, Ayça Seren Ural, Sibel Torunoğlu, Mehmet Kartal"]. Yüksek Lisans Program, 2010.

Coontz, Stephanie. *The Way We Never Were: American Families and the Nostalgia Trap.* Basic Books, 1992.

Corso, Gregory. *Mindfield: New and Selected Poems.* Thunder's Mouth, 1998.

Cran, Rona. "'Everything Is Permitted': William Burroughs' Cut-up Novels and European Art." *Comparative American Studies*, vol. 11, no. 3, 2013, pp. 300–313.

Damon, Maria. *Postliterary America: From Bagel Shop Jazz to Micropoetries.* U of Iowa P, 2011.

———. "Post-Literary Poetry, Counterperformance, and Micropoetries." *Poetry and Pedagogy: The Challenge of the Contemporary*, edited by Joan Retallack and Juliana Spahr. Palgrave Macmillan, 2006, pp. 129–47.

de Haan, Martin. "Letter to Turkish Ministry of Justice." *The European Council of Literary Translators' Associations.* 2011. Web. Feb. 9, 2013. www.ceatl.eu/.

Demac, Donna A. *Liberty Denied: The Current Rise of Censorship in America.* PEN American Center, 1988.

D'Emilio, John. *Sexual Politics, Sexual Communities: The Making of a Homosexual Minority in the United States, 1940–1970.* U of Chicago P, 1983.

Demirsü, Zeynep. "Yolun Bir Yerinde Kerouac" ["Kerouac at Some Point on the Road"]. *Varlık*, vol. 75, no. 1209, 2008, pp. 29–33.

Dilbaz, Bahadır. "Gülemiyorum Seni" ["I Cannot Smile You"]. *Underground Poetix*, vol. 6, 2010, n. pag.

di Prima, Diane. Introduction. *The Floating Bear: A Newsletter*, edited by Diane di Prima and LeRoi Jones. Laurence McGilvery, 1973, pp. vii–xvii.

Doğa. "Röpörtaj: küçük iskender" ["Interview: küçük iskender"]. Nov. 21, 2009, www.turkgayclub.org/tge/kucuk-iskender.htm.

Doğan, Mehmet Onur. "10 Soruda 'Muzır Kurul'" ["The 'Harmful Committee' in 10 Questions"]. *Sabitfikir*, last modified 2011. Accessed Feb. 9, 2013. www.sabitfikir.com/dosyalar/10-soruda-muzir-kurul.

Dorsay, Atilla. "Yalnız Kentin Radyosu" ["The City's Only Radio"]. *Sabah*, Mar. 26, 2011, www.sabah.com.tr/Cumartesi/2011/03/26/yalniz_kentin_radyosu.

Duman, Sevda. "Yaşamayı Seven Isyankarlar" ["Legislation Loving Rebels"]. *Birgün*, Mar. 23, 2008. www.birgun.net/book_index.php?news_code=1208930563&month=04&day=23.

Durmuş, Oya Dinçer. "Popüler Kültürün Kimlik Oluşumuna Etkileri: 'Özgür Kız-Nil Karaibrahimgil' Modeli" ["The Effects of Popular Culture on Identity Formation: The 'Free Girl-Nil Karaibrahimgil' Model"]. *Sosyal Bilimler Enstitüsü Dergisi*, 2006, www.sbed.mu.edu.tr/index.php/asd/article/view/184/190.

Duru, Orhan. "Gezegen Antika Olacak Yakında Ben de Bir Antika Eşya Gibiyim. Buna Karşı Değilim Çünkü Antikalar Çok Değerli" ["The Planet Will Soon Become an Antique. I Am Also Like an Antique Piece. But I Am Not Against This, Because Antiques Are Quite Valuable"]. *Heves*, vol. 23, October 2009, pp. 55–61.

Duru, Sezer. "Allen Ginsberg'le Anılar" ["Memories with Allen Ginsberg"]. *Hürriyet Gösteri*, no. 197–98, 1997, pp. 44–47.

Edgü, Ferit. "Amerika Gözlerin Neden Yaşlı?" ["America, Why Are Your Eyes Full of Tears?"] *Radikal*, Nov. 4, 2003, www.//kitap.radikal.com.tr/Preview /251430-yazdir.

———. "Birinci Basımın Önsöz Gibi'si" ["Like a Preface to the First Edition"]. Edgü and Duru, pp. 7–9.

Edgü, Ferit, and Orhan Duru, translators. *Amerika: Şiirler* [America: Poems]. By Allen Ginsberg and Lawrence Ferlinghetti. Ada Yayınları, 1976.

Edebiyathaber.net. "Yumuşak Makine ve Ölüm Pornosu Davasında Sonuçsuz Karar: Beraat Yok, Erteleme Var!" ["The Decision in *The Soft Machine* and *Snuff*'s Endless Trial: No Acquittal, but Postponement!"] July 6, 2012, www.edebiyathaber.net/yumusak-makine-ve-olum-pornosu-davasinda-sonucsuz -karar-beraat-yok-erteleme-var/.

Edington, Stephen D. *The Beat Face of God: The Beat Generation as Spirit Guides*. Trafford Publishing, 2006.

Edwards, Brian T. *Morocco Bound: Disorienting America's Maghreb, from Casablanca to the Marrakech Express*. Duke UP, 2005.

El-Rouayheb, Khaled. *Before Homosexuality in the Arab-Islamic World, 1500–1800*. U of Chicago P, 2005.

Erdoğan, Özcan. "Küçük İskender'le Söyleşi: Şiirsel Söylemi Kendime Kul Etme" ["A Conversation with Küçük İskender : Making Poetic Expression My Servant"]. Blog repost from *bireylikler*, www.kenanyucel.blogcu.com /kucuk-iskender-le-soylesi-siirsel-soylemi-kendime-kul-etme/3571898. Accessed 2008.

Erdoğan, Şenol. "Giriş" ["Introduction"]. *Beat Kuşağı Antolojisi* [*Beat Generation Anthology*]. 6:45 Publishers, 2011.

———. Interview by author. Translated by Sinan Ünver. Digital recording, Istanbul, May 14, 2010.

———. *Uluma ve Öteki Şiirler* [*Howl and Other Poems*]. Altıkırkbeş Yayın, 2013.

———. "Yeni Garip ve Beat Kuşağı" ["New Strange and the Beat Generation"]. Sept. 8, 2012, www.odeonblog.wordpress.com/2010/12/23/1-yeni -garip-hareketi-ve-beat-kusagi/.

———. "Yerin Dibi!" ["The Very Bottom!"] *Notos*, August-September 2011, pp. 28–30.

Ergin, Murat. "The Racialization of Kurdish Identity in Turkey." *Ethnic and Racial Studies*, vol. 37, no. 2, 2014, pp. 322–41.

Ertem, Ece. "Istanbul'un Orta Yerinde Skandal" ["Istanbul in the Midst of Scandal"]. Apr. 18, 2011. *CNN Turk*. www.cnnturk.com/2011/yasam/diger /04/18/istanbulun.orta.yerinde.skandal/613702.0/index.html.

Evren, Süreyya. "Dosya: Türkiye'de Yeraltı Edebiyatı Var mı?" ["Dossier: Is There an Underground Literature in Turkey?"] *Varlık*, February 2005, pp. 14–24.

Fazzino, Jimmy. *World Beats: Beat Generation Writing and the Worlding of U.S. Literature*. Hanover, N.H.: Dartmouth College P, 2016.

Felek, Özgen. "The Ottoman Empire." *Cultural History of Reading*, vol. 1, *World Literature*, edited by Gabrielle Watling. Greenwood Press, 2009.

Fidan, Burak. "Ginsberg'in İstanbul Günleri" ["The Istanbul Nights of Ginsberg"]. *Heves*, vol. 23, October 2009, pp. 49–50.

Filkins, Dexter. "The Deep State: The Prime Minister Is Revered as a Moderate, but How Far Will He Go to Stay in Power?" *The New Yorker*, Mar. 12, 2012.

Fishkin, Shelley Fisher. "Crossroads of Cultures: The Transnational Turn in American Studies; Presidential Address to the American Studies Association, November 12, 2004." *American Quarterly*, vol. 57, no. 1, 2005, pp. 17–57.

Flood, Alison. "European Court Rules against Turkey's Apollinaire Ban." *The Guardian*, Feb. 17, 2010, www.guardian.co.uk/books/2010/feb/17/european-court-turkey-apollinaire-ban.

Fox, Hugh. "The Living Underground." *The North American Review*, Fall 1969, pp. 57–58.

Gair, Christopher, and Konstantina Georganta. "Greece and the Beat Generation: The Case of Lefteris Poulios." Grace and Skerl, *The Transnational Beat Generation*, pp. 219–29.

García-Robles, Jorge. *At the End of the Road: Jack Kerouac in Mexico.* Translated by Daniel C. Schechter, U of Minnesota P, 2014.

"Genç Bir Don Juan'ın Maceraları Davası Ertelemeyle Sonuçlandı" ["Court Case of 'The Adventures of a Young Don Juan' Ends with a Delay"]. Sel. Last modified 2013, accessed Sept. 25, 2014, www.selyayincilik.com.

Giles, Paul. *Virtual Americas: Transnational Fictions and the Transatlantic Imaginary.* Duke UP, 2002.

Ginsberg, Allen. *Allen Verbatim: Lectures on Poetry, Politics, Consciousness.* Edited by Gordon Ball, McGraw-Hill, 1974.

———. *Collected Poems: 1947–1980.* Harper and Row, 1985.

———. *Deliberate Prose: Selected Essays, 1952–1995.* Edited by Bill Morgan, Harper Collins, 2000.

———. "Notes Written on Finally Recording Howl." *Evergreen Review*, vol. 3, no. 10, 1959, pp. 132–35.

Goodman, Michael B. *Contemporary Literary Censorship: The Case History of Burroughs'* Naked Lunch. Scarecrow, 1981.

Göle, Nilüfer. "The Quest for the Islamic Self within the Context of Modernity." *Rethinking Modernity and National Identity in Turkey*, edited by Sibel Bozdoğan and Reşat Kasaba. U of Washington P, 1997, pp. 81–94.

Gorkemli, Serkan. "'Coming Out of the Internet': Lesbian and Gay Activism and the Internet as a 'Digital Closet' in Turkey." *Journal of Middle East Women's Studies*, vol. 8, no. 3, 2012, pp. 63–88.

Grace, Nancy M., and Jennie Skerl. "Introduction to Transnational Beat: Global Poetics in a Postmodern World." Grace and Skerl, *Transnational Beat Generation*, pp. 1–11.

———, editors. *The Transnational Beat Generation*. Palgrave Macmillan, 2012.

Gray, Timothy. *Gary Snyder and the Pacific Rim: Creating Countercultural Community*. U of Iowa P, 2006.

Gündüz, Zuhal Yeşilyurt. "The Women's Movement in Turkey: From Tanzimat towards European Union Membership." *Perceptions*, Autumn 2004, pp. 115–34.

Güner, Kanat. *Eroin Güncesi* [*Heroin Diary*]. Era Yayıncılık, 1997.

Gürbilek, Nurdan. *The New Cultural Climate in Turkey: Living in a Shop Window*. Translated by Victoria Holbrook, Zed Books, 2011.

Hall, Stuart, and Tony Jefferson. *Resistance through Rituals: Youth Subcultures in Post-war Britain*. Routledge, 2006.

Halman, Talat S. *A Millennium of Turkish Literature*. Edited by Jayne L. Warner, Republic of Turkey Ministry of Culture and Tourism, 2009.

Hardesty, Michele. "'If the Writers of the World Get Together': Allen Ginsberg, Lawrence Ferlinghetti, and Literary Solidarity in Sandinista Nicaragua." Grace and Skerl, *Transnational Beat Generation*, pp. 115–28.

Harris, Oliver. *William Burroughs and the Secret of Fascination*. Southern Illinois UP, 2003.

Hebdige, Dick. *Subculture: The Meaning of Style*. Routledge, 1979.

Heins, Marjorie. *Sex, Sin, and Blasphemy: A Guide to America's Censorship Wars*. The New Press, 1993.

Hippler, Bob. "Fast Times in the Motor City: The First Ten Years of the Fifth Estate, 1965–1975." *Voices from the Underground: Insider Histories of the Vietnam Era Underground Press*, edited by Ken Wachsberger. Mica's Press, 1993, pp. 9–36.

Hofstede, Geert. *Culture's Consequences: Comparing Values, Behaviors, Institutions, and Organizations across Nations*. Sage Publications, 2001.

Höllerer, Walter, and Gregory Corso. *Junge Amerikanische Lyrik* [*New American Poetry*]. Carl Hanser Verlag, 1961.

Horemans, Rudi. *Beat Indeed!* J. H. Weinberg, 1985.

Hutchens, Jack. "Translating the Queer Voice: Problems with Polish Translations of Ginsberg's 'America' and 'Message.'" *The Journal of Popular Culture*, vol. 40, no. 6, 2007, pp. 979–93.

İnce, Özdemir. "Beat Generation ve 'Amerika' Üzerine" ["On the Beat Generation and 'America'"]. *Şiirden Dergisi*, no. 6, July-August 2011, pp. 26–33.

Insel, Ahmet. "The AKP and Normalizing Democracy in Turkey." *The South Atlantic Quarterly*, special issue, vol. 102, no. 2/3, Spring / Summer 2003, pp. 293–308.

International Publishers Association. "IPA Press Release," last modified 2011. www.internationalpublishers.org. Accessed Feb. 9, 2013.

Irzık, Sibel, and Güven Güzeldere. Introduction. "Relocating the Fault Lines: Turkey beyond the East-West Divide." *The South Atlantic Quarterly*, special issue, vol. 102 no. 2/3, Spring / Summer 2003, pp. 283–92.

Iser, Wolfgang. *The Act of Reading: A Theory of Aesthetic Response.* 1978. John Hopkins UP, 1980.

———. *The Implied Reader: Patterns of Communication in Prose Fiction from Bunyan to Beckett.* 1974. John Hopkins UP, 1978.

iskender, küçük. *Periler Ölürken Özür Diler* [*Fairies Apologize as They Die*]. Yapı Kredilan, 1994.

———. "Dosya: Türkiye'de Yeraltı Edebiyatı Var mı?" ["Dossier: Is There an Underground Literature in Turkey?"] *Varlık*, February 2005, pp. 14–24.

———. "Televizyon Okuyan bir Kapitalizme Uluma" [*"A Howl at Capitalism Which Reads Television"*]. *Sabitfikir*, June 13, 2013, www.sabitfikir.com.

Johnson, David K. *The Lavender Scare: The Cold War Persecution of Gays and Lesbians in the Federal Government.* U of Chicago P, 2004.

Johnson, Ronna C., and Nancy M. Grace, eds. *Girls Who Wore Black: Women Writing the Beat Generation.* Rutgers UP, 2002.

———. "Visions and Revisions of the Beat Generation." Johnson and Grace, *Girls Who Wore Black*, pp. 1–24.

———. "Mapping Women Writers of the Beat Generation." *Breaking the Rule of Cool: Interviewing and Reading Women Beat Writers*, edited by Ronna C. Johnson and Nancy M. Grace. U of Mississippi P, 2004, pp. 3–41.

Johnson, Ronna C. "And Then She Went: Beat Departures and Feminine Transgressions in Joyce Johnson's *Come and Join the Dance.*" Johnson and Grace, *Girls Who Wore Black*, pp. 69–95.

Jordan, Ken. "Introduction." *Evergreen Review Reader: 1957–1966*, edited by Barney Rosset. Arcade Publishing, 2011.

Kaçan, Metin. *Ağır Roman* [*Cholera Street*]. Metis Yayınları, 1995.

Kağıtçıbaşı, Çiğdem. "Autonomy and Relatedness in Cultural Context: Implications for Self and Family." *Journal of Cross-Cultural Psychology*, vol. 36, no. 4, July 2005, pp. 403–22.

———. *Gençlerin Tutumları: Kültürler Arası Bir Karşılastırma* [*Youth Attitudes: A Cross-Cultural Comparison*]. Middle East Technical University, 1973.

———. "Social Norms and Authoritarianism: A Turkish-American Comparison." *Journal of Personality and Social Psychology*, vol. 16, no. 3, 1970, pp. 444–51.

Kahraman, Hasan Bülent. "Kötülük, Yeraltı Edebiyatı ve Yerüstü" ["Evil, Underground Literature, and Aboveground"]. *Varlık*, February 2005, pp. 8–13.

———. "Yerüstünden Yer altı Edebiyatına Bakmak" ["Looking at Underground Literature from Aboveground"]. *Notos*, vol. 4, 2011, pp. 22–26.

Kantarcı, Can. Interview with author. E-mail, Nov. 1, 2012. In English.

Kaplan, Amy, and Donald Pease, editors. *Cultures of United States Imperialism.* Duke UP, 1993.

Karataş, Evren. "Türkiye'de Yeraltı Edebiyatı ve Hakan Günday'ın Romanlarında Yeraltı Edebiyatının İzleri" ["Underground Literature in Turkey and the Traces of Underground Literature in Hakan Günday's Novels"]. *Zeitschrift für die Welt der Türken*, vol. 2, no. 1, 2010, pp. 89–113.

Kerouac, Jack. *On the Road.* 1957. London: Penguin Classics, 2000.

———. *Yolda: Orijinal Rulo* [*On the Road: The Original Scroll*]. Translated by Can Kantarcı, Ayrıntı, 2008.

———. *Yolda* [*On the Road*]. Translated by Güzin Özkan and Ferruh Armutçuoğlu, Kıyı Yayınları, 1993.

———. *Zen Kaçıkları* [*The Dharma Bums*]. Translated by Nevzat Erkmen, yol yayınları, 1982.

Kerubi, Medsen. "BENIM ADIM SIK-K-ME BAŞ" ["My Name Is 'Fuck Head'"]. *Kadıköy Underground Poetix*, vol. 99 [but really vol. 2], 2040 [but really 2008], 170–72.

Kinross, Lord. *The Ottoman Centuries: The Rise and Fall of the Turkish Empire.* Harper Perennial, 1979.

"Kirli, Irkiltici ve Çekici" ["Dirty, Startling, and Seductive"]. *Birgun.* 2012. Web. Feb. 6, 2013. www.birgun.net.

Köser, Melda. "Then Mama Says Nö!" *Underground Poetix*, vol. 8, 2011, p. 11.

"Küçük Iskender ile Edebiyat ve Yaşam Üzerine" ["On Life and Literature with Küçük Iskender"]. *Lacivert*, vol. 6, no. 31, January-February 2010, pp. 3–26.

Kulaoğlu, Hüseyin. "İşte Küçük iskender bu!" ["This Is Küçük Iskender!"] Oct. 21, 2008, *Habervaktim.com*, www.habervaktim.com/haber/38557/iste-kucuk-iskender-bu.html.

Kurtar, Büşra. "Üryan geldim" ["I Came Naked"]. *Underground Poetix*, vol. 5, 2010, p. 146.

Lee, Ben. "*Howl and Other Poems*: Is There Old Left in These New Beats?" *American Literature*, vol. 76, no. 2, June 2004, pp. 367–89.

Lee, A. Robert. *Modern American Counter Writing: Beats, Outriders, Ethnics.* Routledge, 2010.

Leland, John. *Why Kerouac Matters: The Lessons of* On the Road *(They're Not What You Think).* Penguin Books, 2008.

Le Pellec, Yves. *Entretiens: Beat Generation.* Editions Subervie, 1975.

Lewis, Felice Flanery. *Literature, Obscenity, and Law.* Southern Illinois UP, 1976.

Lewis, Geoffrey. *The Turkish Language Reform: A Catastrophic Success.* Oxford UP, 2002.

Lipsitz, George. *American Studies in a Moment of Danger.* U of Minnesota P, 2001.

Lundén, Rolf. "The Eternal, Irresoluble Tensions in American Studies." *Beyond the Crisis in US American Studies: Scandinavian Perspectives*, edited by David E. Nye. UP of Southern Denmark, 2007, pp. 25–52.

Lydenberg, Robin. *Word Cultures: Radical Theory and Practice in William S. Burroughs' Fiction.* U of Illinois P, 1987.

Mackay, Polina, and Chad Weidner, editors. *The Beat Generation and Europe. Comparative American Studies*, special issue, vol. 11, no. 3, 2013, pp. 221–342.

Mango, Andrew. *The Turks Today*. John Murray, 2004.

Mardin, Şerif. *Religion, Society, and Modernity in Turkey*. Syracuse UP, 2006.

Marakoğlu, Ozan. "Edebiyatın Edepsizliği Ya Da Tutucu Olmayan Bütün Metinler Üstüne" ["The Impertinence of Literature, or On All the Texts Which Aren't Conservative"]. *Notos*, vol. 4, 2011, pp. 47–49.

Marler, Regina. *Queer Beats: How the Beats Turned America On to Sex*. Cleis Press, 2004.

Martinez, Manuel Luis. *Countering the Counterculture: Rereading Postwar American Dissent from Jack Kerouac to Tomás Rivera*. U of Wisconsin P, 2003.

McMillan, John. *Smoking Typewriters: The Sixties Underground Press and the Rise of Alternative Media in America*. Oxford UP, 2011.

Miles, Barry. *The Beat Hotel: Ginsberg, Burroughs, and Corso in Paris, 1957–1963*. Grove Press, 2001.

Morgan, Bill. *The Beats Abroad: A Global Guide to the Beat Generation*. City Lights Publishers, 2016.

———. "The Censorship Battle Continues." *Howl on Trial: The Battle for Free Expression*, edited by Bill Morgan and Nancy J. Peters. City Lights Books, 2006.

Mortenson, Erik. *Ambiguous Borderlands: Shadow Imagery in Cold War American Culture*. Southern Illinois UP, 2016.

———. *Capturing the Beat Moment: Cultural Politics and the Poetics of Presence*. Southern Illinois UP, 2011.

———. "The 'Underground' Reception of the Beats in Turkey." *Comparative American Studies: An International Journal*, vol. 11, no. 3, 2013, pp. 327–41.

Mortenson, Erik, Duygu Ergun, and Selen Erdoğan. "Underground Literature and Its Influence on Youth in Turkey." *New Perspectives on Turkey*, no. 52, 2015, pp. 77–104.

Mortenson, Erik, and Rafet Karaoğlu. "Diagnosing the National Neurosis: The Underground Journal *Şizofrengi* and Its Critique of 1990s Turkish Society." *Turkish Studies*, vol. 16, no. 1, 2015, pp. 20–35.

Mottram, Eric. *William Burroughs: The Algebra of Need*. Marion Boyars Publishers, 1978.

Mullins, Greg. *Colonial Affairs: Bowles, Burroughs, and Chester Write Tangier*. U of Wisconsin P, 2002.

Murphy, Timothy S. *Wising Up the Marks: The Amodern William Burroughs*. U of California P, 1997.

Myrsiades, Kostas, editor. *The Beat Generation: Critical Essays*. Peter Lang, 2002.

Nadel, Alan. *Containment Culture: American Narratives, Postmodernism, and the Atomic Age*. Duke UP, 1995.

Neish, Alex. Editorial. *Edinburgh University Review*. Jabberwock, 1959.

Neyzi, Leyla. "The Construction of 'Youth' in Public Discourse in Turkey." *Youth and Youth Culture in the Contemporary Middle East*, edited by Jørgen Bœk Simonsen. Proceedings of the Danish Institute in Damascus III, Aarhus UP, 2005, pp. 107–16.

Nicosia, Gerald. *Memory Babe*. Grove Press, 1983.

Öktem, Altay. Interview by author. Translated by Rafet Karaoğlu. Digital recording, Istanbul, Turkey, Mar. 21, 2012.

———. *Şehrin Kötü Çoçukları* [*The Bad Kids of the City*]. Ithaki Yayınları, 2002.

———. *Şeytan Aletleri* [*Satan's Tools*]. Everest Yayınları, 2000.

———. "Yeraltı Edebiyatı" ["Underground Literature"]. *Varlık*, February 2005, pp. 3–7.

———. "Yeraltı Edebiyatının Temel Özellikleri ve Edebiyatımızda Yeraltı" ["The Main Characteristics of Underground Literature and the Underground in Our Literature"]. *Notos*, no. 4, 2011, pp. 16–21.

Önok, Murat. Interview by author. Istanbul, October 2012. In English.

Özgün, Fatih. "Hazlar Bahcesi" ["Garden of Delights"]. *Bir+Bir*, July 8, 2012. http://birdirbir.org/hazlar-bahcesi/.

Özlü, Demir. Interview by author. E-mail, Istanbul, Mar. 10, 2014. In English.

Özyeğin, Gül. "The Doorkeeper, the Maid, and the Tenant: Troubling Encounters in the Turkish Urban Landscape." *Fragments of Culture: The Everyday of Modern Turkey*, edited by Deniz Kandiyoti and Ayşe Saktanber, I. B. Tauris, 2002, pp. 43–72.

Pamuk, Orhan. *Istanbul: Memories and the City*. Translated by Maureen Freely, Vintage Books, 2004.

———. *The New Life*. Translated by Güneli Gün, Faber and Faber, 1997.

Parla, Jale. "Car Narratives: A Subgenre in Turkish Novel Writing." *The South Atlantic Quarterly*, vol. 102, no. 2/3, Spring / Summer 2003, pp. 535–50.

Pease, Donald. "Introduction: Re-Mapping the Transnational Turn." *Re-Framing the Transnational Turn in American Studies*, edited by Pease, Winfried Fluck, and John Carlos Rowe. Dartmouth College P, 2011, pp. 10–49.

Peck, Abe. Foreword. *Voices from the Underground: Insider Histories of the Vietnam Era Underground Press*, edited by Ken Wachsberger. Mica's Press, 1993, pp. xviii–xix.

Peters, Nancy J. "Milestones of Literary Censorship." *Howl on Trial: The Battle for Free Expression*, edited by Bill Morgan and Nancy J. Peters. City Lights Books, 2006, pp. 5–13. The article title is given as it appears in the text; the table of contents has it as "Censorship Milestones."

Pike, David L. *Metropolis on the Styx: The Underworlds of Modern Urban Culture, 1800–2001*. Cornell UP, 2007.

Pivano, Fernanda. *Beat & Pieces: A Complete Story of the Beat Generation in the Words of Fernanda Pivano with Photographs by Allen Ginsberg*. Photology, 2005.

Polat, Tayfun. "Alt Üst Oldu" ["Under Became Above"]. *Notos*, vol. 4, 2011, pp. 44–46.
Pope, Nicole, and Hugh Pope. *Turkey Unveiled: A History of Modern Turkey.* The Overlook Press, 2004.
Radway, Janice A. *Reading the Romance: Women, Patriarchy, and Popular Culture.* U of North Carolina P, 1984.
Renan, Sheldon. *An Introduction to Underground Film.* E. P. Dutton, 1967.
Renaissance. No. 8, supplement. San Francisco, date assumed 1971, no page.
Ring, Kevin. *Beat Scene*, no. 44, Winter 2003.
Rothenberg, Jerome. "Pre-Face." Clay and Phillips, *A Secret Location on the Lower East Side*, pp. 8–11.
Rowe, John Carlos. *The New American Studies.* U of Minnesota P, 2002.
Russell, Jamie. *Queer Burroughs.* Palgrave, 2001.
Sabitfikir. "Ve Burroughs Hakim Karşısında" ["And Burroughs Faces the Judge"]. July 6, 2011, *Sabitfikir.com*, www.sabitfikir.com/haber/ve-burroughs-hakim-karsisinda.
Şahinsoy, Melike Aslı. *İstanbul'da Rock Kültürü: Yeraltından Yeryüzüne* [*Rock Culture in Istanbul: From Underground to the Surface*]. Clinart, 2010.
Said, Edward. *Orientalism.* Vintage Books, 1994.
Sancı, İrfan. Interview by author. Translated by Rafet Karaoğlu. Digital recording, Istanbul, Dec. 27, 2011.
Sarı, Mustafa. *Türkçenin Batı Dilleriyle İlişkisi* [*The Relation of the Turkish Language with Western Languages*]. Türk Dil Kurumu Yayınları, 2008.
Savran, David. *Taking It Like a Man: White Masculinity, Masochism, and Contemporary American Culture.* Princeton UP, 1998.
Schneiderman, Davis, and Philip Walsh, editors. *Retaking the Universe: William S. Burroughs in the Age of Globalization.* Pluto, 2004.
Schober, Rick, editor. *The Whole Shot: Collected Interviews with Gregory Corso.* Tough Poets Press, 2015.
Sertabiboğlu, Süha. Interview by author. Translated by Rafet Karaoğlu. Digital recording, Istanbul, Jan. 26, 2012.
Silier, Yıldız. *Özgürlük Yanılsaması: Rousseau ve Marx* [*The Illusion of Freedom: Rousseau and Marx*]. Yordam Kitap, 2010.
Sinclair, John. "The Alternative Press." Detroit, Nov. 7, 1969, no page.
Skau, Michael. "Jack Kerouac's Rubáiyat: The Influence of Omar Khayyám." *The Journal of Popular Culture*, vol. 48, no. 3, 2015, pp. 487–506.
Solomon, Thomas. "'Living Underground Is Tough': Authenticity and Locality in the Hip-hop Community in Istanbul, Turkey." *Popular Music*, vol. 24, no. 1, 2005, pp. 1–20.
Sorrentino, Gilbert. "*Neon, Kulchur,* Etc." *The Little Magazine in America: A Modern Documentary History*, edited by Elliott Anderson and Mary Kinzie. Pushcart Press, 1978, pp. 298–316.

Stewart, Sean. *On the Ground: An Illustrated Anecdotal History of the Sixties Underground Press in the U.S.* PM Press, 2011.

Stokes, Martin. "The Tearful Public Sphere: Turkey's 'Sun of Art,' Zeki Müren." *Music and Gender: Perspectives from the Mediterranean*, edited by Magrini Tullia. U of Chicago P, 2003, pp. 307–28.

Suárez, Juan A. *Bike Boys, Drag Queens, and Superstars: Avant-Garde, Mass Culture, and Gay Identities in 1960s Underground Cinema.* Indiana UP, 1996.

Sullivan, James D. *On the Walls and in the Streets: American Poetry Broadsides from the 1960s.* U of Illinois P, 1997.

Suner, Asuman. *New Turkish Cinema: Belonging, Identity, and Memory.* I. B. Tauris, 2010.

Tapınç, Hüseyin. "Masculinity, Femininity, and Turkish Male Homosexuality." *Modern Homosexualities*, edited by Ken Plummer. Routledge, 1992, pp. 39–49.

Tapper, Richard. *Islam in Modern Turkey: Religion, Politics and Literature in a Secular State.* I. B. Tauris, 1991.

Tietchen, Todd F. *The Cubalogues: Beat Writers in Revolutionary Havana.* UP of Florida, 2010.

Trigilio, Tony. "The Beat Goes On—But How?" *Phi Kappa Phi Forum*, vol. 94, no. 3, 2014, pp. 12–15.

Turan, Güven. "Allen Ginsberg: Şairin Poetikası, Şairin Politikası" ["Allen Ginsberg: A Poet's Poetics, A Poet's Politics"]. *Gösteri Hürriyet Gösteri*, no. 197–98, 1997, pp. 44–47.

———. Interview by author. Digital recording, Istanbul, Mar. 14, 2014. In English.

Türkeş, Ömer. "Dosya: Türkiye'de Yeraltı Edebiyatı Var mı?" ["Dossier: Is There an Underground Literature in Turkey?"] *Varlık*, February 2005, pp. 14–24.

Turgut, Alper. "Kaybedenler Kulübü: Seçilmiş Yalnızlık ve Kadıköy" ["Losers' Club: Chosen Loneliness and Kadiköy"]. http://www.alperturgut.net. Accessed May 16, 2012.

Turkish Penal Code. Translated by Edward Grieves and Vahit Bıcak. 2007.

Tytell, John. *Naked Angels: The Lives and Literature of the Beat Generation.* McGraw-Hill, 1976.

Uludere, Ferhat. "Interview with Mehmet Öztekin." *Taraf*, May 22, 2008, http://www.uluma-izmir.blogspot.com/2009/01/uluma-film.html.

———. "Kutsal Serserinin Yol Maceraları" ["Holy Bums' Road Adventures"]. *Taraf*, Mar. 12, 2008, www.taraf.com.tr/haber/kutsal-serserinin-yol-maceralari.htm.

Uluma. Directed by Mehmet Ada Öztekin, 2008, Internet distribution.

Uncu, Funda. Interview with author. E-mail, Istanbul, Mar. 29, 2012. In English.

Ural, Ayça Seren. *Pogo.* Stüdyo İmge, 2003.
van der Bent, Jaap. "'Holy Amsterdam Holy Paris': The Beat Generation in Europe." *Beat Culture: The 1950s and Beyond*, edited by Cornelis A. van Minnen, Jaap van der Bent, and Mel van Elteren. VU UP, 1999, pp. 49–60.
Veselka, Vanessa. "Where Are the Women Kerouacs?" *Salon*, Mar. 14, 2013, http://www.salon.com/2013/03/13/where_are_the_women_kerouacs_partner/.
Venuti, Lawrence. "Translation, Community, Utopia." *The Translation Studies Reader*, edited by Lawrence Venuti. Routledge, 2009, pp. 482–502.
Vrchota, Janet. "The Underground Press." *Print*, November-December 1967.
Walsh, Joy, and Michael Basinski, editors. *Moody Street Irregulars: A Kerouac Newsletter*, vol. 1, no. 1, Winter 1978.
Weidner, Chad, and Polina Mackay. "The Beat Generation and Europe." *Comparative American Studies*, vol. 11, no. 3, September 2013, pp. 221–26.
Wills, David S. *Beatdom*. www.beatdom.com/. Accessed Feb. 18, 2014.
Wilson, Meagan. "Your Reputation Precedes You: A Reception Study of *Naked Lunch*." *Journal of Modern Literature*, vol. 35, no. 2, 2012, pp. 98–125.
Yılmaz, Abdullah. Interview by author. Translated by Rafet Karaoğlu. Digital recording, Istanbul, Dec. 27, 2011.
Yılmaz, Çetin. Untitled. *Underground Poetix*, vol. 7, 2010, p. 75.
Ze'evi, Dror. "Hiding Sexuality: The Disappearance of Sexual Discourse in the Late Ottoman Middle East." *Social Analysis*, vol. 49, no. 2, Summer 2005, pp. 34–53.
Zürcher, Erik J. *Turkey: A Modern History.* I. B. Tauris, 1993.

COVER ILLUSTRATION AND TEXT CREDITS

COVER ILLUSTRATION

Cover design by Jack Prange.

ON THE ROAD Copyright © 1955, 1957 by Jon Sampas, Literary representative, the Estate of Stella Sampas Kerouac; John Lash, Executor of the Estate of Jan Kerouac; Nancy Bump; and Anthony M. Sampas, used by permission of The Wylie Agency LLC. DHARMA BUMS copyright © 1958 Jon Sampas, Literary representative, the Estate of Stella Sampas Kerouac; John Lash, Executor of the Estate of Jan Kerouac; Nancy Bump; and Anthony M. Sampas, used by permission of The Wylie Agency LLC.

Excerpt from "Letter from a Master Addict to Dangerous Drugs" Copyright © William S. Burroughs 1957, used by permission of The Wylie Agency LLC. Excerpt from "The Letters of William S. Burroughs, Vol. 1: 1945–1959" Copyright © William S. Burroughs 1993, used by permission The Wylie Agency LLC.

"A Supermarket in California," "An Eastern Ballad," "A Western Ballad," and "Kiss Ass" currently collected in *Collected Poems, 1947–1997*, by Allen Ginsberg. Copyright © 2006 Allen Ginsberg, LLC, used by permission of The Wylie Agency LLC.

TEXT

Portion of "Reclaiming the Underground: Turkish Women Writers and Their Beat Women Counterparts," pp. 25–39 in *Out of the Shadows: Beat Women Are Not Beaten Women*, reprinted in chapter 1 with permission from Portal forlag, Norway; poem, "The Alternative Press," by John Sinclair, quoted in chapter 2 with permission of the poet; earlier version of chapter 3 published as "Importing Counterculture: *On the Road*'s Turkish Reception," pp. 119–40 in *The Transnational Turn in American Studies: Turkey and the United States* (ISBN 978-3-0343-0552-5; DOI: http://dx.doi.org/10.3726/978-3-0351-0390-8), reproduced with permission of Peter Lang; portion of chapter 4 previously published as "Turkish Censorship, Cultural Translation, and the Trial of William S. Burroughs's *The Soft Machine*," *Arizona Quarterly: A Journal of American Literature, Culture, and Theory*, vol. 72, no. 3, 2016, pp. 47–73 (© 2016 Arizona Board of Regents), reprinted with permission of Johns Hopkins University Press; Erik Mortenson's "Howling in Turkish: The Cultural Appropriation of Allen Ginsburg in Turkey," *CLCWeb: Comparative Literature and Culture*, vol. 18, no. 5, December 2016, reprinted in part in chapter 5 courtesy of Purdue University Press (all rights reserved); poem, "Bir Kumkapı Gecesi" ("Mirrors are not people . . ."), by Allen Ginsberg and Can Yücel (copyright © 2018 by Allen Ginsberg) used in chapter 5 by permission of the Wylie Agency (UK), Limited; and poem, "Uygunsuzerler" ("Misfits"), by Can Yücel, reproduced in chapter 5 with permission of the poet's daughter, Su Yücel.

INDEX

Page numbers in italics indicate illustrations.

Erik Mortenson spent ten years as an assistant professor in the Department of English and Comparative Literature at Koç University in Istanbul, and is now a senior lecturer at Wayne State University's Honors College in Detroit. He is the author of *Ambiguous Borderlands: Shadow Imagery in Cold War American Culture* (2016) and *Capturing the Beat Moment: Cultural Politics and the Poetics of Presence*, which was selected as a *Choice* outstanding academic title in 2011.